Summarizing the message of a c
short, and coherent sentence is v
every book of the Bible, and every chapter of every book of the Bible in this way is at once a monumental accomplishment and an enormous gift to all who love the Word of God. Together with its invaluable appendices, this book is designed to serve the average Christian who wishes to understand what they read as they open the Book of God. It's apparent simplicity and immediate accessibility doubtless belie the difficulty of producing it, and we are deeply grateful to Dr. McGraw for loving both the Bible and the church enough to write it. Keep *A Divine Tapestry* at hand when you open your Bible and you will be better equipped to grasp God's truth and live in its light.

DAVID STRAIN,
Senior Minister at First Presbyterian Church, Jackson, Mississippi

There is no book more important to read than the Bible, and there is hardly a book more intimidating to read than the Bible. We may be thankful to Ryan McGraw for producing such a practical and user-friendly help to the study of Scripture. Concise summaries and memorization verses from each chapter serve not only beginning readers but also seasoned readers. Read this book, and then read the Bible!

GUY WATERS,
James M. Baird, Jr. Professor of New Testament
at Reformed Theological Seminary

We are ever laboring to cultivate the discipline of reading and understanding God's Word, as it is the spiritual nourishment given to us by our Lord. I am always glad to find helpful resources that can encourage and assist believers toward this end. Thankfully, Ryan McGraw has provided a valuable book for the church that will serve as a companion in Bible study. *A Divine Tapestry* is aptly titled, as it skillfully demonstrates the woven thread of God's providential workings through His covenant people. I sincerely hope this becomes a well-used resource for years to come.

NATE PICKOWICZ,
Teaching Pastor of Harvest Bible Church, Gilmanton Iron Works,
New Hampshire; Author of *How to Eat Your Bible*

Scripture instructs us to write God's word and wisdom upon the tablets of our hearts – Ryan McGraw has given the church a useful resource for this very purpose. Not only does he provide a treasury of Scripture verses ripe for memorization but he summarizes each chapter of the Bible so we can see the scope of the whole of Scripture, which is to give all glory to God, by which we can behold the many incomparable excellencies of the mercies of our triune God.

J. V. Fesko
Harriet Barbour Professor of Systematic and Historical Theology
Reformed Theological Seminary
Jackson, Mississippi

A DIVINE TAPESTRY

Summaries and Memory Verses from Every Chapter of Scripture

RYAN M. McGRAW

paperback ISBN 978-1-5271-0940-7
ebook ISBN 978-1-5271-0998-8

10 9 8 7 6 5 4 3 2

Published in 2023 and reprinted in 2023
by
Christian Focus Publications Ltd,
Geanies House, Fearn, Ross-shire,
IV20 1TW, Great Britain.

www.christianfocus.com

Cover design by Pete Barnsley

Printed by Bell and Bain, Glasgow

CONTENTS

To Owen, Calvin, Jonathan, and Callie, who have heard everything in this book many times over. May you pass it on to your children one day.

Introduction

The Bible is a big book. Yet it is God's book and it is worth knowing. As Thomas Manton (1620–1677) wrote, 'A Christian is to be a walking bible, to have a good stock and treasure in himself.'[1] Yet how do we get to know God's Word? Appearing over many centuries through many authors, getting to know the Bible can be a daunting task. Many start reading through the Bible only to get lost and lose heart early on. Others memorize large collections of seemingly random verses, missing their contexts and the scope of the whole book. Still others persevere and read the whole thing, failing to see the interconnectedness of the parts and where the narrative is going.

This book aims to help readers become more familiar with the storyline of the Bible, through summarizing the content of every chapter in Scripture, and by singling out key verses that epitomize each chapter. Seeking to show the argument of each biblical book in its context, the summaries indicate what happens and why in each chapter, paving the way for letting the Bible tell its own story in its own words.

In order to understand what this book is more fully and how it works, it may help to explain its target audience, the nature of

1. Thomas Manton, *Several Sermons upon the 119th Psalm*, in, *The Complete Works* (London: Nisbet, 1870), 6:101.

the summaries and the selection of verses, why it uses the NKJV translation, and some suggestions on how to use it.

Audience

This book is for everyone. Initially, the author intended to give his children targeted memory verses to help them memorize more of the language of Scripture and to understand the meaning of the whole. However, seminary students began to express interest in the book in order to prepare for ordination exams, and to know Scripture better as they prepared to teach the church. Yet as word of this project spread, church members began asking for incomplete copies of the text, longing for a means of getting to know the Bible better and to navigate its voluminous pages in a single book. People wanted summaries, and they wanted memory verses, but they wanted understanding as well. These things made it clear that this book had potential to reach everyone from children to seminary students, pulling along everyone in between.

Summaries and Verses

How does one summarize every chapter in the Bible, reflecting progression of thought, and which verses should stand out to readers? Admittedly, this is a hard task, which is far from perfect. Some of the summaries are long, especially when chapters of Scripture are long. Old Testament narrative texts often have one main point, making analysis relatively easy and targeting verses obvious. Yet other parts of the Bible, like the gospels and Acts, while having a main point and flow of thought, contained so much material in each chapter that the summaries became paragraphs. The summaries use the verses to explain content, illustrating that they accomplish more than headings in English Bible translations. They illustrate that each chapter of the Bible builds the broader argument of each book. Such progression and logical ordering is what most Bible readers miss at first glance. Aiming at logical coherence, 'summaries' thus teach people how to read and understand the Scriptures.

The memory verses enable readers to see first-hand that the ideas presented in the summaries lie on the surface of the text. The author initially sought one verse for every chapter of the Bible. However, this became untenable, since key ideas were often distributed through several verses. As a general rule, each chapter includes 1 to 4 verses, epitomizing key ideas. Sometimes, such as with the gospels, the author chose different verses than those listed already in parallels elsewhere, maintaining a focus on meaning. Readers should notice that some Old Testament selections, and more New Testament ones, are Trinitarian in tone. This itself reflects how the Bible gradually reveals God as it reveals the gospel.

A single sentence introduces every book of the Bible as well. Encapsulating the main idea presented in that book, these statements can aid memory as people read the summaries and verses, which flesh out the details.

Highlighting progression and overarching unity, covenant became a natural path for explaining the Bible's message on its own terms. Covenant language looms large in Scripture, with covenant ideas carrying through both testaments, even where the word does not appear. Selecting additional things that readers should become familiar with, the appendices augment the text with key themes and parts of Scripture, such as the states of God's covenant, what each book says about Christ, and where to find the Ten Commandments, the Beatitudes, and the Lord's Prayer.

Bible Translation

In light of the popularity of more modern Bible translations, why the NKJV? The KJV has dominated the language of exegesis and theology since the early seventeenth century. Being displaced only recently by newer translations, such as the NIV and ESV, the language of the KJV shaped the language of theology, prayer, and devotion in a way that no other English Bible translation has. The NKJV retains most of the words and feel of the KJV, relying on similar manuscripts, while updating enough expressions for modern readers to retain readability.

Whether or not readers agree with every instance of this translation, it is important to be familiar with wording in it that is often lost in other translations. For instance, in the KJV, Haggai 2:7 reads, 'I will shake all the nations, and the Desire of nations shall come.' The NKJV, altering the translation slightly, says, 'they shall come to the Desire of all nations.' However, the ESV and the HCSB say, 'the treasures of all nations shall come in,' while the NIV has, 'what is desired by all nations will come.' Yet when we sing, 'O Come, O Come, Immanuel,' we say, 'O come Desire of Nations bind, in one the hearts of all mankind.' Familiarity with the older strand of translations makes the Christological reference to this verse intelligible, even though other versions pick up the overarching sense of the verse. Of course, the Christological reading of the text relies more on the context of Haggai 2 than the translation of this particular verse does. Without the older translation, however, we lose some of the background for the devotional language of the English-speaking world. The same thing is true in relation to James 5:4, where the KJV and NKJV retain the title, 'Lord of Sabaoth,' while the NIV has, 'Lord Almighty,' and the ESV and others have, 'Lord of hosts.' While the meaning remains the same in some of these translations, only the KJV and NKJV pick up the transliteration of the Hebrew term for 'hosts.' This explains why, in the famous hymn, 'A Mighty Fortress is our God,' we sing, 'Lord Sabaoth His name, from age to age the same.' The NKJV is often more readable than the KJV, while keeping us familiar with the devotional language carried over from preceding centuries.

The same comments apply to the theological language of the church. Using creeds and confessions as a standard of unity, and a means of continuity with the church in all ages, historic creeds often incorporated verbal allusions to the text of Scripture in their statements. This point stands out in the Westminster Confession of Faith and Catechisms, which continue to be some of the most widely used Protestant confessional documents. For instance, WCF 8.3 states:

> The Lord Jesus Christ, in his human nature thus united to the divine, was sanctified, and anointed with the Holy Spirit, above measure,

> having in him all the treasures of wisdom and knowledge; in whom it pleased the Father that all fulness should dwell; to the end that, being holy, harmless, undefiled, and full of grace and truth, he might be thoroughly furnished to execute the office of a mediator, and surety. Which office he took not unto himself, but was thereunto called by his Father, who put all power and judgment into his hand, and gave him commandment to execute the same.

This paragraph includes verbal allusions to John 3:34, Col. 2:3, Col. 1:19, Heb. 7:26, 7:22, 5:4-5, and John 5:22, 27. Retaining the language of the KJV via the NKJV brings the biblical allusions to the surface more easily than other modern translations might. While no Bible translation is faultless, the NKJV has devotional and confessional advantages with respect to language.

How to use this Book

The best way to use this book is to have it open while reading through the whole Bible. Each chapter can encourage readers to keep going as the summaries and memory verses train them what to look for and how to read better. Reading through the Bible in families, with this book as a companion and guide, can also help parents pass along what they learn to their children. Older children and students can work through it themselves. While few will likely memorize all of the chosen verses, people can select sections in order to memorize Scripture in a targeted and meaningful way. The book headings and the first two appendices can also be handy for cultivating a "big picture" view of the Bible's storyline. There are other possible uses for this material, which some prayerful creativity can bring out.

Conclusion

In writing this book, the breathtaking unity of Scripture stood out perhaps above all things. Written over many centuries, through many authors, from differing backgrounds, in different languages, epitomizing the message of each chapter shows organically how the entire Bible hangs together. Since God is the ultimate author of Scripture, readers have a vested interest in getting to know the author as they read His Word. Readers should not only read, but pray for the Holy Spirit to illumine their hearts as they seek to know the God of the Word through the Word of God. Eternal life is knowing the only true God, and Jesus Christ whom He has sent (John 17:3). God's book is well-spoken and well-suited to this end. May readers by faith see the God whom no man has seen nor can see, as they behold His glory in the face of Jesus Christ.

Genesis

God covenants with fallen human beings, promising to undo the ruin Satan brought on the human race, dividing mankind into the seed of the woman and the seed of the serpent.

Chapter 1
God Creates the Heavens and the Earth in Six Days, and Makes Man After His Own Image as the Capstone of Creation

> 'Then God said, "Let Us make man in Our image, according to Our likeness; let them have dominion over the fish of the sea, over the birds of the air, and over the cattle, over all the earth and over every creeping thing that creeps on the earth."' Gen. 1:26.

Chapter 2
God Institutes the Sabbath, Resting from His Work of Creation, and Places Man in a Covenant Relationship with Himself, Instituting Marriage

> 'And the LORD God commanded the man, saying, "Of every tree of the garden you may freely eat; but of the tree of the knowledge of good and evil you shall not eat, for in the day you eat of it you shall surely die."' Gen. 2:16-17.

Chapter 3
Mankind Falls through Adam Breaking the Covenant, and Amidst the Curse, God Promises to Preserve a Seed from the Woman Until the Great Seed of the Woman Saves His People By Crushing the Serpent's Head

> 'And I will put enmity between you and the woman, and between your seed and her seed; He shall bruise your head, and you shall bruise His heel.' Gen. 3:15.

Chapter **4**

The Lord Divides the Seed of the Woman from the Seed of the Serpent, Cain Murders Abel, and the Promise Goes to the Sons of Seth

> 'And as for Seth, to him also a son was born; and he named him Enosh. Then men began to call on the name of the LORD.' Gen. 4:26.

Chapter **5**

God Preserves the Seed of the Woman and Gives Hope in the Face of the First List of Deaths

> 'And Enoch walked with God; and he was not, for God took him.' Gen. 5:24.

Chapter **6**

The Seed of the Woman Mixes with the Seed of the Serpent and God Promises to Preserve the Covenant Line in Spite of Man's Wickedness

> 'But I will establish My covenant with you; and you shall go into the ark – you, your sons, your wife, and your sons wives with you.' Gen. 6:18.

Chapter **7**

God Judges Man's Universal Rebellion by a Universal Flood

> 'Then the LORD said to Noah, "Come into the ark, you and your household, because I have seen that you are righteous before Me in this generation."' Gen. 7:1.

Chapter **8**

God Restores the Earth and Promises to Preserve Mankind for the Sake of Preserving His Covenant People

> 'Then Noah built an altar to the LORD, and took of every clean animal and of every clean bird, and offered burnt offerings on the altar. And the LORD smelled a soothing aroma. Then the LORD said in His heart, "I will never again curse the ground for man's sake, although the imagination of man's heart is evil from his youth; nor will I again destroy every living thing as I have done. While the earth remains, seedtime and harvest, cold and heat, winter and summer, and day and night shall not cease."' Gen. 8:20-22.

CHAPTER **9**

God Preserves His Covenant with the Seed of the Woman through Noah, Showing the Difference Between Animal and Human Life, Giving the Rainbow as a Covenant Sign, and cursing the Canaanites

> 'And as for Me, behold, I establish My covenant with you and with your descendants after you, and with every living creature that is with you: the birds, the cattle, and every beast of the earth with you, of all that go out of the ark, every beast of the earth. Thus I will establish My covenant with you: Never again shall all flesh be cut off by the waters of the flood; never again shall there be a flood to destroy the earth.' Gen. 9:9-10.

CHAPTER **10**

God Divides the Nations by Covenant, Separating the Children of Shem from the Seed of the Serpent

> 'These were the sons of Shem, according to their families, according to their languages, in their lands, according to their nations. These were the families of the sons of Noah, according to their generations, in their nations; and from these the nations were divided on the earth after the flood.' Gen. 10:31-32.

CHAPTER **11**

God Divides the Nations by Cursing Rebellion at Babel, Preventing Unity in Wickedness as Before the Flood, and Preserving the Seed of the Woman up to Abram

> 'Come, let Us go down and there confuse their language, that they may not understand one another's speech.' Gen. 11:7.

CHAPTER **12**

God Narrows the Promise to the Seed of the Woman to Abram by Calling him Out of Ur of the Chaldees, and God Tests Abram's Faith in Egypt

> 'Now the LORD had said to Abram: "Get out of your country, from your family and from your father's house, to a land that I will show you. I will make you a great nation; I will bless you and make your name great; and you shall be a blessing. I will bless those who bless you, and I will curse him who curses you; and in you all the families of the earth shall be blessed."' Gen. 12:1-3.

Chapter 13
Abram and Lot Go Separate Ways and God Gives the Land of Canaan to Abram as a Pledge that He Would Fulfill His Covenant Promises to the Seed of the Woman

> 'And the LORD said to Abram, after Lot had separated from him: "Lift your eyes now and look from the place where you are – northward, southward, eastward, and westward; for all the land which you see I will give to you and to your descendants forever. And I will make your descendants as the dust of the earth; so that if a man could number the dust of the earth, then your descendants could be numbered. Arise, walk in the land through its length and its width, for I give it to you."' Gen. 13:14-17.

Chapter 14
Abram Becomes a Blessing to Lot by Rescuing him From his Enemies, and Melchizedek Blesses Abram as a Type of the Christ, Anticipating Psalm 110

> 'Then Melchizedek king of Salem brought out bread and wine; he was the priest of God Most High. And he blessed him and said: "Blessed be Abram of God Most High, Possessor of heaven and earth; And blessed be God Most High, who has delivered your enemies into your hand." And he gave him a tithe of all.' Gen. 14:18-20.

Chapter 15
God Strengthens Abram's Faith by Reaffirming His Covenant With him, Showing that the Land Promise Would Be Long in Coming

> 'And he believed in the LORD, and He accounted it to him for righteousness.' Gen. 15:6.

Chapter 16
Abram Lapses in Faith and Begets Ishmael Through Hagar

> 'Then she called the name of the LORD who spoke to her, You-Are-The-God-Who-Sees; for she said, "Have I also seen Him who sees me?"' Gen. 16:13.

Chapter 17
God Confirms His Covenant with Abram Again by Giving Circumcision as a Sign of the Covenant and by Changing his Name to Abraham

'And I will establish My covenant between Me and you and your descendants after you in their generations, for an everlasting covenant, to be God to you and your descendants after you ... This is My covenant which you shall keep, between Me and you and your descendants after you: Every male child among you shall be circumcised; and you shall be circumcised in the flesh of your foreskins, and it shall be a sign of the covenant between Me and you.' Gen. 17:7, 10-11.

Genesis **18**

God Reassures Abraham that Sarah Will Bear a Son, and Abraham Intercedes With the Divine Angel of the Lord for Sodom in Order to Save Lot

'Is anything too hard for the LORD? At the appointed time I will return to you, according to the time of life, and Sarah shall have a son.' Gen. 18:14.

Chapter **19**

God Answers Abraham's Prayer to Save Lot While Denying his Request to Spare Sodom, and Lot's Descendants Come Through Incest

'And it came to pass, when God destroyed the cities of the plain, that God remembered Abraham, and sent Lot out of the midst of the overthrow, when He overthrew the cities in which Lot had dwelt.' Gen. 19:29.

Chapter **20**

God Remembers His Covenant with Abraham even though Abraham's Faith Falters and he Lies to Abimelech About his Wife

'And Abraham said, "Because I thought, surely the fear of God is not in this place; and they will kill me on account of my wife."' Gen. 20:11.

Chapter **21**

God Fulfills His Promise in the Birth of Isaac, and Separates the Seed of the Serpent from the Seed of the Woman by Sending Ishmael Away, Preserving Abraham Under Tensions with Abimelech

> 'Now Abraham was one hundred years old when his son Isaac was born to him. And Sarah said, "God has made me laugh, and all who hear will laugh with me."' Gen. 21:5-6.

Chapter 22
God Tests Abraham's Faith by Commanding him to Sacrifice Isaac and Confirms His Covenant to the Seed of the Woman

> 'Then the Angel of the LORD called to Abraham a second time out of heaven, and said, "By Myself I have sworn, says the LORD, because you have done this thing, and have not withheld your son, your only son – blessing I will bless you, and multiplying I will multiply your descendants as the stars of heaven and as the sand which is on the seashore; and your descendants shall possess the gate of their enemies. In your seed all the nations of the earth shall be blessed, because you have obeyed My voice."' Gen. 22:15-18.

Chapter 23
Sarah Dies and Abraham Purchases the Cave of Machpelah as a Pledge of God's Covenant Promises

> 'I am a foreigner and a visitor among you. Give me property for a burial place among you, that I may bury my dead out of my sight.' Gen. 23:4.

Chapter 24
Abraham Seeks a Bride for Isaac to Preserve the Covenant Line

> 'The LORD God of heaven, who took me from my father's house and from the land of my family, and who spoke to me and swore to me, saying, "To your descendants I give this land," He will send His Angel before you, and you shall take a wife for my son from there.' Gen. 24:7.

Chapter 25
Abraham Marries Keturah and then Dies, the Lord Separating the Seed of the Woman from the Seed of the Serpent in Isaac and Ishmael and Jacob and Esau

> 'And the LORD said to her: "Two nations are in your womb, two peoples shall be separated from your body; One people shall be stronger than the other, and the older shall serve the younger."' Gen. 25:23.

Chapter 26

God Assures Isaac that the Promise of the Seed of the Woman Has Passed to him and Tests his Faith through Abimelech, while Esau Solidifies his Departure from the Covenant by Marrying Foreign Wives

> 'Then the LORD appeared to him and said: "Do not go down to Egypt; live in the land of which I shall tell you. Dwell in this land, and I will be with you and bless you; for to you and your descendants I give all these lands, and I will perform the oath which I swore to Abraham your father. And I will make your descendants multiply as the stars of heaven; I will give to your descendants all these lands; and in your seed all the nations of the earth shall be blessed; because Abraham obeyed My voice and kept My charge, My commandments, My statutes, and My laws."' Gen. 26:2-5.

Chapter 27

God Passes the Covenant Promise to Jacob in Spite of his Deception

> 'Let peoples serve you, and nations bow down to you. Be master over your brethren, and let your mother's sons bow down to you. Cursed be everyone who curses you, and blessed be those who bless you.' Gen. 27:29.

Chapter 28

Jacob Vows to Worship God After Dreaming of a Ladder Between Heaven and Earth and Bethel, Esau Marries Ishmaelites, and God Reaffirms the Covenant with Jacob

> 'And behold, the LORD stood above it and said: "I am the LORD God of Abraham your father and the God of Isaac; the land on which you lie I will give to you and your descendants. Also your descendants shall be as the dust of the earth; you shall spread abroad to the west and the east, to the north and the south; and in you and in your seed all the families of the earth shall be blessed. Behold, I am with you and will keep you wherever you go, and will bring you back to this land; for I will not leave you until I have done what I have spoken to you."' Gen. 28:13-15.

Chapter 29

Jacob Marries Rachel and Leah and God Begins to Build the Twelve Tribes of Israel

'When the LORD saw that Leah was unloved, He opened her womb; but Rachel was barren.' Gen. 29:31.

Chapter 30

Leah, Rachel, and their Maidservants Bear the Rest of the Heads of the Tribes of Israel to Jacob, and Jacob Negotiates his Wages With Laban

'Then God remembered Rachel, and God listened to her and opened her womb.' Gen. 30:22.

Chapter 31

Jacob Flees From Laban, Rachel Steals her Father's Idols, and God Protects Jacob According to His Covenant Promises in Spite of Jacob's Foolishness

'I am the God of Bethel, where you anointed the pillar and where you made a vow to Me. Now arise, get out of this land, and return to the land of your family.' Gen. 31:13.

Chapter 32

God Humbles Jacob as he Prepares to Meet Esau and Jacob Wrestles in Prayer with the Angel of the Lord, the Lord Changing his Name to Israel

'Then Jacob said, "O God of my father Abraham and God of my father Isaac, the LORD who said to me, 'Return to your country and to your family, and I will deal well with you.' I am not worthy of the least of all the mercies and of all the truth which You have shown Your servant; for I crossed over this Jordan with my staff, and now I have become two companies. Deliver me, I pray, from the hand of Esau; for I fear him, lest he come and attack me and the mother with the children. For You said, 'I will surely treat you well, and make your descendants as the sand of the sea, which cannot be numbered for multitude.'"' Gen. 32:9-12.

Chapter 33

God Answers Jacob's Prayer, Delivering him from Esau, and Jacob Worships God

'And Jacob said, "No, please, if I have now found favor in your sight, then receive my present from my hand, inasmuch as I have seen your face as though I had seen the face of God, and you were pleased with me."' Gen. 33:10.

Chapter 34

Shechem Takes Dinah, Threatening to Mix the Seed of the Serpent with the Seed of the Woman, Simeon and Levi Retaliate by Killing all the Men of Shechem, and Jacob Fears that the Covenant Promise Will Fail

'Then Jacob said to Simeon and Levi, "You have troubled me by making me obnoxious among the inhabitants of the land, among the Canaanites and Perizzites; and since I am few in number, they will gather themselves together against me and kill me. I shall be destroyed, my household and I."' Gen. 34:30.

Chapter 35

God Renews His Covenant with Jacob and Jacob Renews Covenant with God, and Isaac Dies

'And Jacob said to his household and to all who were with him, "Put away the foreign gods that are among you, purify yourselves, and change your garments. Then let us arise and to up to Bethel; and I will make an altar there to God, who answered me in the day of my distress and has been with me in the way which I have gone."' Gen. 35:2-3.

Chapter 36

God Relegates Esau to the Seed of the Serpent, Separating the Edomites from the Seed of the Woman

'Now this is the genealogy of Esau, who is Edom.' Gen. 36:1.

Chapter 37

Jacob Favors Joseph, Joseph Dreams that God Will Exalt him, and Joseph's Brother's Sell him into Slavery

'Now the Midianites had sold him in Egypt to Potiphar, an officer of Pharaoh and captain of the guard.' Gen. 37:36.

Chapter 38

Judah Mixes with the Canaanites and God Begins to Humble Judah Through his Incestuous Relationship with Tamar, Bearing Perez and Zerah

'So Judah acknowledged them and said, "She has been more righteous than I, because I did not give her to Shelah my son." And he never knew her again.' Gen. 38:26.

Chapter 39
The Lord Exalts Joseph in his Humiliation by Blessing him and Others Through him, While he is Humbled Further Under False Accusations by Potiphar's Wife

'And his master saw that the LORD was with him and that the LORD made all that he did to prosper in his hand ... The keeper of the prison did not look into anything that was under Joseph's authority, because the LORD was with him; and whatever he did, the LORD made it prosper.' Gen. 39:3, 23.

Chapter 40
The Lord Enables Joseph to Interpret the Butler and Baker's Dreams in Prison, but the Time for his Exaltation in Egypt Had not Yet Come

'So Joseph said to them, "Do not interpretations belong to God? Tell them to me, please."' Gen. 40:8b.

Chapter 41
Joseph Interprets Pharoah's Dreams and Becomes Savior of the World to Preserve the Seed of the Woman, as the Man Who Reveals Mysteries (Zaphnath Paaneah)

'And Pharaoh called Joseph's name Zaphnath-Paaneah. And he gave him as a wife Asenath, the daughter of Poti-Pherah priest of On. So Joseph went out over all the land of Egypt.' Gen. 41:45.

Chapter 42
Joseph's Brothers Make their First Trip to Egypt to Buy Food, and God Humbles them Further Through Joseph Testing them, Jacob Wrongly Concluding that God is Against him

'And Jacob their father said to them, "You have bereaved me: Joseph is no more, Simeon is no more, and you want to take Benjamin. All these things are against me."' Gen. 42:36.

Chapter 43
The Brothers Return to Egypt as Jacob Resolves to Trust God's Providence, and Joseph Hints at his Knowledge of his Brothers

'And may God Almighty give you mercy before the man, that he may release your other brother and Benjamin. If I am bereaved, I am bereaved!' Gen. 43:14.

Chapter 44
Joseph Deceives his Brothers, Judah Takes Responsibility Before God

'Then Judah said, "What shall we say to my lord? What shall we speak? Or how shall we clear ourselves? God has found out the iniquity of your servants; here we are, my lord's slaves, both we and he also with whom the cup was found."' Gen. 44:16.

Chapter 45
God Saves the Seed of the Woman Through His Providence in Directing Joseph's Life

'And God sent me before you to preserve a posterity before you in the earth, and to save your lives by a great deliverance. So now it was not you who sent me here, but God; and He has made me a father to Pharaoh, and lord of all his house, and a ruler throughout all the land of Egypt.' Gen. 45:7-8.

Chapter 46
God Brings Jacob to Egypt and Reassures him of His Covenant Promises

'So He said, "I am God, the God of your father; do not fear to go down to Egypt, for I will make of you a great nation there. I will go down with you to Egypt, and I will also surely bring you up again; and Joseph will put his hand on your eyes."' Gen. 46:3-4.

Chapter 47
Jacob Prepares for Death Hoping in God's Covenant Promises

'Please do not bury me in Egypt, but let me lie with my fathers; you shall carry me out of Egypt and bury me in their burial place.' And he said, 'I will do as you have said.' Gen. 47:29b-30.

Chapter 48
Jacob Blesses Joseph's Sons with God's Covenant Promise

> 'And he blessed Joseph, and said: "God, before whom my fathers Abraham and Isaac walked, the God who has fed me all my life long to this day, the Angel who has redeemed me from all evil, bless the lads; let my name be named upon them, and the name of my fathers Abraham and Isaac; and let them grow into a multitude in the midst of the earth."' Gen. 48:15-16.

Chapter **49**

God Predicts Through Jacob that the Covenant Promise Will Narrow to Judah

> 'The scepter shall not depart from Judah, nor a lawgiver from between his feet, until Shiloh comes; and to Him shall be the obedience of the people.' Gen. 49:10.

Chapter **50**

Joseph Buries Jacob in the Land of Canaan in Pledge of his Faith in God's Providence and Faithfulness to his Covenant

> 'Joseph said to them, "Do not be afraid, for am I in the place of God? But as for you, you meant evil against me; but God meant it for good, in order to bring it about as it is this day, to save many people alive. Now therefore, do not be afraid; I will provide for you and your little ones." And he comforted them and spoke kindly to them.' Gen. 50:19-21.

Exodus

God remembers His covenant with His people, redeeming them out of the land of Egypt.

Chapter 1

God Multiplies Israel Under Affliction and Remembers His Covenant with them

> 'But the more they afflicted them, the more they multiplied and grew. And they were in dread of the children of Israel.' Exod. 1:12.

Chapter 2

God Preserves Moses in Order to Remember His Covenant with Afflicted Israel

> 'Now it happened in the process of time that the king of Egypt died. Then the children of Israel groaned because of the bondage, and they cried out; and their cry came up to God because of the bondage. So God heard their groaning, and God remembered his covenant with Abraham, with Isaac, and with Jacob. And God looked upon the children of Israel, and God acknowledged them.' Exod. 2:23-25.

Chapter 3

God Appears as the Angel of the Lord in the Burning Bush, Revealing His Covenant Name in Order to Fulfill His Covenant with Abraham, Isaac, and Jacob Through Moses

> 'And God said to Moses, "I AM WHO I AM." And He said, "Thus you shall say to the children of Israel, I AM has sent me to you." Moreover God said to Moses, 'Thus you shall say to the children of Israel': "The LORD God of your fathers, the God of Abraham, the God of Isaac, and the God of Jacob, has sent

me to you. This is My name forever, and this is My memorial to all generations."' Exod. 3:14-15.

Chapter 4

God Gives Moses Signs to Prove that he is God's Prophet, God Appoints Aaron to Speak for Moses, and the People Believe in the God of Israel

'Then you shall say to Pharaoh, "Thus says the LORD: Israel is My son, my firstborn. So I say to you, let My son go that he may serve Me. But if you refuse to let him go, indeed I will kill your son, your firstborn."' Exod. 4:22.

Chapter 5

Moses Tells Pharaoh to Let the People Worship in the Wilderness, Pharaoh Retaliates, and Moses Forgets that God Predicted Opposition in Fulfilling His Covenant Promises

'So Moses returned to the LORD and said, "LORD, why have You brought trouble on this people? Why is it You have sent me? For since I came to Pharaoh to speak in Your name, he has done evil to this people; neither have You delivered Your people at all."' Exod. 5:22-23.

Chapter 6

God Reiterates His Faithfulness to the Covenant with Abraham, Isaac, and Jacob as the Reason for the Mosaic Covenant, Moses Doubts Again, and God Reaffirms that Aaron Will be His Prophet

'I appeared to Abraham, to Isaac, and to Jacob, as God Almighty, but by My name the LORD I was not known to them. I have also established My covenant with them, to give them the land of Canaan, the land of their pilgrimage, in which they were strangers.' Exod. 6:3-4.

Chapter 7

Aaron as Moses' Prophet Turns the Rod into a Serpent and the Waters into Blood (the First Plague), and God Declares that the Egyptians Will Know That He is the Lord Through His Signs

'And the Egyptians shall know that I am LORD, when I stretch out My hand on Egypt and bring out the children of Israel from among them.' Exod. 7:5

Chapter 8

God Brings the Second, Third, and Fourth Plagues of Frogs, Lice, and Flies to Show that He Alone is God and that He Protects His Covenant People, While Pharaoh Hardens his Heart

> 'So he said, "Tomorrow." And he said, "Let it be according to your word, that you may know that there is no one like the LORD our God." … "And in that day I will set apart the land of Goshen, in which My people dwell, that no swarms of flies shall be there, in order that you may know that I am the LORD in the midst of the land."' Exod. 8:10, 22.

Chapter 9

God Brings the Fifth, Sixth, and Seventh Plagues, Striking Livestock, and Bringing Boils and Hail on Egypt, and the Lord Explains Why He Hardened Pharaoh's Heart

> 'For at this time I will send my plagues to your very heart, and on your servants and on your people, that you may know that there is none like Me in all the earth. Now if I had stretched out My hand and struck you and your people with pestilence, then you would have been cut off from the earth. But indeed for this purpose I have raised you up, that I may show My power in you, and that My name may be declared in all the earth.' Exod. 9:14-16.

Chapter 10

God Sends the Eighth and Ninth Plagues of Locusts and Darkness, and Expands the Explanation for Hardening Pharaoh's Heart

> 'Now the LORD said to Moses, "Go in to Pharaoh; for I have hardened his heart and the hearts of his servants, that I may show these signs of Mine before him, and that you may tell in the hearing of your son and your son's son the mighty things I have done in Egypt, and My signs which I have done among them, that you may know that I am the LORD."' Exod. 10:1-2.

Chapter 11

The Lord Announces the Final Plague in the Death of the Firstborn of Egypt, Preparing to Fulfill God's Promise from Chapter 4

> 'But the LORD said to Moses, "Pharaoh will not heed you, so that My wonders may be multiplied in the land of Egypt."' Exod. 11:9

Chapter 12

The Lord Institutes the Passover to Commemorate His Redemptive Work, Bringing the Tenth Plague Killing the Firstborn of Egypt, and Fulfilling His Promise that Israel Would Plunder the Egyptians

> 'For the LORD will pass through to strike the Egyptians; and when He sees the blood on the lintel and on the two doorposts, the LORD will pass over the door and not allow the destroyer to come into your houses to strike you.' Exod. 12:23.

Chapter 13

The Lord Consecrates Israel's Firstborn to Himself and Regulates the Feast of Unleavened Bread, Leading Israel to the Red Sea in Order to Show His Mighty Works

> 'It shall be as a sign to you on your hand and as a memorial between your eyes, that the LORD's law may be in your mouth; for with a strong hand the LORD has brought you out of Egypt.' Exod. 13:9.

Chapter 14

The Lord Brings Israel Through the Red Sea

> 'And indeed I will harden the hearts of the Egyptians, and they shall follow them. So I will gain honor over Pharaoh and over all his army, his chariots, and his horsemen. Then the Egyptians shall know that I am the LORD, when I have gained honor for Myself over Pharaoh, his chariots, and his horsemen.' And the Angel of God, who went before the camp of Israel, moved and went behind them; and the pillar of cloud went before them and stood behind them.' Exod. 14:17-19.

Chapter 15

Moses and Miriam Lead Israel in Song to Celebrate God's Covenant Faithfulness, and the Lord Tests Israel with the Bitter Waters

> 'Who is like You, O LORD, among the gods? Who is like you, glorious in holiness, fearful in praises, doing wonders? ... He tested them, and said, "If you diligently heed the voice of the LORD your God and do what is right in His sight, give ear to His commandments and keep all His statutes, I will put none

of the diseases on you which I have brought on the Egyptians. For I am the LORD who heals you."' Exod. 15:11, 26.

CHAPTER 16

The People Complain Against Moses, but the Lord, Stating that their Complaint is Against Him, Graciously Provides Manna from Heaven, even as the People Respond with Sabbath Breaking

'And in the morning you shall see the glory of the LORD; for He hears your complaints against the LORD. But what are we, that you complain against us?' Exod. 16:7.

CHAPTER 17

The Lord Tests the People with Thirst, they Distrust the Lord, He Brings them Water from the Rock, and Delivers them from the Amalekites

'So he called the name of the place Massah and Meribah, because of the contention of the children of Israel, and because they tempted the LORD, saying, "Is the LORD among us or not?"' Exod. 17:7.

CHAPTER 18

Jethro, Moses' Father in Law, Declares God's Purpose in the Exodus Regarding the gods of Egypt, and Counsels Moses to Appoint Elders to Help him Judge Israel

'Now I know that the LORD is greater than all the gods; for in the very thing in which they behaved proudly, He was above them.' Exod. 18:11.

CHAPTER 19

The Lord Prepares Israel to Receive His Covenant Through Moses, Fulfilling the Covenant with Abraham and Appearing on the Mountain in Darkness and Fire, Warning the People Not to Come Up to God

'Now therefore, if you will indeed obey my voice and keep My covenant, then you shall be a special treasure to Me above all people; for all the earth is Mine. And you shall be to Me a kingdom of priests and a holy nation. These are the words which you shall speak to the children of Israel.' Exod. 19:5-6.

Chapter 20
God Summarizes His Covenant By Giving Israel the Ten Commandments, as the Lord, as Their God, and as Their Redeemer

> 'Now all the people witnessed the thunderings, the lightning flashes, the sound of the trumpet, and the mountain smoking; and when the people saw it, they trembled and stood afar off. Then they said to Moses, "You speak with us, and we will hear; but let not God speak with us, lest we die." And Moses said to the people, "Do not fear; for God has come to test you, and that His fear may be before you, so that you may not sin." So the people stood afar off, but Moses drew near the thick darkness where God was.' Exod. 20:18-21.

Chapter 21
God Regulates the Holiness of His Covenant People in Relation to Slavery, Violence, and Animals

> 'But if any harm follows, then you shall give life for life, eye for eye, tooth for tooth, hand for hand, foot for foot, burn for burn, wound for wound, stripe for stripe.' Exod. 21:23-25.

Chapter 22
God Gives Directions for Restitution of Stolen Property and Various Principles of Moral and Ceremonial Uprightness

> 'He who sacrifices to any god, except to the LORD only, he shall be utterly destroyed.' Exod. 22:20.

Chapter 23
God Exhorts His Covenant People to Imitate His Character in Justice, Kindness to Strangers, Sabbath Keeping, and Feast Days, Promising to Lead and Bless them Through the Divine Angel of the Lord

> 'Behold, I sent an Angel before you to keep you in the way and to bring you into the place which I have prepared. Beware of Him and obey His voice; do not provoke Him, or He will not pardon your transgressions; for My name is in Him. But if you indeed obey His voice and do all that I speak, then I will be an enemy to your enemies and an adversary to your adversaries. For My Angel will go before you and bring you in to the Amorites and the Hittites and the Perizzites and the

Canaanites and the Hivites and the Jebusites; and I will cut them off.' Exod. 23:20-23.

Chapter 24
Moses Writes the Words of the Covenant and Stands Before God as Israel's Mediator for Forty Days and Forty Nights

'Now the glory of the LORD rested on Mount Sinai, and the cloud covered it six days. And on the seventh day He called to Moses out of the midst of the cloud. The sight of the glory of the LORD was like a consuming fire on the top of the mountain in the eyes of the children of Israel. So Moses went into the midst of the cloud and went up into the mountain. And Moses was on the mountain forty days and forty nights.' Exod. 25:16-18.

Chapter 25
The Lord Instructs Moses to Take Offerings to Build the Tabernacle, Giving him Instructions to Build the Ark of the Covenant, the Table of Showbread, and the Lampstand, According to the Pattern Shown him on the Mountain

'And there I will meet with you, and I will speak with you from above the mercy seat, from between the two cherubim which are on the ark of the Testimony, about everything which I will give you in commandment to the children of Israel.' Exod. 25:22.

Chapter 26
The Lord Gives Moses Instructions for the Curtains of the Tabernacle, Separating the People from the Most Holy Place by a Veil

'And you shall hang the veil from the clasps. Then you shall bring the ark of the Testimony in there, behind the veil. The veil shall be a divider for you between the holy place and the Most Holy.' Exod. 26:33.

Chapter 27
God Instructs Moses to Build the Altar, the Court, and to Care for the Lampstand

'In the tabernacle of meeting, outside the veil which is before the Testimony, Aaron and his sons shall tend it from evening until morning before the LORD. It shall be a statute forever to their generations on behalf of the children of Israel.' Exod. 27:21.

Chapter 28
The Lord Instructs Moses to Make Garments for the High Priest and the Priests Generally, in Order to Maintain Holiness Before the Lord

> 'You shall also make a plate of pure gold and engrave on it, like the engraving of a signet: HOLINESS TO THE LORD.' Exod. 28:36.

Chapter 29
Moses Will Act as Priest to Consecrate the Priests, Who Will Consecrate the People through Daily Offerings to the Lord

> 'And they shall know that I am the LORD their God, who brought them up out of the land of Egypt, that I may dwell among them. I am the LORD their God.' Exod. 29:46.

Chapter 30
The Lord Establishes the Altar of Incense, Provides Ransom for the Firstborn, and Instructs Moses to Make the Bronze Laver and Anointing Oil and Incense

> 'You shall not offer strange incense on it, or a burnt offering, or a grain offering; nor shall you pour out a drink offering on it.' Exod. 30:9.

Chapter 31
The Lord Gifts Artisans with the Holy Spirit in Order to Build the Tabernacle, Stressing the Sabbath as a Sign of Covenant Sanctification to the Lord, and Giving Moses Two Tablets Written with His Own Finger

> 'See, I have called by name Bezalel the son of Uri, the son of Hur, of the tribe of Judah. And I have filled him with the Spirit of God, in wisdom, in understanding, and in all manner of workmanship.' Exod. 31:2-3.

Chapter 32
In the Meantime, Israel Breaks God's Covenant by Making a Golden Calf to Represent their God, and Moses Pleads for Mercy Based on the Abrahamic Covenant

> 'Remember Abraham, Isaac, and Israel, Your servants, to whom You swore by Your own self, and said to them, "I will multiply your descendants as the stars of heaven; and all

this land that I have spoken of I give to your descendants, that they shall inherit it forever." So the LORD relented from the harm which he said He would do to His people.' Exod. 32:13-14.

Chapter 33

God Promises to Send His Angel Before the People in Spite of their Sins, Moses Pleads the Terms of the Covenant, and he Asks to See God's Glory

'Then he said to Him, "If Your Presence does not go with us, do not bring us up from here. For how then will it be known that Your people and I have found grace in Your sight, except You go with us? So we shall be separate, Your people and I, from all the people who are upon the face of the earth."' Exod. 33:15-16.

Chapter 34

God Renews His Covenant with Israel, Expanding the Meaning of His Covenant Name with Words that Pervade the Rest of Scripture, and Moses Serves as Mediator Between the People and God

'Now the LORD descended in the cloud and stood with him there, and proclaimed the name of the LORD. And the LORD passed before him and proclaimed, "The LORD, the LORD God, merciful and gracious, longsuffering, and abounding in goodness and truth, keeping mercy for thousands, forgiving iniquity and transgression and sin, by no means clearing the guilty, visiting the iniquity of the fathers upon the children and the children's children to the third and fourth generation."' Exod. 34:5-7.

Chapter 35

Moses Stresses Sabbath Worship as the Expression of Covenant Faithfulness to God, Taking Offerings to Build the Tabernacle, the People Offering Willingly, the Spirit of God Equipping Bezalel to Lead in the Work

'Then everyone came whose heart was stirred, and everyone whose spirit was willing, and they brought the LORD's offering for the work of the tabernacle of meeting, for all its service, and for the holy garments.' Exod. 35:21.

Chapter 36
Bezalel and Oholiab Begins Building the Tabernacle for God's Presence, and the People Give More than Enough for the Work

> 'Then Moses called Bezalel and Oholiab, and every gifted artisan in whose heart the LORD had put wisdom, everyone whose heart was stirred, to come and do the work.' Exod. 36:2.

Chapter 37
They Make the Ark of the Testimony, the Table for Showbread, the Gold Lampstand, the Incense Altar, and the Anointing Oil

> 'The cherubim spread out their wings above, and covered the mercy seat with their wings. They faced one another; the faces of the cherubim were toward the mercy seat.' Exod. 37:9.

Chapter 38
They Make the Altar for Burnt Offerings, the Bronze Laver, the Tabernacle Court, and the Rest of the Materials for the Tabernacle

> 'He made the altar of burnt offering of acacia wood; five cubits was its length and five cubits its width – it was square – and its height was three cubits.' Exod. 38:1.

Chapter 39
They Make the Garments for the Priests and the High Priest in Order for the Levites to Lead God's People into His Covenant Presence, Completing the Work

> 'Then they made the plate of the holy crown of pure gold, and wrote on it an inscription like the engraving of a signet: HOLINESS TO THE LORD. And they tied it to a blue cord, to fasten it above the turban, as the LORD had commanded Moses.' Exod. 39:30-31.

Chapter 40
The People Erect the Tabernacle and God Fills it with His Covenant Presence, Directing the People Through the Wilderness at His Direction

> 'Then the cloud covered the tabernacle of meeting, and the glory of the LORD filled the tabernacle. And Moses was not able to enter the tabernacle of meeting, because the cloud rested above it, and the glory of the LORD filled the tabernacle.' Exod. 40:34-35.

Leviticus

God in covenant provides a way to return to Him through the priesthood and sacrifices.

Chapter **1**

The Lord Consecrates the Priests and the People for Tabernacle Worship through the Burnt Offering

'It is a burnt sacrifice, an offering made by fire, a sweet aroma to the LORD.' Lev. 1:17b.

Chapter **2**

The Grain Offering

'When anyone offers a grain offering to the LORD, his offering shall be of fine flour. And he shall pour oil on it, and put frankincense on it.' Lev. 2:1.

Chapter **3**

The Peace Offering

'This shall be a perpetual statute throughout your generations in all your dwellings: you shall eat neither fat nor blood.' Lev. 3:17.

Chapter **4**

The Sin Offering

'Now if the whole congregation of Israel sins unintentionally, and the thing is hidden from the eyes of the assembly, and they have done something against any of the commandments of the LORD in anything which should not be done, and are guilty; when the sin which they have committed becomes known, then the assembly shall offer a young bull for the sin, and bring it before the tabernacle of meeting.' Lev. 4:13-14.

Chapter 5
The Sin Offering Continued, and the Guilt Offering Introduced

'If a person sins, and commits any of these things which are forbidden to be done by the commandments of the LORD, though he does not know it, yet he is guilty and shall bear his iniquity.' Lev. 5:17.

Chapter 6
The Priests and the Offerings

'A fire shall always be burning on the altar; it shall never go out.' Lev. 6:13.

Chapter 7
The Laws of the Trespass and Peace Offerings

'Moreover you shall not eat any blood in any of your dwellings, whether of bird or beast. Whoever eats any blood, that person shall be cut off from his people.' Lev. 7:26-27.

Chapter 8
Moses Consecrates Aaron and his Sons in Order to Lead Tabernacle Worship

'So Aaron and his sons did all the things that the LORD had commanded by the hand of Moses.' Lev. 8:36.

Chapter 9
The Consecrated Priests Offer the First Sacrifices and God Shows His Approval by Consuming the Offerings with Fire from Heaven

'Then Aaron lifted his hand toward the people, blessed them, and came down from offering the sin offering, the burnt offering, and peace offerings. And Moses and Aaron went into the tabernacle of meeting, and came out and blessed the people. Then the glory of the LORD appeared to all the people, and fire came out from before the LORD and consumed the burnt offering and the fat on the altar. When all the people saw it, they shouted and fell on their faces.' Lev. 9:22-24.

Chapter 10
Fire From Heaven Now Consumes Nadab and Abihu When they Violate the Lord's Holiness, and Moses Reiterates the Need for Holiness Among the Priests

'Then Nadab and Abihu, the sons of Aaron, each took his censer and put fire in it, put incense on it, and offered profane fire before the LORD, which He had not commanded them. So fire went out from the LORD and devoured them, and they died before the LORD. And Moses said to Aaron, "This is what the LORD spoke, saying: By those who come near Me I must be regarded as holy; and before all the people I must be glorified." So Aaron held his peace.' Lev. 10:1-3.

Chapter 11
Distinguishing Clean and Unclean Animals Illustrates the Separation of Israel from the Nations by Covenant

'For I am the LORD who brings you up out of the land of Egypt, to be your God. You shall therefore be holy, for I am holy.' Lev. 11:45.

Chapter 12
Uncleanness Following Childbirth Illustrating Mankind's Uncleanness Through Sin

'And if she is not able to bring a lamb, then she may bring two turtledoves or two young pigeons – one as a burnt offering and the other as a sin offering. So the priest shall make atonement for her, and she will be clean.' Lev. 12:8.

Chapter 13
Procedures for the Separation of Lepers from the Camp, Illustrating the Need for Holiness Among the People

'Now the leper on whom the sore is, his clothes shall be torn and his head bare; and he shall cover his mustache, and cry, "Unclean! Unclean!" He shall be unclean. All the days he has the sore he shall be unclean. He is unclean, and he shall dwell alone; his dwelling shall be outside the camp.' Lev. 13: 45-46.

Chapter 14
Rules for the Cleansing of Lepers and of Dealing with Leprous Houses

'Then the priest shall offer the sin offering, and make atonement for him who is to be cleansed from his uncleanness. Afterward he shall kill the burnt offering. And the priest shall offer the burnt offering and the grain offering on the altar. So the priest shall make atonement for him, and he shall be clean.' Lev. 14:19-20.

Chapter 15

Laws Concerning Sexual Purity and Uncleanness

> 'Thus you shall separate the children of Israel from their uncleanness, lest they die in their uncleanness when they defile My tabernacle that is among them.' Lev. 15:31.

Chapter 16

The Day of Atonement as the High Point of Priestly Service, Tabernacle Worship, and Consecration

> 'Now the LORD spoke to Moses after the death of the two sons of Aaron, when they offered profane fire before the LORD, and died; and the LORD said to Moses: "Tell Aaron your brother not to come at just any time into the Holy Place inside the veil, before the mercy seat which is on the ark, lest he die; for I will appear in the cloud above the mercy seat."' Lev. 16:1-2.

Chapter 17

The Priests Must Sanctify All Things with Blood Because the Life is in the Blood, and People Must Bring Blood to the Door of the Tabernacle

> 'Whatever man of the children of Israel, or of the strangers who dwell among you, who hunts and catches any animal or bird that may be eaten, he shall pour out its blood and cover it with dust; for it is the life of all flesh. Its blood sustains its life. Therefore I said to the children of Israel, "You shall not eat the blood of any flesh, for the life of all flesh is its blood. Whoever eats it shall be cut off."' Lev. 17:13-14.

Chapter 18

Laws of Sexual Purity and Marriage, Illustrating General Principles of Living by God's Law in Holiness

> 'You shall therefore keep My statutes and My judgments, which if a man does, he shall live by them: I am the LORD.' Lev. 18:5.

Chapter 19

Various Moral and Ceremonial Laws Illustrating the Holiness of the People Before the Lord

> 'And the LORD spoke to Moses, saying, "Speak to all the congregation of the children of Israel, and say to them: You

shall be holy, for I the LORD your God am holy. Every one of you shall revere his mother and his father, and keep My Sabbaths: I am the LORD your God.'" Lev. 19:1-3.

Chapter 20
The Lord Imposes Penalties for Breaking the Law and Rejecting the Covenant, Reinforcing the Need for Covenant Holiness

'And you shall keep My statutes, and perform them: I am the LORD who sanctifies you … And you shall be holy to Me, for I the LORD am holy, and have separated you from the peoples, that you should be Mine.' Lev. 20:8, 26.

Chapter 21
Special Regulations Regarding the Holiness of the Priests in Order to Maintain the Covenant Holiness of the People

'Therefore you shall consecrate him, for he offers the bread of your God. He shall be holy to you, for I the LORD, who sanctify you, am holy.' Lev. 21:8.

Chapter 22
The Need for the Priests to Lead in Worship by Maintaining Ceremonial Holiness

'You shall not profane My holy name, but I will be hallowed among the children of Israel. I am the LORD who sanctifies you, who brought you out of the land of Egypt, to be your God: I am the LORD.' Lev. 22:32-33.

Chapter 23
The Feasts of the Lord Mark the High Point of Covenant Worship, the Sabbath Serving as their Pattern

'Six days shall work be done, but the seventh day is a Sabbath of solemn rest, a holy convocation. You shall do no work on it; it is the Sabbath of the LORD in all your dwellings.' Lev. 23:3.

Chapter 24
The Priests Must Maintain Worship by Caring for the Lamps and the Showbread, and Those Who Blaspheme God's Holy Name Shall Die

'Whoever kills any man shall surely be put to death. Whoever kills an animal shall make it good, animal for animal. If a man causes disfigurement of his neighbor, as he has done, so shall it be done to him – fracture for fracture, eye for eye, tooth for tooth; as he has caused disfigurement of a man, so shall it be done to him. And whoever kills an animal shall restore it; but whoever kills a man shall be put to death. You shall have the same law for the stranger and for one from your own country; for I am the LORD your God.' Lev. 24:19-21.

Chapter 25
The Seventh Year Sabbath, the Jubilee Sabbath, Redemption, and Caring for the Poor

'Therefore you shall not oppress one another, but you shall fear your God; for I am the LORD your God … For the children of Israel are servants to Me; they are My servants whom I brought out of the land of Egypt: I am the LORD your God.' Lev. 25:17, 55.

Chapter 26
The Lord Summarizes Covenant Holiness and Consecration by Summarizing Covenant Blessings and Curses

'But if they confess their iniquity and the iniquity of their fathers, with their unfaithfulness in which they were unfaithful to Me, and that they also have walked contrary to Me, and that I also have walked contrary to them and have brought them into the land of their enemies; if their uncircumcised hearts are humbled, and they accept their guilt – then I will remember My covenant with Jacob, and My covenant with Isaac and My covenant with Abraham I will remember; I will remember the land.' Lev. 26:40-42.

Chapter 27
Leviticus Concludes with an Appendix on Dedicating People, Things, and Objects as Holy to the Lord

'These are the commandments which the LORD commanded Moses for the children of Israel on Mount Sinai.' Lev. 27:34.

Numbers

Applying the terms of the covenant, God chastens His rebellious people, and restores them, preparing them to enter the Promised Land

Chapter 1

The Lord Prepares the People to Travel in the Wilderness With His Covenant Presence in the Midst of Them

> '"The children of Israel shall pitch their tents, everyone by his own camp, everyone by his own standard, according to their armies; but the Levites shall camp around the tabernacle of the Testimony, that there may be no wrath on the congregation of the children of Israel; and the Levites shall keep charge of the tabernacle of the Testimony." Thus the children of Israel did; according to all that the LORD commanded Moses, so they did.' Num. 1:52-54.

Chapter 2

The Lord Orders the Camp According to the Tribes Around His Covenant Presence

> 'Thus the children of Israel did according to all that the LORD commanded Moses; so they camped by their standards and so they broke camp, each one by his family.' Num. 2:34.

Chapter 3

The Lord Establishes the High Priests and the Levites to Mediate Between God and the People, Taking the Levites in Place of the Firstborn of the People

> 'Then the LORD spoke to Moses, saying, "Now behold, I Myself have taken the Levites from among the children of Israel instead of every firstborn who opens the womb among

the children of Israel. Therefore the Levites shall be Mine, because all the firstborn are Mine. On the day that I struck all the firstborn in the land of Egypt, I sanctified to Myself all the firstborn in Israel, both man and beast. They shall be Mine: I am the LORD."' Num. 3:11-13.

Chapter 4
The Kohathites, Gershonites, and Merarites Prepare the Tabernacle to Move When the People Break Camp, Guarding the Holiness of the Lord

'And when Aaron and his sons have finished covering the sanctuary and all the furnishings of the sanctuary, when the camp is set to go, then the sons of Kohath shall come to carry them; but they shall not touch any holy thing lest they die. These are the things in the tabernacle of meeting which the sons of Kohath are to carry.' Num. 4:15.

Chapter 5
The Lord Maintains the Holiness of the Camp by Separating Unclean Persons, Making Restitution, and Preserving the Sanctity of Marriage

'Every offering of all the holy things of the children of Israel, which they bring to the priest, shall be his. And every man's holy things shall be his; whatever any man gives the priest shall be his.' Num. 5:9-10.

Chapter 6
The Nazarites Dedicate Themselves to the Lord, and the Lord Dedicates His People to Himself By Setting His Name Upon Them and Blessing Them Through the Priests

'And the LORD spoke to Moses, saying: "Speak to Aaron and his sons, saying, This is the way you shall bless the children of Israel. Say to them: The LORD bless you and keep you; the LORD make His face shine upon you, and be gracious to you; the LORD lift His countenance upon you, and give you peace. So they shall put My name on the children of Israel, and I will bless them."' Num. 6:22-27.

Chapter 7
The Leaders of the Twelve Tribes Present Offerings for Twelve Days for Service in the Consecrated Tabernacle

'Now when Moses went into the tabernacle of meeting to speak with Him, he heard the voice of One speaking to him from above the mercy seat that was on the ark of the Testimony, from between the two cherubim; thus He spoke to him.' Num. 7:89.

Chapter 8

The Lord Arranges the Lamps and Dedicates the Levites to His Service

'So you shall bring the Levites before the LORD, and the children of Israel shall lay their hands on the Levites; and Aaron shall offer the Levites before the LORD like a wave offering from the children of Israel, that they may perform the work of the LORD. Then the Levites shall lay their hands on the heads of the young bulls, and you shall offer one as a sin offering and the other as a burnt offering to the LORD, to make atonement for the Levites.' Num. 8:10-12.

Chapter 9

Israel Observes the First Annual Passover, Providing Opportunity for Those Who Were not Consecrated in Time to Participate in the Second Month, and the Pillar of Cloud of Fire Goes Up to Lead Them

'So it was, when the cloud remained only from evening until morning: when the cloud was taken up in the morning, then they would journal; whether by day or by night, whenever the cloud was taken up they would journey. Whether it was two days, a month, of a year that the cloud remained above the tabernacle, the children of Israel would remain encamped and not journey; but when it was taken up, they would journey. At the command of the LORD they remained encamped, and at the command of the LORD they journeyed; they kept the charge of the LORD, at the command of the LORD by the hand of Moses.' Num. 9:21-23.

Chapter 10

The Lord Instructs the People to Construct Trumpets by Which They Go to War and Feast Before the Lord, the Congregation Breaks Camp for the First Time, and God Proclaims His Presence With Them

'So it was, whenever the ark set out, that Moses said: "Rise up, O LORD! Let your enemies be scattered, and let those who hate You flee before You." And when it rested, he said: "Return, O LORD, to the many thousands of Israel."' Num. 10:35-36.

Chapter 11

The Mixed Multitude Leads Israel to Complain that they Have No Food, the Lord Places His Spirit on the Seventy Elders to Help Moses, and the Lord Sends Quail

> 'Now when the people complained, it displeased the LORD; for the LORD heard it, and His anger was aroused. So the fire of the LORD burned among them, and consumed some in the outskirts of the camp.' Num. 11:1.

Chapter 12

Miriam and Aaron Complain Against Moses, the Lord Shows Moses' Special Place as Prophet, and Moses Intercedes for Miriam's Leprosy

> 'Not so with My servant Moses; He is faithful in all My house. I speak with him face to face, even plainly, and not in dark sayings; and he sees the form of the LORD. Why then were you not afraid to speak against My servant Moses?' Num. 12:7-8.

Chapter 13

The People Send the Twelve Spies into the Land, and Only Joshua and Caleb Trust the Lord

> 'Then Caleb quieted the people before Moses, and said, "Let us go up at once and take possession, for we are able to overcome it."' Num. 13:30.

Chapter 14

Israel Refuses to Enter the Land, Moses Intercedes for them, and the Lord Promises to Secure His Own Glory Even Though the People Would Wander in the Wilderness Forty Years and Fail to Enter the Land, Blessing Joshua and Caleb

> 'And now, I pray, let the power of my Lord be great, just as You have spoken, saying, "The LORD is longsuffering and abundant in mercy, forgiving iniquity and transgression; but He by no means clears the guilty, visiting the iniquity of the fathers on the children to the third and fourth generation.' Pardon the iniquity of this people, I pray, according to the

greatness of Your mercy, just as You have forgiven this people, from Egypt even until now."' Num. 14:17-19.

CHAPTER 15
Free Will Offerings, Offerings for Unintentional Sins, and Presumptuous Sins, with the Sabbath Breaker as a Pattern of Dealing with Presumptuous Sins

'You shall have one law for him who sins unintentionally, for him who is native-born among the children of Israel and for the stranger who dwells among them.' Num. 15:29.

CHAPTER 16
Korah, Dathan, and Abiram Rebel Against Moses and Aaron and the Lord Consumes them with Fire as they Offer Incense to Him, the People Complaining Against Moses Again

'And Moses said: "By this you shall know that the LORD has sent me to do all these works, for I have not done them of my own will. If these men die naturally like all men, or if they are visited by the common fate of all men, then the LORD has not sent me. But if the LORD creates a new thing, and the earth opens its mouth and swallows them up with all that belongs to them, and they go down alive into the pit, then you will understand that these men have rejected the LORD"' Num. 16:28-30.

CHAPTER 17
Aaron's Rod Blossoms, Showing that he was the Lord's High Priest

'And the LORD said to Moses, "Bring Aaron's rod back before the Testimony, to be kept as a sign against the rebels, that you may put their complaints away from Me, lest they die."' Num. 17:10.

CHAPTER 18
The Priests and Levites Shall Bear the Iniquity of the People, the People Shall Support them by Tithes, and the Levites Shall Pay Tithes to the Lord

'All the heave offerings of the holy things, which the children of Israel offer to the LORD, I have given to you and your sons and daughters with you as an ordinance forever; it is a covenant of salt forever before the LORD with you and your descendants with you.' Num. 18:19.

Chapter 19
The Lord Sets Apart the Ashes of a Red Heifer to Sanctify All Things

'Whatever the unclean person touches shall be unclean; and the person who touches it shall be unclean until evening.' Num. 19:22.

Chapter 20
Miriam Dies, the People Have no Water, Moses Disbelieves the Lord, Edom Refuses Israel Passage, and Aaron Dies

'Then the LORD spoke to Moses and Aaron, "Because you did not believe Me, to hallow Me in the eyes of the children of Israel, therefore you shall not bring this assembly into the land which I have given them."' Num. 20:12.

Chapter 21
The Lord Delivers Israel from the Canaanites, the Lord Sends Fiery Serpents to Curse the Complaining Israelites, the Lord Defeats Sihon and Og

'Then the LORD said to Moses, "Make a fiery serpent, and set it on a pole; and it shall be that everyone who is bitten, when he looks at it, shall live." So Moses made a bronze serpent, and put it on a pole; and so it was, if a serpent had bitten anyone, when he looked at the bronze serpent, he lived.' Num. 21:8-9.

Chapter 22
Balak Sends for Balaam to Curse Israel, and Balaam's Donkey Speaks to Warn the Prophet to Speak God's Word Only

'And Balaam said to Balak, "Look, I have come to you! Now, have I any power at all to say anything? The word that God puts in my mouth, that I must speak."' Num. 22:38.

Chapter 23
Balaam's First and Second Prophecies Pronounce Greater Blessings on Israel the Less he Sees of their Camp, Paving the Way for the Third Prophecy

'God is not a man, that He should lie, nor a son of man, that He should repent. Has He said, and will He not do? Or has He spoken, and will He not make it good? Behold, I have received a command to bless; He has blessed, and I cannot reverse it. He has not observed iniquity in Jacob, nor has He seen wickedness in Israel. The LORD his God is with him, and the shout of a King is among them.' Num. 23:19-21.

Chapter 24

Balaam Filled With the Spirit of God Pronounces the Abrahamic Blessings on Israel and Proclaims Israel's Dominion Over the Nations Through a Coming Ruler

'I see Him, but not now; I behold Him, but not near; a Star shall come out of Jacob; a Scepter shall arise out of Israel, and batter the brow of Moab, and destroy all the sons of tumult.' Num. 24:17.

Chapter 25

Israel Commits Harlotry with Moab, Phinehas Turns Back God's Wrath, and the Lord Pronounces a Curse on the Midianites

'Therefore say, "Behold, I give to him My covenant of peace; and it shall be to him and to his descendants after him a covenant of an everlasting priesthood, because he was zealous for his God, and made atonement for the children of Israel."' Num. 25:12-13.

Chapter 26

The Lord Takes a Second Census of Israel After the Wilderness Wanderings and their Numbers are Virtually the Same as When they Started

'For the LORD had said of them, "They shall surely die in the wilderness." So there was not left a man of them, except Caleb the son of Jephunneh and Joshua the son of Nun.' Num. 26:65.

Chapter 27

The Daughters of Zelophehad Secure their Inheritance in the Land with the Lord's Blessings and in Faithfulness to His Covenant, and Joshua will become the Next Spirit-Filled Leader in Place of Moses

'So Moses did as the LORD commanded him. He took Joshua and set him before Eleazar the priest and before all the congregation. And he laid hands on him and inaugurated him, just as the LORD had commanded by the hand of Moses.' Num. 27:22-23.

Chapter **28**

The Lord Reinstates the Daily, Sabbath, and Monthly Offerings, as Well as the Passover and the Feast of Weeks

'On the first day you shall have a holy convocation. You shall do no customary work ... And on the seventh day you shall have a holy convocation. You shall do no customary work.' Num. 28:18, 25.

Chapter **29**

The Feast of Trumpets, the Day of Atonement, and the Feast of Tabernacles

'And in the seventh month, on the first day of the month, you shall have a holy convocation. You shall do no customary work. For you it is a day of blowing the trumpets.' Num. 29:1.

Chapter **30**

Regulations for Vows of Men and Women, with a Focus on Husbands and Fathers, With Possible Respect to the Daughters of Zelophehad

'These are the statutes which the LORD commanded Moses, between a man and his wife, and between a father and his daughter in her youth in her father's house.' Num. 30:16.

Chapter **31**

The Lord Commands Israel to Take Vengeance on the Midianites for Leading them into Idolatry and Immorality, Dividing the Spoil

'Therefore we have brought an offering for the LORD, what every man found of ornaments of gold: armlets and bracelets and signet rings and earrings and necklaces, to make atonement for ourselves before the LORD.' Num. 31:50.

Chapter **32**

Reuben, Gad, and Half of Manasseh Seek to Settle East of the Jordan, Moses Warns them Against Apostasy, and they Resolve to Remain Faithful to the Lord

'But if you do not do so, then take note, you have sinned against the LORD; and be sure your sin will find you out.' Num. 32:23.

Chapter 33

The Lord Reminds Israel of the Redemption from Egypt and their Wilderness Wanderings in Order to Prepare them to Enter the Land

'But if you do not drive out the inhabitants of the land from before you, then it shall be that those whom you let remain shall be irritants in your eyes and thorns in your sides, and they shall harass you in the land where you dwell. Moreover it shall be that I will do to you as I thought to do to them.' Num. 33:55-56.

Chapter 34

The Lord Appoints the Borders of the Land and a New Generation of Leaders in Israel

'These are the ones the LORD commanded to divide the inheritance among the children of Israel in the land of Canaan.' Num. 34:29.

Chapter 35

The Lord Appoints Cities for the Levites and Cities of Refuge, Promoting His Covenant Presence Among them

'Therefore do not defile the land which you inhabit, in the midst of which I dwell; for I the LORD dwell among the children of Israel.' Num. 35:34.

Chapter 36

The Lord Gives Instructions for Female Heirs in the Land, With Special Reference to the Daughters of Zelophehad

'These are the commandments and the judgments which the LORD commanded the children of Israel by the hand of Moses in the plains of Moab by the Jordan, across from Jericho.' Num. 36:13.

Deuteronomy

God gives covenant promises and threats, preparing generations to come to remain in covenant with Him

Chapter **1**

Moses Reviews God's Faithfulness to His Covenant with Abraham, and Israel's Refusal to Enter the Land Due to their Unbelief

> 'Yet, for all that, you did not believe the LORD your God.' Deut. 1:32.

Chapter **2**

Moses Reminds them of God's Faithfulness to them even in the Wilderness, Promising to Put the Dread of the New Generation in the Hearts of their Enemies, Encouraging them with His Victory Over Sihon King of Heshbon

> 'For the LORD your God has blessed you in all the work of your hand. He knows your trudging through this great wilderness. These forty years the LORD your God has been with you; you have lacked nothing.' Deut. 2:7.

Chapter **3**

The Lord Further Encourages them with His Defeat of Og king of Bashan, the Division of the Land East of the Jordan, and His Refusal to Let Moses Enter the Land

> 'You must not fear them, for the LORD your God Himself fights for you.' Deut. 3:22.

Chapter **4**

Israel's Unique Witness to God's Covenant Nearness to them, Warnings Against Making Image of the True God, and Warnings Against Covenant Breaking and Encouragements to Return

'Therefore know this day, and consider it in your heart, that the LORD Himself is God in heaven above and on the earth beneath; there is no other. You shall therefore keep His statutes and His commandments which I command today, that it may go well with you and with your children after you, and that you may prolong your days in the land which the LORD your God is giving you for all time.' Deut. 4:39-40.

Chapter 5

The Lord Renews the Covenant by Repeating the Ten Commandments, the People Need a Mediator Between them and God, and the Lord Urges them to Renewed Obedience

'Therefore you shall be careful to do as the LORD your God has commanded you; you shall not turn aside to the right hand or to the left.' Deut. 5:32.

Chapter 6

The Lord Exhorts Israel to Humility and Love to God, Passing Down the Knowledge of God to Coming Generations

'Hear, O Israel: the LORD our God, the LORD is one! You shall love the LORD your God with all your heart, with all your soul, and with all your strength.' Deut. 6:4.

Chapter 7

God Warns Israel Against Turning to Idolatry by Making Alliances with the Nations in the Land, Promising to Bless their Obedience and Bring them into the Land

'The LORD did not set His love on you nor choose you because you were more in number than any other people, for you were the least of all peoples; but because the LORD loves you, and because He would keep the oath which He swore to your fathers, the Lord has brought you out with a mighty hand, and redeemed you from the house of bondage, from the hand of Pharaoh king of Egypt.' Deut. 7:7-8.

Chapter 8

The Lord Reminds them that He Led them Through the Wilderness to Test their Faith in His Providence and their Obedience to His Commands, Warning them Against Forgetting Him in their Prosperity

'So He humbled you, allowed you to hunger, and fed you with manna which you did not know nor did your fathers know, that He might make you know that man shall not live by bread alone, but man lives by every word that proceeds from the mouth of the LORD.' Deut. 8:3.

Chapter 9

The Lord Will not Bring Israel into the Land for their Righteousness, but Because of His Covenant Faithfulness, and Moses Recounts the Renewal of the Abrahamic Covenant with them After their Rebellion with the Golden Calf

'Do you not think in your heart, after the LORD your God has cast them out before you saying, "Because of my righteousness the LORD has brought me in to possess this land;" but it is because of the wickedness of these nations that the LORD is driving them out before you. It is not because of your righteousness or the uprightness of your heart that you go in to possess their land, but because of the wickedness of these nations that the LORD your God drives them out from before you, and that He may fulfill the word which the LORD swore to your fathers, to Abraham, Isaac, and Jacob. Therefore understand that the LORD your God is not giving you this good land to possess because of your righteousness, for you are a stiff-necked people.' Deut. 9:4-6.

Chapter 10

Moses Makes New Tablets of the Covenant and Places them in the Ark of the Covenant, Summarizing Love for the Lord Again

'And now, Israel, what does the LORD your God require of you, but to fear the LORD your God, to walk in all His ways and to love Him, to serve the LORD your God with all your heart and with all your soul, and to keep the commandments of the LORD and His statutes which I command you today for your good?' Deut. 10:12-13.

Chapter 11

The Lord Presses the People to Faith and Obedience, Reminding them both of His Faithfulness and their Rebellion, Promising Victory Over the Enemies, and Summarizing Covenant Blessings and Curses

'Therefore you shall lay up these words of mine in your heart and in your soul, and bind them as a sign on your hand, and they shall be as frontlets between your eyes. You shall teach them to your children, speaking of them when you sit in your house, when you walk by the way, when you lie down, and when you rise up. And you shall write them on the doorposts of your house and on your gates, that your days and the days of your children may be multiplied in the land of which the LORD swore to your fathers to give them, like the days of the heavens above the earth.' Deut. 11:18-21.

Chapter **12**

The Lord Prescribes the Place for Worship, and Urges His People not to Worship Him as the Nations Worship their gods, but According to His Word Only

'When the LORD your God cuts off from before you the nations which you go to dispossess, and you displace them and dwell in their land, take heed to yourself that you are not ensnared to follow them, after they are destroyed from before you, and that you do not inquire after their gods, saying, "How did these nations serve their gods? I will also do likewise." You shall not worship the LORD your God in that way; for every abomination to the LORD which He hates they have done to their gods; for they burn even their sons and daughters in the fire to their gods. Whatever I command you, be careful to observe it; you shall not add to it nor take away from it.' Deut. 12:29-32.

Chapter **13**

The Lord Warns them Against False Prophets Who do Signs and Wonders, yet Divert them from the Word of the Lord

'You shall not listen to the words of that prophet or that dreamer of dreams, for the LORD your God is testing you to know whether you love the LORD your God with all your heart and with all your soul.' Deut. 13:3.

Chapter **14**

The People Must be Holy, Avoid Unclean Foods, and Pay the Tithe

'For you are a holy people to the LORD your God, and the LORD has chosen you to be a people for Himself, a special treasure above all the peoples who are on the face of the earth.' Deut. 14:2.

CHAPTER **15**
Debts Should be Cancelled Every Seven Years, the People Must Care for the Poor and Bondservants, and Dedicate Firstborn Animals to the Lord

> 'Only you shall not eat its blood; you shall pour it out on the ground like water.' Deut. 15:23.

CHAPTER **16**
The Lord Reviews the Passover, the Feast of Weeks, and the Feast of Tabernacles in Order to Maintain Covenant Fellowship with Himself, and Establishes Just Judgment

> 'Every man shall give as he is able, according to the blessing of the LORD your God which He has given you.' Deut. 16:17.

CHAPTER **17**
Principles of Justice Continued in Crimes Deserving Death, and the Lord Gives Provisions for Future Kings of Israel

> 'When you come to the land which the LORD your God is giving you, and possess in it and dwell in it, and say, "I will set a king over me like all the nations that are around me," you shall surely set a king over you whom the LORD your God chooses; one from among your brethren you shall set as king over you; you may not set a foreigner over you, who is not your brother.' Deut. 17:14-15.

CHAPTER **18**
The Lord Provides for the Levites Who Teach the Law and the Knowledge of God, He Prohibits the Customs of the Nations, and the Lord Promises a Line of Prophets Leading to a Great Prophet

> 'The LORD your God will raise up for you a Prophet like me from your midst, from your brethren. Him you shall hear, according to all you desired of the LORD your God in Horeb in the day of the assembly, saying, "Let me not hear again the voice of the LORD my God, nor let me see this great fire anymore, lest I die."' Deut. 18:15-16.

CHAPTER **19**
The People Must Appoint Cities of Refuge, Respect Property Boundaries, and Have Just Witnesses

> 'One witness shall not rise against a man concerning any iniquity or any sin that he commits; by the mouth of two or three witnesses the matter shall be established.' Deut. 19:15.

Chapter 20
The Lord Encourages the People to Fight for the Land with Assurance of His Covenant Presence Among them

> 'For the LORD your God is He who goes with you, to fight for you against your enemies, to save you.' Deut. 20:4.

Chapter 21
Laws Concerning Unsolved Murders, Female Captives, the Inheritance Rights of Firstborn, Rebellious Sons, and the Curse of Hanging Someone on a Tree

> 'If a man has committed a sin deserving of death, and he is put to death, and you hang him on a tree, his body shall not remain overnight on the tree, but you shall surely bury him that day, so that you do not defile the land which the LORD your God is giving you as an inheritance; for he who is hanged is accursed of God.' Deut. 21:22-23.

Chapter 22
Miscellaneous Laws and Laws Governing Sexuality

> 'A woman shall not wear anything that pertains to a man, nor shall a man put on a woman's garment, for all who do so are an abomination to the LORD your God.' Deut. 22:5.

Chapter 23
Ammonites, Moabites, and Edomites Excluded from the Congregation to the Tenth and Third Generations, a Place Outside the Camp for those Unclean, and Maintaining Justice Between Neighbors

> 'When you make a vow to the LORD your God, you shall not delay to pay it; for the LORD your God will surely require it of you, and it would be sin to you. But if you abstain from vowing, it shall not be sin to you. That which has gone from your lips you shall keep and perform, for you voluntarily vowed to the LORD your God what you have promised with your mouth.' Deut. 23:21-23.

Chapter 24
Laws Governing Divorce, and Justice Towards Others in Light of the Lord's Covenant Kindness to His People

'Fathers shall not be put to death for their children, nor shall children be put to death for their fathers; a person shall be put to death for his own sin.' Deut. 24:16.

CHAPTER 25

Marriage Duties for the Wife of a Dead Brother, Various Laws, and the Command to Destroy the Amalekites

'You shall not muzzle an ox while it treads out the grain.' Deut. 25:4.

CHAPTER 26

Firstfruits and Tithes, and Remembering God's Call to be a Special People in Covenant with Himself

'Also today the LORD has proclaimed you to be His special people, just as He promised you, that you should keep all His commandments, and He will set you high above all nations which He has made, in praise, in name, and in honor, and that you may be a holy people to the LORD your God, just as He has spoken.' Deut. 26:18-19.

CHAPTER 27

The Covenant Blessings and Curses Summarized on Mount Gerizim and Mount Ebal

'Then Moses and the priests, the Levites, spoke to all Israel, saying, "Take heed and listen, O Israel: This day you have become the people of the LORD your God. Therefore you shall obey the voice of the LORD your God, and observe His commandments and His statutes which I command you today."' Deut. 27:9-10.

CHAPTER 28

The Lord Summarizes Covenant Blessings and Covenant Curses

'Because you did not serve the LORD your God with joy and gladness of heart, for the abundance of everything, therefore you shall serve your enemies, whom the LORD will send against you, in hunger, in thirst, in nakedness, and in need of everything; and He will put a yoke of iron on your neck until He has destroyed you.' Deut. 28:47-48.

CHAPTER 29

The Lord Reviews His Covenant Faithfulness in Leading Them Through the Wilderness, Fulfilling His Promises to Abraham,

Isaac, and Jacob, Warning Against Apostasy, and Summarizing Their Duty to Hold to God's Law

'The secret things belong to the LORD our God, but those things which are revealed belong to us and to our children forever, that we may do all the words of this law.' Deut. 29:29.

Chapter **30**

The Lord Promises to Bring them Back from Captivity, Circumcising their Hearts and those of their Descendants, and Reminding them that the Law is in their Reach

'And the LORD your God will circumcise your heart and the heart of your descendants, to love the LORD your God with all your heart and with all your soul, that you may live.' Deut. 30:6.

Chapter **31**

Moses Charges Joshua to Trust the Lord as he Leads the People into the Land, to Read the Law to the People at the Feast of Tabernacles Every Seven Years, and Predicts that the People Will Rebel Against the Covenant

'Be strong and of good courage, do not fear nor be afraid of them; for the LORD your God, He is the One who goes with you. He will not leave you nor forsake you.' Deut. 31:6.

Chapter **32**

The Song of Moses Stands as a Testimony Against Israel as Well as an Encouragement to Future Faith and Repentance

'They have corrupted themselves; they are not His children, because of their blemish: a perverse and crooked generation. Do you thus deal with the LORD, O foolish and unwise people? Is He not your Father, who bought you? Has He not made you and established you? … Now see that I, even I, am He, and there is no God besides Me; I kill and I make alive; I wound and I heal; nor is there any who can deliver from My hand.' Deut. 32:5-6, 39.

Chapter **33**

Moses Pronounces Final Blessings on the Twelve Tribes as he Prepares for Death

'There is no one like the God of Jeshurun, who rides the heavens to help you, and in His excellency on the clouds. The eternal God is your refuge, and underneath are the everlasting arms; He will thrust out the enemy from before you, and will say, "Destroy!"' Deut. 33:26-27.

Chapter 34

Moses Dies and No Prophet Like him Had Yet Arisen in Israel

'But since then there has not arisen a prophet like Moses, whom the LORD knew face to face, in all the signs and wonders which the LORD sent him to do in the land of Egypt, before Pharaoh, before all his servants, and in all his land, and by all that mighty power and all the great terror which Moses performed in the sight of all Israel.' Deut. 34:10-12.

Joshua

God's covenant presence goes with His people, leading them into the Promised Land

Chapter **1**

The Lord Encourages Joshua with Faith in His Covenant Promises, and the People Agree to Follow Joshua

> 'Just as we heeded Moses in all things, so we will heed you. Only the LORD your God be with you as He was with Moses. Whoever rebels against your command and does not heed your words, in all that you command him, shall be put to death. Only be strong and of good courage.' Josh. 1:17 18.

Chapter **2**

The Lord Puts the Fear of Israel in the Nations, and Rahab Delivers the Spies

> 'And as soon as we heard these things, our hearts melted; neither did there remain any more courage in anyone because of you, for the LORD your God, He is God in heaven above and on earth beneath.' Josh. 2:11.

Chapter **3**

The Lord Parts the Jordan Before Joshua, Showing His Presence with Joshua and Approval of His Call

> 'And the LORD said to Joshua, "This day I will begin to exalt you in the sight of all Israel, that they may know that, as I was with Moses, so I will be with you."' Josh. 3:7.

Chapter **4**

Israel Places Memorial Stones in the Midst of the Parted Jordan in Order to Remember the Works of the Lord

> 'On that day the LORD exalted Joshua in the sight of all Israel; and they feared him, as they had feared Moses, all the days of his life ... that all the peoples of the earth may know the hand of the LORD, that it is mighty, that you may fear the LORD your God forever.' Josh. 4:14, 24.

Chapter 5

The Lord Renews Covenant with Israel by Circumcising the New Generation, Sending the Commander of the Armies of the Lord Before them and Leading them, Just as the Angel of the Lord Appeared to Moses and Led him

> 'And it came to pass, when Joshua was by Jericho, that he lifted his eyes and looked, and behold, a Man stood opposite him with His sword drawn in His hand. And Joshua went to Him and said to Him, "Are You for us or for our adversaries?" So He said to him, "No, but as Commander of the army of the LORD I have now come." And Joshua fell on his face to the earth and worshiped, and said to Him, "What does my Lord say to His servant?" Then the Commander of the LORD's army said to Joshua, "Take your sandal off your foot, for the place where you stand is holy." And Joshua did so.' Josh. 5:13-15.

Chapter 6

The Lord Brings Israel Victory Against Jericho by Making the Walls Fall

> 'Then Joshua charged them at that time, saying, "Cursed be the man before the LORD who rises up and builds this city Jericho; he shall lay its foundation with his firstborn, and with his youngest he shall set up its gates." So the LORD was with Joshua, and his fame spread throughout all the country.' Josh. 6:26-27.

Chapter 7

Israel Suffers Defeat at Ai, Achan's Sin in Taking Spoils from Jericho is Revealed, and the Lord Humbles Israel

> 'Then they raised over him a great heap of stones, still there to this day. So the LORD turned from the fierceness of His anger. Therefore the name of that place has been called the Valley of Achor to this day.' Josh. 7:26.

Chapter 8
The Lord Defeats Ai and Israel Renews Covenant with Him

'And afterward he read all the words of the law, the blessings and the cursings, according to all that is written in the Book of the Law. There was not a word of all that Moses had commanded which Joshua did not read before all the assembly of Israel, with the women, the little ones, and the strangers who were living among them.' Josh. 8:34-35.

Chapter 9
Israel Hastily Makes a Covenant with the Gibeonites, Seeing the Folly of Not Consulting the Lord

'But the children of Israel did not attack them, because the rulers of the congregation had sworn to them by the LORD God of Israel. And all the congregation complained against the rulers.' Josh. 9:18.

Chapter 10
The Lord Makes the Sun Stand Still as Israel Defends the Gibeonites from the Surrounding Nations, and Israel Gains Victory Over Many Kings

'Then Joshua said to them, "Do not be afraid, nor be dismayed; be strong and of good courage, for thus the LORD will do to all your enemies against whom you fight … And these kings and their land Joshua took at one time, because the LORD God of Israel fought for Israel."' Josh. 10:25, 42.

Chapter 11
Conquest of the Northern Land and Summary of the Conquests Under Joshua

'So Joshua took the whole land, according to all that the LORD had said to Moses; and Joshua gave it as an inheritance to Israel according to their divisions by their tribes. Then the land rested from war.' Josh. 11:23.

Chapter 12
The Lord Reviews Kings Conquered by Moses and by Joshua

'These Moses the servant of the LORD and the children of Israel had conquered; and Moses the servant of the LORD had given it as a possession to the Reubenites, the Gadites, and half the tribe of Manasseh.' Josh. 12:6.

Chapter 13

The Lord Charges Joshua with the Remaining Land to Possess, Reviews the Division of the Land East of the Jordan, and Stresses that the Levites Have the Lord as their Inheritance

'The children of Israel also killed with the sword Balaam the son of Beor, the soothsayer, among those who were killed by them.' Josh. 13:22.

Chapter 14

The Lord Divides the Land West of the Jordan, Beginning with Caleb's Inheritance of Hebron

'As yet I am as strong this day as on the day that Moses sent me; just as my strength was then, so now is my strength for war, both for going out and for coming in. Now therefore, give me this mountain of which the LORD spoke in that day; for you heard in that day how the Anakim were there, and that the cities were great and fortified. It may be that the LORD will be with me, and I shall be able to drive them out as the LORD said.' Josh. 14:11-12.

Chapter 15

The Land of Judah, Including Caleb's Inheritance, and the Cities of Judah

'As for the Jebusites, the inhabitants of Jerusalem, the children of Judah could not drive them out; but the Jebusites dwell with the children of Judah at Jerusalem to this day.' Josh. 15:63.

Chapter 16

The Land of Ephraim and West Manasseh

'And they did not drive out the Canaanites who dwelt in Gezer; but the Canaanites dwell among the Ephraimites to this day and have become forced laborers.' Josh. 16:10.

Chapter 17

The Other Half Tribe of Manasseh and the Daughters of Zelophehad, and the Need to Expand these Territories

'Yet the children of Manasseh could not drive out the inhabitants of those cities, but the Canaanites were determined to dwell in that land. And it happened, when the children of Israel grew strong, that they put the Canaanites to force labor, but did not utterly drive them out.' Josh. 17:12-13.

Chapter 18

The Lord Divides the Land of the Seven Remaining Tribes, Beginning with Benjamin

'Now the whole congregation of the children of Israel assembled together at Shiloh, and set up the tabernacle of meeting there. And the land was subdued before them. But there remained among the children of Israel seven tribes which had not yet received their inheritance.' Josh. 18:1-2.

Chapter 19

Simeon's Inheritance Included in Judah's Territory, Zebulun, Issachar, Asher, Naphtali, and Dan Receive their Land by Lot, While Joshua's Inheritance is Singled Out

'When they had made an end of dividing the land as an inheritance according to their borders, the children of Israel gave an inheritance among them to Joshua the son of Nun. According to the word of the LORD they gave him the city which he asked for, Timnath Serah in the mountains of Ephraim; and he built the city and dwelt in it.' Josh. 19:49-50.

Chapter 20

Cities of Refuge Appointed

'These were the cities appointed for all the children of Israel and for the stranger who dwelt among them, that whoever killed a person accidentally might flee there, and not die by the hand of the avenger of blood.' Josh. 20:9.

Chapter 21

Cities for the Levites and the Lord's Faithfulness in Fulfilling His Covenant Promises

'So the LORD gave to Israel all the land of which He had sworn to give to their fathers, and they took possession of it and dwelt in it. The LORD gave them rest all around, according to all that He had sworn to their fathers. And not a man of all their enemies stood against them; the LORD delivered all their enemies into their hand. Not a word failed of any good thing which the LORD had spoken to the house of Israel. All came to pass.' Josh. 21:43-45.

Chapter 22

The Tribes East of the Jordan Return to their Inheritance and Build a Large Memorial Altar, While Joshua and the Rest of Israel Warn them Against Apostasy

'Then Phinehas the son of Eleazar the priest said to the children of Reuben, the children of Gad, and the children of Manasseh, "This day we perceive that the LORD is among us, because you have not committed this treachery against the LORD. Now you have delivered the children of Israel out of the hand of the LORD."' Josh. 22:31.

Chapter 23

Joshua Exhorts the People to Trust in the Lord in the Next Generation and Remain Faithful to the Covenant

'Therefore be very courageous to keep and to do all that is written in the Book of the Law of Moses, lest you turn aside from it to the right hand or to the left, and lest you go among these nations, these who remain among you. You shall not make mention of the name of their gods, nor cause anyone to swear by them; you shall not serve them nor bow down to them, but you shall hold fast to the LORD your God, as you have done to this day.' Josh. 23:6-8.

Chapter 24

The Lord Recounts God's Covenant Faithfulness to Israel from Abraham Through Moses, Exhorting them to Love the Lord and Serve Him

'But as for me and my house, we will serve the LORD ... Israel served the LORD all the days of Joshua, and all the days of the elders who outlived Joshua, who had known all the works of the LORD which He had done for Israel. The bones of Joseph, which the children of Israel had brought up out of Egypt, they buried at Shechem, in the plot of ground which Jacob had bought from the sons of Hamor the father of Shechem for one hundred pieces of silver, and which had become an inheritance of the children of Joseph.' Josh. 24:15b, 31-32.

Judges

God faithfully preserves His covenant people, even though they bring covenant curses on themselves

CHAPTER 1

After the Death of Joshua, the People Cast Lots for Judah to Go up First Against the People Remaining in the Land, but they Cannot Drive them Out Entirely

> 'So the LORD was with Judah. And they drove out the mountaineers, but they could not drive out the inhabitants of the lowland, because they had chariots of iron.' Judg. 1:19.

CHAPTER 2

The Angel of the Lord Indicts Israel for Covenant Unfaithfulness, a Generation that Did not Know the Lord's Works Rises After Joshua, and the Lord Begins a Cycle of Raising Up Judges to Deliver them in their Distress

> 'Then the anger of the LORD was hot against Israel; and he said, "Because this nation has transgressed My covenant which I commanded their fathers, and has not heeded My voice, I also will no longer drive them out before them any of the nations which Joshua left when he died, so that through them I may test Israel, whether they will keep the ways of the LORD, to walk in them as their fathers kept them, or not." Therefore the LORD left those nations, without driving them out immediately; nor did He deliver them into the hand of Joshua.' Judg. 2:20-23.

CHAPTER 3

The Lord Leaves People in the Land to Test Israel's Heart, and Othniel, Ehud, and Shamgar are the First Judges

> 'When the children of Israel cried out to the LORD, the LORD raised up a deliverer for the children of Israel, who delivered them: Othniel the son of Kenaz, Caleb's younger brother. The Spirit of the LORD came upon him, and he judged Israel. He went out to war, and the LORD delivered Cushan-Rishathaim king of Mesopotamia into his hand; and his hand prevailed over Cushan-Rishathaim.' Judg. 3:9-10.

Chapter 4
Israel Turns from the Lord When Ehud Dies, and Deborah Judges Israel, Shaming Barak, Who Should Have Been Judge, the Lord Giving Victory into the Hand of Jael

> 'And Barak said to her, "If you will go with me, then I will go; but if you will not go with me, I will not go!" So she said, "I will surely go with you; nevertheless there will be no glory for you in the journey you are taking, for the LORD will sell Sisera into the hand of a woman."' Judg. 4:8-9.

Chapter 5
Deborah and Barak Praise the Lord for Showing His Covenant Faithfulness in Victory

> 'Thus let all Your enemies perish, O Lord! But let those who love Him be like the sun when it comes out in full strength. So the land had rest for forty years.' Judg. 5:31.

Chapter 6
The Midianites Oppress Israel for Seven Years, the Lord Explaining Why, and He Calls Gideon to Save Israel, Though He Does not Understand Why Israel Suffers, Gideon Destroys the Altar of Baal, and Tests God with the Fleece

> 'Now Gideon perceived that He was the Angel of the LORD. So Gideon said, "Alas, O LORD God! For I have seen the Angel of the LORD face to face ... But the Spirit of the LORD came upon Gideon; then he blew the trumpet, and the Abiezrites gathered behind him."' Judg. 6:22, 34.

Chapter 7
The Lord Reassures Gideon Again, Strengthening his Weak Faith, and Delivering Oreb and Zeeb into his Hands by Three Hundred Men in Order to Give All Glory to God

'But the LORD said to Gideon, "The people are still too many; bring them down to the water, and I will test them for you there."' Judg. 7:4a.

CHAPTER **8**

The Lord Delivers Zebah and Zalmunna into Gideon's Hands, Gideon Disciplines the Men of Succoth for Doubting Him, Gideon Refuses to Become King but Turns to Idolatry, and Israel Returns to Baal Worship at Gideon's Death

'So it was, as soon as Gideon was dead, that the children of Israel again played the harlot with the Baals, and made Baal-Berith their god.' Judg. 8:33.

CHAPTER **9**

Abimelech Son of Gideon Conspires to be King with the Men of Shechem, Kills All Gideon's Other Sons, Jotham Escapes and Condemns Abimelech and the Men of Shechem, and God Destroys them in the Temple of the False god Baal-Berith

'Now when all the men of the tower of Shechem had heard that, they entered the stronghold of the temple of the god Berith ... Thus God repaid the wickedness of Abimelech, which he had done to his father by killing his seventy brothers. And all the evil of the men of Shechem God returned on their own heads, and on them came the curse of Jotham the son of Jerubbaal.' Judg. 9:46, 56-57.

CHAPTER **10**

Tola and Jair Judge Israel, Israel Returns to Idolatry, God Judges them, and God has Pity on them

'Then the children of Israel again did evil in the sight of the LORD, and served the Baals and Ashtoreths, the gods of Syria, the gods of Sidon, the gods of Moab, the gods of the people of Ammon, and the gods of the Philistines; and they forsook the LORD and did not serve Him ... So they put away the foreign gods from among them and served the LORD. And His soul could no longer endure the misery of Israel.' Judg. 10:6, 16.

CHAPTER **11**

Jephthah Judges Israel, Leads Israel in Victory by the Spirit, and Rashly Dedicates his Daughter to Die Childless

> 'Then the Spirit of the LORD came upon Jephthah, and he passed through Gilead and Manasseh, and passed through Mizpah of Gilead; and from Mizpah of Gilead he advanced toward the people of Ammon.' Judg. 11:29.

Chapter **12**

Jephthah Falls into Conflict with Ephraim, Foreshadowing Future Divisions in Israel, and Ibzan, Elon, and Abdon Judge Israel

> 'And Jephthah judged Israel six years. Then Jephthah the Gileadite died and was buried in among the cities of Gilead.' Judg. 12:7.

Chapter **13**

The Angel of the Lord Predicts the Birth of Samson, and the Spirit of the Lord Begins to Strengthen him to Judge Israel

> 'And the Angel of the LORD said to him, "Why do you ask My name, seeing it is wonderful?" ... When the Angel of the LORD appeared no more to Manoah and his wife, then Manoah knew that He was the Angel of the LORD. And Manoah said to his wife, "We shall surely die, because we have seen God!" ... And the Spirit of the LORD began to move upon him at Mahaneh Dan between Zorah and Eshtaol.' Judg. 13:18, 21-22, 25.

Chapter **14**

The Lord Uses Samson's Inappropriate Desire for a Philistine Woman to Move him Against the Philistines, Samson Kills a Lion, Tells his Parable to his Wife, Who Tells the Philistines, and Samson Kills Thirty Philistines

> 'Then the Spirt of the LORD came upon him mightily, and he went down to Ashkelon and killed thirty of their men, took their apparel, and gave them the changes of clothing to those who had explained the riddle. So his anger was aroused, and he went back up to his father's house. And Samson's wife was given to his companion, who had been his best man.' Judg. 14:19-20.

Chapter **15**

Samson Returns to the Philistines to Reclaim his Wife, Burns Down their Field When he Discovers that they Gave her to Another Man, and he Kills One Thousand Philistines with the Jawbone of a Donkey

'When he came to Lehi, the Philistines came shouting against him. Then the Spirit of the LORD came mightily upon him; and the ropes that were on his arms became like flax that is burned with fire, and his bonds broke loose from his hands. He found a fresh jawbone of a donkey, reached out his hand and took it, and killed a thousand men with it.' Judg. 15:14-15.

Chapter 16

Delilah Manipulates Samson to Reveal the Secret of his Strength to the Philistines, they Capture him and Put out his Eyes, Giving Glory to their gods, and the Lord Strengthens Samson to Take Vengeance for his Eyes

'Then Samson called to the LORD, saying, "O LORD God, remember me, I pray! Strengthen me, I pray, just this once, O God, that I may with one blow take vengeance on the Philistines for my two eyes!"' Judg. 16:28.

Chapter 17

Micah Illustrates Israel's Blindness by Stealing Money from his Mother to Make an Image of the Lord, Consecrates his Son as Priest, then Replaces him with a Levite, Presuming that the Lord Will Bless him in Spite of his Ignorance of the Law

'In those days there was no king in Israel; everyone did what was right in his own eyes.' Judg. 17:6.

Chapter 18

The Tribe of Dan Steals Micah's Image and his Priest, as the Danites Seek their Inheritance Among People at Ease Rather than in the Promised Land

'Then the children of Dan set up for themselves the carved image; and Jonathan the son of Gershom, the son of Manasseh, and his sons were priests to the tribe of Dan until the day of captivity of the land. So they set up for themselves Micah's carved image which he made, all the time that the house of God was at Shiloh.' Judg. 18:30-31.

Chapter 19

A Levite Chases his Concubine Back to Bethlehem, and After Several Delays, Stays the Night in Gibeah Instead of Jebus, Yet the Men of Gibeah do Worse with the Woman than the Men of Sodom Were Able to do with Lot

> 'And so it was that all who saw it said, "No such deed has been done or seen from the day that the children of Israel came up from the land of Egypt until this day. Consider it, confer, and speak up!"' Judg. 19:30.

Chapter **20**

All Israel Gathers to War Against the Benjamites, Echoing Chapter 1 They Cast Lots and Judah Goes up Against them First, the Lord Humbles them with Defeat, but Eventually Gives them Victory

> 'Then all the children of Israel, that is, all the people, went up and came to the house of God and wept. They sat there before the LORD and fasted that day until evening; and they offered burnt offerings and peace offerings before the LORD.' Judg. 20:26.

Chapter **21**

The People Mourn Over the Loss of the Tribe of Benjamin and Find a Dishonest Way Around their Oath not to Give them Wives

> 'In those days there was no king in Israel; everyone did what was right in his own eyes.' Judg. 21:25.

Ruth

God gives examples of covenant loyalty and redemption in distress, preparing the way for His covenant with David

Chapter 1

Elimelech's Family Leaves the House of Bread (Bethlehem) in Order to Find Bread, he Dies, and Ruth Shows Covenant Loyalty to Naomi and to the God of Israel

> 'But Ruth said: "Entreat me not to leave you, or to turn back from following after you; for wherever you go, I will go; and wherever you lodge, I will lodge; your people shall be my people, and your God, my God. Where you die I will die, and there I will be buried. The LORD do so to me, and more also, if anything but death parts you and me."' Ruth 1:16-17.

Chapter 2

Ruth Gleans From Boaz's Field, Whom the Lord Uses to Provide for and Save the Family

> 'Then Naomi said to her daughter-in-law, "Blessed be he of the LORD, who has not forsaken His kindness to the living and the dead!' And Naomi said to her, "This man is a relation of ours, one of our close relatives."' Ruth 2:20.

Chapter 3

Boaz Agrees to be the Kinsman Redeemer of Naomi's Family and to Marry Ruth

> 'Then he said, "Blessed are you of the LORD, my daughter! For you have shown more kindness at the end than at the beginning, in that you did not go after young men, whether poor or rich."' Ruth 3:10.

Chapter 4
Boaz Claims the Right of Redemption from the Other Close Relative, Redeeming Naomi's Family, and Preparing the Way for the Davidic Covenant

> 'Now this is the genealogy of Perez: Perez begot Hezron, Hezron begot Ram, Ram begot Amminadab; Amminadab begot Nashon, and Nashon begot Salmon; Salmon begot Boaz, and Boaz begot Obed; Obed begot Jesse, and Jesse begot David.' Ruth 4:18-21.

1 Samuel

God shows that He is covenant Lord over Israel, showing the insufficiency of placing hope in anything or anyone else

Chapter 1

Elkanah's Wife Hannah is Barren, While his Other Wife Peninnah has Children, Hannah Vows to Dedicate a Son to God, and Returns to Eli the Priest After Samuel is Born

> '"For this child I prayed, and the LORD has granted me my petition which I asked of Him. Therefore I have also lent him to the LORD; as long as he lives he shall be lent to the LORD." So they worshipped the LORD there.' 1 Sam. 1:27-28.

Chapter 2

Hannah Praises God for His Salvation, Setting the Tone for the Book with the Lord Remembering His Covenant with His Anointed King, God Rejects Eli's Sons While Samuel Grows in Stature and in Favor both with God and Men

> 'The Adversaries of the LORD shall be broken in pieces; from heaven He will thunder against them. The LORD will judge the ends of the earth. He will give strength to His king, and exalt the horn of His anointed.' 1 Sam. 2:10.

Chapter 3

Samuel's First Prophecy Confirms the Fall of Eli's House, and the Lord Establishes Samuel as a Prophet

> 'So Samuel grew, and the LORD was with him and let none of his words fall to the ground.' 1 Sam. 3:19.

Chapter 4

Israel Trusts in the Ark Rather than in the Lord, the Lord Humiliates them by Delivering the Ark to the Philistines, Eli Dies in Shame, and the Glory Departs from Israel

'Then she named the child Ichabod, saying, "The glory has departed from Israel!" because the ark of God had been captured and because of her father-in-law and her husband. And she said, "The glory has departed from Israel, for the ark of God has been captured."' 1 Sam. 4:21-22.

Chapter 5
The Lord Humiliates Dagon and the Philistines Without Israel, Reiterating the Need to Trust Nothing Besides the Lord for Safety

'And when they arose early the next morning, there was Dagon, fallen on its face to the ground before the ark of the LORD. The head of Dagon and both the palms of its hands were broken off on the threshold; only Dagon's torso was left of it.' 1 Sam. 5:4.

Chapter 6
The Philistines Return to the Ark to Israel, God Strikes the Men of Beth Shemesh for Looking into the Ark, and the Lord Maintains His Own Holiness in Spite of Israel's Misplaced Trust

'And the men of Beth Shemesh said, "Who is able to stand before this holy LORD God? And to whom shall it go up from us?" So they sent messengers to the inhabitants of Kirjath Jearim, saying, "The Philistines have brought back the ark of the LORD; come down and take it up with you."' 1 Sam. 6:20-21.

Chapter 7
Samuel Judges Israel, Leading Israel Away from Idols and Leading them to Victory over the Philistines

'So the children of Israel put away the Baals and the Ashtoreths, and served the LORD only.' 1 Sam. 7:4.

Chapter 8
Israel Rejects God and Samuel by Placing their Trust in a King Instead of the Lord, Making the Same Mistake that they Did by Trusting in the Ark

'And the LORD said to Samuel, "Heed the voice of the people in all that they say to you; for they have not rejected you, but they have rejected Me, that I should not reign over them."' 1 Sam. 8:7.

Chapter 9
The Lord Chooses Saul to be King

'But as for your donkeys that were lost three days ago, do not be anxious about them, for they have been found. And on whom is all the desire of Israel? Is it not on you and on all your father's house?' 1 Sam. 9:20.

Chapter 10

Samuel Anoints Saul as Israel's First King, the Spirit of the Lord Seals Saul's Kingship, and Samuel Rebukes Israel for Trusting in a King Instead of the Lord

'But you have today rejected your God, who Himself saved you from all your adversities and your tribulations; and you have said to Him, "No, set a king over us!" Now therefore, present yourselves before the LORD by your tribes and by your clans.' 1 Sam. 10:19.

Chapter 11

Saul Saves Jabesh Gilead Against the Ammonites

'Then Samuel said to the people, "Come, let us go to Gilgal and renew the kingdom there." So all the people went to Gilgal, and there they made Saul king before the LORD in Gilgal. There they made sacrifices of peace offerings before the LORD, and there Saul and the men of Israel rejoiced greatly.' 1 Sam. 11:14-15.

Chapter 12

Samuel Gives One Final Rebuke to the People for Trusting in a King Instead of in the Lord

'Moreover, as for me, far be it from me that I should sin against the LORD in ceasing to pray for you; but I will teach you the good and right way. Only fear the LORD, and serve Him in truth with all your heart; for consider what great things He has done for you. But if you still do wickedly, you shall be swept away, both you and your king.' 1 Sam. 12:23-24.

Chapter 13

Saul Offers an Unlawful Sacrifice When he Sees the People Leaving him in the Face of the Philistines, Samuel Proclaims that he Will Lose the Kingdom as a Result, and the Army has no Weapons

'And Samuel said to Saul, "You have done foolishly. You have not kept the commandment of the LORD your God, which He commanded you. For now the LORD would have established your kingdom over Israel forever. But now your kingdom shall not continue. The LORD has sought for Himself a man after His own heart, and the LORD has commanded him to be commander over His people, because you have not kept what the LORD commanded you."' 1 Sam. 13:13-14.

CHAPTER **14**

Jonathan and his Armor Bearer Defeat the Philistines, God Does not Answer Saul, Saul Makes a Rash Vow, and the People Deliver Jonathan

'Then Saul built an altar to the LORD. This was the first altar that he built to the LORD.' 1 Sam. 14:35.

CHAPTER **15**

Saul Spares King Agag, and the Lord Does not Spare King Saul from Judgment

'So Samuel said: "Has the LORD as great delight in burnt offerings and sacrifices, as in obeying the voice of the LORD? Behold, to obey is better than sacrifice, and to heed than the fat of rams. For rebellion is as the sin of witchcraft, and stubbornness is as iniquity and idolatry. Because you have rejected the word of the LORD, He also has rejected you from being king … And also the Strength of Israel will not lie or relent. For He is not a man, that He should relent."' 1 Sam. 15:22-23, 29.

CHAPTER **16**

God Directs Samuel to Anoint David as King in Saul's Place

'But the LORD said to Samuel, "Do not look at his appearance or at his physical stature, because I have refused him. For the LORD does not see as man sees; for man looks at the outward appearance, but the LORD looks at the heart"… Then Samuel took the horn of oil and anointed him in the midst of his brothers; and the Spirit of the LORD came upon David from that day forward. So Samuel arose and went to Ramah. But the Spirit of the LORD departed from Saul, and a distressing spirit from the LORD troubled him.' 1 Sam. 16:7, 13-14.

CHAPTER **17**

David Delivers Israel by Challenging Goliath, Illustrating that the Lord Brings Victory for His People Rather than Men

'Then David said to the Philistine, "You come to me with a sword, with a spear, and with a javelin. But I come to you in the name of the LORD of hosts, the God of the armies of Israel, whom you have defied. This day the LORD will deliver you into my hand, and I will strike you and take your head from you. And this day I will give the carcasses of the camp of the Philistines to the birds of air and the wild beasts of the earth, that all the earth may know that there is a God in Israel. Then all this assembly shall know that the LORD does not save with sword or spear; for the battle is the LORD's, and He will give you into our hands."' 1 Sam. 17:45-47.

Chapter **18**

David and Jonathan Grow in Friendship, Saul Grows Jealous of David, David Marries Michal Saul's Daughter, and the Lord is With David

'Then the princes of the Philistines went out to war. And so it was, whenever they went out, that David behaved more wisely than all the servants of Saul, so that his name became highly esteemed.' 1 Sam. 18:30.

Chapter **19**

Jonathan Warns David that Saul Seeks to Kill him, and Saul Continues to Plot to Kill David in Spite of his Promises

'So he went there to Naioth in Ramah. Then the Spirit of God was upon him also, and he went on and prophesied until he came to Naioth in Ramah.' 1 Sam. 19:23.

Chapter **20**

Jonathan Makes a Covenant with David to Save his Life and to Transfer the Kingdom to him

'Then Jonathan said to David, "Go in peace, since we have both sworn in the name of the LORD, saying, May the LORD be between you and me, and between your descendants and my descendants, forever." So he arose and departed, and Jonathan went into the city.' 1 Sam. 20:42.

Chapter **21**

David Eats the Showbread, Takes Goliath's Sword, and Flees from Saul to Gath, Pretending Madness to Escape with his Life

> 'Now a certain man of the servants of Saul was there that day, detained before the LORD. And his name was Doeg, an Edomite, the chief of the herdsman who belonged to Saul.' 1 Sam. 21:7.

Chapter 22
David Gathers Four Hundred to himself, Saul Murders the Priests After Hearing Doeg's Report, and David Takes Responsibility for the Results

> 'So David said to Abiathar, "I knew that day, when Doeg the Edomite was there, that he would surely tell Saul. I have caused the death of all the persons of your father's house. Stay with me; do not fear. For he who seeks my life seeks your life, but with me you shall be safe."' 1 Sam. 22:22-23.

Chapter 23
David Saves the City of Keilah from the Philistines, While Saul is Consumed with Killing David Instead of Saving the People, David then Dwelling in the Wilderness

> 'But a messenger came to Saul, saying, "Hurry and come, for the Philistines have invaded the land!" Therefore Saul returned from pursuing David, and went against the Philistines; so they called that place the Rock of Escape.' 1 Sam. 23:27.

Chapter 24
David Spares Saul in the Cave, Saul Lets David Go, and David Promises to Spare Saul's Descendants

> 'Therefore let the LORD judge, and judge between you and me, and see and plead my case, and deliver me out of your hand.' 1 Sam. 24:15.

Chapter 25
Samuel Dies and David Falls into Temptation to Avenge himself on Nabal Even Though he would Not Against Saul, and Abigail Prevents him from Doing so and Becomes his Wife

> 'That this will be no grief to you, nor offense of heart to my lord, either that you have shed blood without cause, or that my lord has avenged himself. But when the LORD has dealt well with my lord, then remember your maidservant.' 1 Sam. 25:31.

Chapter 26
David Spares Saul's Life a Second Time, Committing his Cause to the Lord

> 'May the LORD repay every man for his righteousness and his faithfulness; for the LORD delivered you into my hand today, but I would not stretch out my hand against the LORD's anointed. And indeed, as your life was valued much this day in my eyes, so let my life be valued much in the eyes of the LORD, and let Him deliver me out of all tribulation.' 1 Sam. 26:23-24.

Chapter 27
David Allies himself with the Philistines, and Achish Believes that David Fights Against Israel

> 'Now the time that David dwelt in the country of the Philistines was one full year and four months.' 1 Sam. 27:7.

Chapter 28
David Prepares to Go to War Along with the Philistines, While Saul Consults a Medium and the Lord Assures him of his Destruction

> 'Moreover the LORD will also deliver Israel with you into the hand of the Philistines. And tomorrow you and your sons will be with me. The LORD will also deliver the army of Israel into the hand of the Philistines.' 1 Sam. 28:19.

Chapter 29
The Philistines Refuse to Let David go to Battle with them

> '... then the princes of the Philistines said, "What are these Hebrews doing here?"' 1 Sam. 29:3a.

Chapter 30
David Strengthens himself in the Lord to Rescue his Family and Other Captives from the Amalekites

> 'But David strengthened himself in the LORD his God.' 1 Sam. 30:6c.

Chapter 31
In Contrast to David, Saul Dies in Shame Apart from the Lord's Help

'And they cut off his head and stripped off his armor, and send word throughout the land of the Philistines, to proclaim it in the temple of their idols and among the people. Then they put his armor in the temple of the Ashtoreths, and they fastened his body to the wall of Beth Shan.' 1 Sam. 31:9-10.

2 Samuel

God establishes David as His anointed Christ, directing Israel to hope in David's greater Son, according to the terms of the covenant

Chapter 1

David Hears the News of Saul's Death, Executes the Messenger, and Laments Saul and his Sons

> "Tell it not in Gath, proclaim it not in the streets of Ashkelon – lest the daughters of the Philistines rejoice, lest the daughters of the uncircumcised triumph.' 2 Sam. 1:20.

Chapter 2

David is Anointed King in Hebron, Ishbosheth Becomes a Rival King, and Israel and Judah are at War Over David

> 'But the servants of David had struck down, of Benjamin and Abner's men, three hundred and sixty men who died.' 2 Sam. 2:31.

Chapter 3

The Lord Strengthens David's Kingdom Further by Giving him Sons and Abner Joining him, While Joab Threatens the Stability of the Kingdom by Killing Abner

> 'And I am weak today, though anointed king; and these men, the sons of Zeruiah, are too harsh for me. The LORD shall repay the evildoer according to his wickedness.' 2 Sam. 3:39.

Chapter 4

Ishbosheth is Murdered and the Lord Establishes David as King

> 'So David commanded his young men, and they executed them, and cut off their hands and feet, and hanged them by

> the pool in Hebron. But they took the head of Ishbosheth and buried it in the tomb of Abner in Hebron.' 2 Sam. 4:12.

Chapter 5
David Reigns Over All Israel, Conquers Jerusalem, and Defeats the Philistines Because the Lord is with him

> 'So David knew that the LORD had established him as king over Israel, and that He had exalted His kingdom for the sake of His people Israel.' 2 Sam. 5:12.

Chapter 6
David Seeks to Bring the Ark to Jerusalem, but Uzzah Dies While Mishandling the Ark, and David then Brings the Ark Properly to Jerusalem While Saul's Daughter is Cursed

> 'And David became angry because of the LORD's outbreak against Uzzah; and he called the name of the place Perez Uzzah to this day.' 2 Sam. 6:8.

Chapter 7
God Establishes His Covenant with David and His Descendants, and David Prays for God's Covenant Presence with His People

> 'When your days are fulfilled and you rest with your fathers, I will set up your seed after you, who will come from your body, and I will establish his kingdom. He shall build a house for My name, and I will establish the throne of his kingdom forever. I will be his Father, and he shall be My son. If he commits iniquity, I will chasten him with the rod of men and with the blows of the sons of men. But My mercy shall not depart from him, as I took it from Saul, whom I removed from before you. And your house and your kingdom shall be established forever before you. Your throne shall be established forever.' 2 Sam. 7:12-16.

Chapter 8
The Lord Further Strengthens David Against his Enemies as David Governs the Kingdom

> 'King David also dedicated these to the LORD, along with the silver and gold that he had dedicated from all the nations which he had subdued – from Syria, from Moab, from the people of Ammon, from the Philistines, from Amalek, and

from the spoil of Hadadezer the son of Rehob, king of Zobah.' 2 Sam. 8:11-12.

Chapter 9
David Shows Kindness to Mephibosheth, Remembering his Oath to Saul

'So Mephibosheth dwelt in Jerusalem, for he ate continually at the king's table. And he was lame in both his feet.' 2 Sam. 9:13.

Chapter 10
The Lord Delivers David from the Ammonites and the Syrians

'And when the kings who were servants to Hadaezer saw that they were defeated by Israel, they made peace with Israel and served them. So the Syrians were afraid to help the people of Ammon anymore.' 2 Sam. 10:19.

Chapter 11
David Neglects his Kingly Duties, Sins with Bathsheba, and Murders Uriah the Hittite to Cover his Sin

'But the thing that David had done displeased the LORD.' 2 Sam. 11:27b.

Chapter 12
Nathan the Prophet Confronts David with his Sin After David has Covered it for Nearly a Year, his Child Dies, Solomon is Born, and David Captures Rabbah

'And he said, "While the child was alive, I fasted and wept; for I said, Who can tell whether the LORD will be gracious to me, that the child may live? But now he is dead; why should I fast? Can I bring him back again? I shall go to him, but he shall not return to me."' 2 Sam. 12:22-23.

Chapter 13
Amnon Defiles Tamar and Absalom Murders Amnon, Going into Exile, Fulfilling the Lord's Curse Against David

'And David longed to go to Absalom. For he had been comforted concerning Amnon, because he was dead.' 2 Sam. 13:39.

Chapter 14
Absalom Returns to Jerusalem and David Receives him

'So Joab went to the king and told him. And when he had called for Absalom, he came to the king and bowed himself on his face to the ground before the king. Then the king kissed Absalom.' 2 Sam. 14:33.

Chapter 15
Absalom Conspires Against David and David Flees, Praying for the Lord's Protection

'Then someone told David, saying, "Ahithophel is among the conspirators with Absalom." And David said, "O LORD, I pray, turn the counsel of Ahithophel into foolishness!"' 2 Sam. 15:31.

Chapter 16
David Gives Mephibosheth's Portion to Zeba, Shimei Curses David, and Ahithophel Gives Absalom Counsel, Sealing his Rebellion Against his Father

'But the king said, "What have I to do with you, you sons of Zeruiah? So let him curse, because the LORD has said to him, Curse David. Who then shall say, Why have you done so?"' 2 Sam. 16:10.

Chapter 17
The Lord Answers David's Prayer for Protection, Ahithophel Commits Suicide, and Absalom Replaces Joab with Amasa as Captain of the Army

'And Absalom made Amasa captain of the army instead of Joab. This Amasa was the son of a man whose name was Jithra, an Israelite, who had gone into Abigail the son of Nahash, sister of Zeruiah, Joab's mother.' 2 Sam. 17:25.

Chapter 18
Joab Kills Absalom and David Mourns his Death

'Then the king was deeply moved, and went up to the chamber over the gate, and wept. And as he went, he said thus: "O my son Absalom – my son, my son Absalom – if only I had died in your place! O Absalom my son, my son!"' 2 Sam. 18:33.

Chapter 19
David Almost Loses the Kingdom in Mourning for Absalom, he Replaces Joab with Amasa as Captain of the Army, he Spares

Shimei, Meets Mephibosheth, and Cares for Barzillai, while Division Continues Among Judah and Israel

> 'And the men of Israel answered the men of Judah, "We have ten shares in the king; therefore we also have more right to David than you. Why then do you despise us – were we not the first to advise bringing back our king?" Yet the words of the men of Judah were fiercer than the words of the men of Israel.' 2 Sam. 19:43.

Chapter 20

The Division in Israel Leads Sheba to Lead a Rebellion Against David, Joab Murders Amasa and Becomes Captain Again, Lead the People to Victory, and David Appoints New Officers

> 'And there happened to be there a rebel, whose name was Sheba the son of Bichri, a Benjamite. And he blew a trumpet, and said: "We have no share in David, nor do we have an inheritance in the son of Jesse; every man to his tents, O Israel!"' 2 Sam. 20:1.

Chapter 21

David Remembers Israel's Covenant with the Gibeonites from Joshua, Avenging Saul's Violence Against them, and then Defeats Philistine Giants, God Again Strengthening his Kingdom

> 'But the king spared Mephibosheth the son of Jonathan, the son of Saul, because of the LORD's oath that was between them, between David and Jonathan the son of Saul.' 2 Sam. 21:7.

Chapter 22

David Praises God for All of His Covenant Faithfulness and Deliverance, Echoing Psalm 18

> 'As for God, His way is perfect; the word of the LORD is proven; He is a shield to all who trust in Him.' 2 Sam. 22:31.

Chapter 23

David Speaks by the Spirit of the Lord, Praising God for His Covenant Faithfulness in Spite of David's Failings, and David's Mighty Men Illustrate the Lord's Protection

> 'Although my house is not so with God, yet He has made with me an everlasting covenant, ordered in all things and secure. For this is all my salvation and all my desire; will He not make it increase?' 2 Sam. 23:5.

CHAPTER 24

David Sins by Taking a Census of Israel, Illustrating the Folly of Trusting Military Might Instead of the Lord, and David Obtains the Threshing Floor of Ornan Where the Temple Would Later be Built

> 'Then the king said to Araunah, "No, but I will surely buy it from you for a price; nor will I offer burnt offerings to the LORD my God with that which costs me nothing." So David bought the threshing floor and the oxen for fifty shekels of silver.' 2 Sam. 24:24.

1 Kings

God sustains His covenant people, showing that the fulfillment of His promises to David are not yet complete

Chapter **1**

Adonijah Presumes to Take David's Place as King, While David Confirms Solomon as his Successor

> 'Benaiah the son of Jehoiada answered the king and said, Amen! May the LORD God of my lord the king say so too. As the LORD has been with my lord the king, even so may He be with Solomon, and make his throne greater than the throne of my lord King David."' 1 Kings 1:36-37.

Chapter **2**

David Encourages Solomon with God's Covenant Promises, Giving him Instructions Regarding Joab, Barzillai, and Shimei, David Dies, and Solomon Executes Adonijah, Exiles Abiathar, and Kills Joab and Shimei

> 'And keep the charge of the LORD your God: to walk in His ways, to keep His statutes, His commandments, His judgments, and His testimonies, as it is written in the Law of Moses, that you may prosper in all that you do and wherever you turn; that the LORD may fulfill His word which He spoke concerning me, saying, "If your sons take heed to their way, to walk before Me in truth with all their heart and with all their soul," He said, "you shall not lack a man on the throne of Israel."' 1 Kings 2:3-4.

Chapter **3**

Solomon Wisely Asks the Lord for Wisdom to Lead the Covenant People, God Promises Wisdom and Wealth, and God Shows Solomon's Wisdom with Two Women

> 'Behold, I have done according to your words; see, I have given you a wise and understanding heart, so that there has not been anyone like you before you, nor shall any like you arise after you. And I have also given you what you have not asked: both riches and honor, so that there shall not be anyone like you among the kings all your days. So if you walk in My ways to keep My statutes and My commandments, as your father David walked, then I will lengthen your days.' 1 Kings 3:12-14.

Chapter 4
God Establishes Solomon's Reign in Wisdom and Prosperity According to His Promise

> 'For he had dominion over all the region on this side of the River from Tiphsah even to Gaza, namely over all the kings on this side of the River; and he had peace on every side all around him. And Judah dwelt safely, each man under his vine and under his fig tree, from Dan as far as Beersheba, all the days of Solomon.' 1 Kings 4:24-25.

Chapter 5
Solomon Enlists Hiram of Tyre to Help him Build a House for the Lord, Appealing to the Davidic Covenant, While God Continues to Increase Solomon's Wisdom and Wealth

> 'So the LORD gave Solomon wisdom, as He had promised him; and there was peace between Hiram and Solomon, and the two of them made a treaty together.' 1 Kings 5:12.

Chapter 6
Solomon Builds the Lord's Temple

> 'So he was seven years in building it.' 1 Kings 6:38c.

Chapter 7
Solomon's Other Building Projects and the Implements and Furnishings for the Temple

> 'So all the work that King Solomon had done for the house of the LORD was finished; and Solomon brought the things which his father David had dedicated; the silver and the gold and the furnishings. He put them in the treasuries of the house of the LORD.' 1 Kings 7:51.

Chapter 8

After the Lord's Glory Fills the Temple, Solomon Prays for the Lord's Blessings on the Temple According to the Terms of the Covenant with David, Blessing the People

> 'Then Solomon spoke: "The LORD said He would dwell in the dark cloud. I have surely built You an exalted house, and a place for You to dwell in forever."' 1 Kings 8:12-13.

Chapter 9

God Appears to Solomon a Second Time, Urging him to Covenant Faithfulness, and Solomon Completes Other Building Projects

> 'Then I will establish the throne of your kingdom over Israel forever, as I promised David your father, saying, "You shall not fail to have a man on the throne of Israel."' 1 Kings 9:5.

Chapter 10

The Queen of Sheba is Overwhelmed by Solomon's Wisdom, Praising his God, While Solomon Continues to Accumulate Wealth

> 'Blessed be the LORD your God, who delighted in you, setting you on the throne of Israel! Because the LORD loved Israel forever, therefore He made you king, to do justice and righteousness.' 1 Kings 10:9.

Chapter 11

Solomon Forgets the Covenant, Marrying Many Foreign Women and Worshiping their gods, and God Promises to Divide the Kingdom, Raising up Enemies Against Solomon and Ending Israel's Time of Peace

> 'Therefore the LORD said to Solomon, "Because you have done this, and have not kept My covenant and My statutes, which I have commanded you, I will surely tear the kingdom away from you and give it to your servant. Nevertheless I will not do it in your days, for the sake of your father David; I will tear it out of the hands of your son. However I will not tear away the whole kingdom; I will give one tribe to your son for the sake of My servant David, and for the sake of Jerusalem which I have chosen."' 1 Kings 11:11-13.

Chapter 12

The Lord Divides the Kingdom Under Rehoboam by Leaving him to Follow the Bad Advice of his Friends, and Jeroboam Makes two Golden Calves to Worship the Lord

'Therefore the king asked advice, made two calves of gold, and said to the people, "It is too much for you to go up to Jerusalem. Here are your gods, O Israel, which brought you up from the land of Egypt!"' 1 Kings 12:28.

Chapter 13

A Man of God Prophesies that Josiah Will Desecrate Jeroboam's Altar at Bethel, but then Disobeys the Word of the Lord and Dies, Illustrated the Consequences of Disobedience to the Lord

'Then he cried out against the altar by the word of the LORD, and said, "O altar, altar! Thus says the LORD: Behold, a child, Josiah by name, shall be born to the house of David; and on you he shall sacrifice the priests of the high places who burn incense on you, and men's bones shall be burned on you."' 1 Kings 13:2.

Chapter 14

Ahijah the Prophet Proclaims Judgment Against Abijah, Son of Jeroboam, While Jeroboam Dies and Rehoboam Reigns in Judah

'Now Judah did evil in the sight of the LORD, and they provoked Him to jealousy with their sins which they committed, more than all their fathers had done. For they also built for themselves high places, sacred pillars, and wooden images on every hill and under every green tree.' 1 Kings 14:22-23.

Chapter 15

Abijam Reigns in Rehoboam's Place, Followed by Asa, While Nadab of Israel is Killed by Baasha, Who Takes Over the Kingdom, and the Lord Remembers His Covenant with Judah

'And he walked in all the sins of his father, which he had done before him; his heart was not loyal to the LORD his God, as was the heart of his father David. Nevertheless for David's sake the LORD his God gave him a lamp in Jerusalem, by setting up his son after him and by establishing Jerusalem … Asa did what was right in the eyes of the LORD, as did his father David.' 1 Kings 15:3-4, 11.

Chapter 16

The Lord Proclaims Judgment Against Baasha, and Zimri Kills Baasha's Son Elah, then Omri Takes the Kingdom, Passing it to Ahab his Son

'Now Ahab the son of Omri did evil in the sight of the LORD more than all who were before him. And it came to pass, as though it had been a trivial thing for him to walk in the sins of Jeroboam the son of Nebat, that he took as wife Jezebel the daughter of Ethbaal, king of the Sidonians; and he went and served Baal and worshiped him.' 1 Kings 16:30-31.

Chapter **17**

The Lord Sends Elijah to Prophesy a Drought in Israel, Establishing him as Prophet through Miraculously Saving a Widow and her Son, and Raising the Widow's Son from the Dead

'Then the woman said to Elijah, "Now by this I know that you are a man of God, and that the word of the LORD in your mouth is the truth."' 1 Kings 17:24.

Chapter **18**

Elijah Shows that the Lord is God by Sending Fire from Heaven and Killing the Prophets of Baal, and Brings the Drought to an End

'And Elijah came to all the people, and said, "How long will you falter between two opinions? If the LORD is God, follow Him; but if Baal, follow him." But the people answered him not a word ... Now when all the people saw it, they fell on their faces; and said, "The LORD, He is God! The LORD, He is God!"' 1 Kings 18:21, 39.

Chapter **19**

Elijah Flees When Jezebel Seeks to Kill him, he Complains that he Alone is Left as a Prophet, and Elijah Passes the Mantle to Elisha as Prophet

'Yet I have reserved seven thousand in Israel, all whose knees have not bowed to Baal, and every mouth that has not kissed him.' 1 Kings 19:18.

Chapter **20**

Ahab Defeats the Assyrians, but God Curses him for Making Friendship with Ben-Hadad

'Then he said to him, "Thus says the LORD: Because you have let slip out of your hand the man whom I appointed to utter destruction, therefore your life shall go for his life, and your people for his people."' 1 Kings 20:42.

Chapter 21

Jezebel Incites Ahab to Murder Naboth and Take his Inheritance, the Lord Pronounces Judgment Against him, but Delays the Punishment When Ahab Humbles himself

> 'See how Ahab has humbled himself before Me? Because he has humbled himself before Me, I will not bring the calamity in his days. In the days of his son I will bring calamity on his house.' 1 Kings 21:29.

Chapter 22

Micaiah Warns Ahab not to Fight the Syrians, Relating a Vision in which the Lord Sent Lying Spirits into Ahab's Prophets, Ahab Dies in Battle, and Jehoshaphat Reigns in Judah

> 'And he walked in all the ways of his father Asa. He did not turn aside from them, doing what was right in the eyes of the LORD. Nevertheless the high places were not taken away, for the people offered sacrifices and burned incense on the high places. Also Jehoshaphat made peace with the king of Israel.' 1 Kings 22:43-44.

2 Kings

God preserves David's line due to His covenant with him, even though his sons rebel and end in exile

Chapter 1

Elijah Predicts Judgment Against Ahab's Son Ahaziah, God shows that Elijah is a Prophet by Calling Fire from Heaven on Ahaziah's Messengers, and Ahaziah Dies According to his Word

> 'Then he said to him, "Thus says the LORD: Because you have sent messengers to inquire of Baal-Zebub, the god of Ekron, is it because there is no God in Israel to inquire of His word? Therefore you shall not come down from the bed to which you have gone up, but you shall surely die."' 2 Kings 1:16.

Chapter 2

Elisha Asks for a Double Portion of the Spirit of Elijah, the Lord Takes Elijah into Heaven in a Chariot of Fire, and God Shows that Elisha Received What he Asked by Parting the Jordan, Healing Poisoned Waters, and Sending Bears Against Children who Mocked him

> 'Then he took the mantle of Elijah that had fallen from him, and struck the water, and said, "Where is the LORD God of Elijah?" And when he had struck the water, it was divided this way and that; and Elisha crossed over.' 2 Kings 2:14.

Chapter 3

Jehoram of Israel Enlists Jehoshaphat of Judah to Help Fight the Moabites, and the Lord Delivers them for the Sake of Jehoshaphat

> 'Then Elisha said, "As the LORD of hosts lives, before whom I stand, surely were it not that I regard the presence of

Jehoshaphat king of Judah, I would not look at you, nor see you."' 2 Kings 3:14.

Chapter 4

The Lord Confirms Elisha's Call as Prophet by Multiplying a Widow's Oil, Raising a Woman's Son from the Dead, Purifying a Pot of Stew, and Feeding One Hundred Men

'So he set it before them; and they ate and had some left over, according to the word of the LORD.' 2 Kings 4:44.

Chapter 5

The Lord Continues to Show that Elisha has a Double Portion of the Spirit of Elijah by Healing Naaman's Leprosy, While he Curses Gehazi with Leprosy for his Greed

'So it was, when Elisha the man of God heard that the king of Israel had torn his clothes, that he sent to the king, saying, "Why have you torn your clothes? Please let him come to me, and he shall know that there is a prophet in Israel."' 2 Kings 5:8.

Chapter 6

The Lord Continues to Testify to Elisha's Prophetic Call by Making an Ax Head Float, by Capturing the Blinded Assyrians, and the King of Israel Seeks to Kill Elisha for a Famine in Anger Against the Lord

'So he answered, "Do not fear, for those who are with us are more than those who are with them."' 2 Kings 6:16.

Chapter 7

Elisha Promises the End of the Famine, an Officer Mocks him, Two Lepers Discover that the Syrians Have Fled, the Man who Mocked Elisha Dies, and the Lord Confirms Elisha's Prophetic Ministry

'So it happened just as the man of God had spoken to the king, saying, "Two seahs of barley for a shekel, and a seah of fine flower for a shekel, shall be sold tomorrow about this time at the gate of Samaria."' 2 Kings 7:18.

Chapter 8

The King Restores the Shunammite Woman's Land Through Elisha's Intervention, Elisha Anoints Hazael King of Syria, Jehoram Reigns in Judah, Followed by his Son Ahaziah

'And he walked in the way of the house of Ahab, and did evil in the sight of the LORD, like the house of Ahab, for he was the son-in-law of the house of Ahab.' 2 Kings 8:27.

Chapter 9
Elisha Anoints Jehu King of Israel, Who Kills Joram of Israel and Ahaziah of Judah, as Well as Jezebel

'Therefore they came back and told him. And he said, "This is the word of the LORD, which He spoke by His servant Elijah the Tishbite, saying, On the plot of ground at Jezreel dogs shall eat the flesh of Jezebel; and the corpse of Jezebel shall be as refuse on the surface of the field, in the plot at Jezreel, so that they shall not say, Here lies Jezebel."' 2 Kings 9:36-37.

Chapter 10
Jehu Kills Ahab's Seventy Sons, Ahaziah's Forty-Two Brothers, the Rest of Ahab's Family, and the Worshipers of Baal, and Jehoahaz Reigns in his Father's Place in Israel

'And when he came to Samaria, he killed all who remained to Ahab in Samaria, till he had destroyed them, according to the word of the LORD which He spoke to Elijah.' 2 Kings 10:17.

Chapter 11
Athaliah Kills her Grandchildren, the Heirs of the Throne of Judah, Filling the Power Vaccum, but Jehoiada the Priest Saves Joash, Kills Athaliah, and Places Joash on the Throne, Preserving David's Line and Renewing the Covenant

'Then Jehoiada made a covenant between the LORD, the king, and the people, that they should be the LORD's people, and also between the king and the people.' 2 Kings 11:17.

Chapter 12
Joash Repairs the Temple and Restores Worship, Hazael of Syria Attacks Jerusalem, and Joash's Servants Kill him

'So he died, and they buried him with his fathers in the City of David. Then Amaziah his son reigned in his place.' 2 Kings 12:21b.

Chapter 13
Jehoahaz Jehu's Son Reigns in Israel, God Delivers him into the Hands of Syria for Continuing Jeroboam's Calf Worship, Jehoash

Reigns in his Place, and Elisha Dies After Announcing a Partial Victory Against Syria

> 'Then Elisha died, and they buried him. And the raiding bands from Moab invaded the land in the spring of the year. So it was, as they were burying a man, that suddenly they spied a band of raiders; and they put the man in the tomb of Elisha; and when the man was let down and touched the bones of Elisha, he revived and stood on his feet.' 2 Kings 13:20-21.

Chapter 14

Amaziah Reigns in Judah, Loses in Battle Against the King of Israel, is Killed by Conspirators but Succeeded by his Son Azariah, While Jeroboam II Reigns in Israel

> 'And he did what was right in the sight of the LORD, yet not like his father David; he did everything as his father Joash had done.' 2 Kings 14:3.

Chapter 15

Azariah (Uzziah) Reigns in Judah, Zechariah is the End of Jehu's Line, then Shallum, then Menahem, then Pekahiah then Pekah Reign Successively in Israel, While Jothan Reigns in Judah after Azariah

> 'And he did what was right in the sight of the LORD, according to all that his father Amaziah had done, except that the high places were not removed; the people still sacrificed and burned incense on the high places…And he did what was right in the sight of the LORD; he did according to all that his father Uzziah had done.' 2 Kings 15:3-4, 34.

Chapter 16

Ahaz Reigns in Judah, and God Raises Rezin and Pekah to Punish him for his Sins, While Ahaz Seeks Help from Assyria and Builds an Idolatrous Altar

> 'Ahaz was twenty years old when he became king, and he reigned sixteen years in Jerusalem; and he did not do what was right in the sight of the LORD his God, as his father David had done.' 2 Kings 16:2.

Chapter 17

Hoshea Reigns in Israel, Assyria Takes Israel Captive, the Lord Reviews their History of Sin and Idolatry, Giving Warnings to

Judah, While the Samaritans Whom Assyria Placed in the Land Invent their Own Idolatrous Worship

> 'They feared the LORD, yet served their own gods – according to the rituals of the nations from among whom they were carried away. To this day they continue practicing the former rituals; they do not fear the LORD, nor do they follow their statutes or their ordinances, or the law and commandment which the LORD had commanded the children of Jacob, whom He named Israel…So these nations feared the LORD, yet served their carved images; also their children and their children's children have continued doing as their fathers did, even to this day.' 2 Kings 17:33-34, 41.

Chapter **18**

Hezekiah Reigns in Judah, Finally Removing Most of the High Places, and Assyria Threatens to Take Jerusalem

> 'Who among all the gods of the lands have delivered their counsels from my hand, that the LORD should deliver Jerusalem from my hand?' 2 Kings 18:35.

Chapter **19**

Hezekiah Prays and Asks Isaiah for Help, and Isaiah Prophesies Deliverance for Those Who Trust in the Lord

> 'Truly, LORD, the kings of Assyria have laid waste the nations and their lands, and have cast their gods into the fire; for they were not gods, but the work of men's hands – wood and stone. Therefore they destroyed them. Now therefore, O LORD our God, I pray, save us from his hand, that all the kingdoms of the earth may know that You are the LORD God, You alone.' 2 Kings 19:17-19.

Chapter **20**

Hezekiah Prays that the Lord Would Extend his Life, but Then Falls into Pride with the Babylonian Envoys, Illustrating the Lord's Mercies to those Who Seek Him and the Consequences of Pride

> 'And I will add to your days fifteen years. I will deliver you and this city from the hand of the king of Assyria; and I will defend this city for My own sake, and for the sake of My servant David.' 2 Kings 20:6.

Chapter 21

Manasseh Reigns in Hezekiah's Place and is Judah's Worst King, Resulting in the Lord Announcing the Babylonian Captivity, and Amon Reigns After his Father Manasseh

> 'Therefore thus says the LORD God of Israel: "Behold, I am bringing such calamity upon Jerusalem and Judah, that whoever hears of it, both his ears will tingle. And I will stretch over Jerusalem the measuring line of Samaria and the plummet of the house of Ahab; I will wipe Jerusalem as one wipes a dish, wiping it and turning it upside down."' 2 Kings 21:12-13.

Chapter 22

Josiah Reigns in Judah, and is Israel's Best King Since David, Recovering the Book of the Law, and Humbling himself to Seek the Lord

> 'And he did what was right in the sight of the LORD, and walked in all the ways of his father David; he did not turn aside to the right hand or to the left.' 2 Kings 22:2.

Chapter 23

Josiah Renews Covenant with God, Restores Temple Worship, Destroys the Altar at Bethel According to the Promise of 1 Kings 12, and Restores the Passover, Even in the Face of Impending Doom, the Captivity Beginning with Jehoahaz and Jehoiakim

> 'Then the king stood by a pillar and made a covenant before the LORD, to follow the LORD and to keep His commandments and His testimonies and His statutes, with all his heart and all his soul, to perform the words of this covenant that were written in this book. And all the people took a stand for the covenant.' 2 Kings 23:3.

Chapter 24

The Lord Begins to Deliver Judah to Babylon for the Sins of Manasseh, Jehoiachin Goes into Captivity, Nebuchadnezzar Captures Jerusalem, and Appoints Zedekiah to Reign in the Line of David

> 'Surely at the commandment of the LORD this came upon Judah, to remove them from His sight because of the sins of Manasseh, according to all that he had done, and also because of the innocent blood that he had shed; for he had filled

Jerusalem with innocent blood, which the LORD would not pardon.' 2 Kings 24:3-4.

CHAPTER **25**

Nebuchadnezzar Finally Destroys Jerusalem and the Temple, Ends the Line of Zedekiah, Appoints Gedaliah as Governor, and Gives Judah Hope by Releasing Jehoiachin in the Line of David from Prison

'So Jehoiachin changed from his prison garments, and he ate bread regularly before the king all the days of his life. And as for his provisions, there was a regular ration given him by the king, a portion for each day, all the days of his life.' 2 Kings 25:29-30.

1 Chronicles

God encourages His people in exile with His past covenant faithfulness

Chapter **1**

God Separates the Seed of the Woman and the Seed of the Serpent from Adam to Esau

> 'And Abraham begot Isaac. The sons of Isaac were Esau and Israel.' 1 Chron. 1:34.

Chapter **2**

God Narrows the Covenant Promise through from the Tribes of Israel, to Judah, to David

> 'There were the sons of Israel: Reuben, Simeon, Levi, Judah, Issachar, Zebulun, Dan, Joseph, Benjamin, Naphtali, Gad, and Asher.' 1 Chron. 2:1.

Chapter **3**

God Confirms His Covenant Promises Through David and his Sons

> 'Now these were the sons of David who were born to him in Hebron.' 1 Chron. 3:1a.

Chapter **4**

God Preserves His Covenant Through Preserving the Tribes of Israel

> 'Now Jabez was more honorable than his brothers, and his mother called his name Jabez, saying, "Because I bore him in pain." And Jabez called on the God of Israel saying, "Oh, that You would bless me indeed, and enlarge my territory, that Your

hand would be with me, and that You would keep me from evil, that I might not cause pain!" God granted him what he requested.' 1 Chron. 4:9-10.

Chapter 5
The Lord Transfers the Promise of the Seed of the Woman from Reuben, to Joseph, to Judah, Fulfilling Genesis 35 and 49

'Now the sons of Reuben the firstborn of Israel – he was indeed the firstborn, but because he defiled his father's bed, his birthright was given to the sons of Joseph, the Son of Israel, so that the genealogy is not listed according to the birthright; yet Judah prevailed over his brothers, and from him came a ruler, although the birthright was Joseph's.' 1 Chron. 5:1-2.

Chapter 6
The Sons of Levi Lead God's Covenant People in Worship as Priests and Musicians

'Jehozadak went into captivity when the LORD carried Judah and Jerusalem into captivity by the hand of Nebuchadnezzar.' 1 Chron. 6:15.

Chapter 7
God Preserves the Tribes of Issachar, Benjamin, Naphtali, Manasseh, Ephraim, and Asher, as Numbered by David

'The sons of Tola were mighty men of valor in their generations; their number in the days of David was twenty-two thousand six hundred.' 1 Chron. 7:2b.

Chapter 8
God Raises up Saul as the First King of Israel

'Ner begot Kish, Kish begot Saul, and Saul begot Jonathan, Malchishua, Abinadab, and Esh-Baal. The son of Jonathan was Merib-Baal, and Merib-Baal begot Micah.' 1 Chron. 8:33-34.

Chapter 9
God Preserved Priests and Levites in Jerusalem, Through Saul's Reign and Up to the Captivity in Babylon

'So all Israel was recorded by genealogies, and indeed, they were inscribed in the book of the kings of Israel. But

Judah was carried away captive to Babylon because of their unfaithfulness.' 1 Chron. 9:1.

Chapter **10**

Saul Embodies Israel's Unfaithfulness to God's Covenant and God Rejects him (as He Would Israel)

'So Saul died for his unfaithfulness which he had committed against the LORD, because he did not keep the word of the LORD, and also because he consulted a medium for guidance. But he did not inquire of the LORD; therefore He killed him, and turned the kingdom over to David the son of Jesse.' 1 Chron. 10:13-14.

Chapter **11**

God Establishes David's Throne and Strengthens it with Mighty Men

'Then all Israel came together to David at Hebron, saying, "Indeed we are your bone and your flesh. Also, in time past, even when Saul was king, you were the one who led Israel out and brought them in; and the LORD your God said to you, "You shall shepherd My people Israel, and be ruler over My people Israel."' 1 Chron. 11:1-2.

Chapter **12**

The Lord Fulfills His Covenant With David by Strengthening his Army at Hebron, Even Bringing Loyal Benjamites to Join him

'Then the Spirit came upon Amasai, chief of the captains, and he said: "We are yours, O David; we are on your side, O son of Jesse! Peace, peace to you, and peace to your helpers! For your God helps you." So David received them, and made them captains of the troop.' 1 Chron. 12:18.

Chapter **13**

God Reminds David of His Holiness by Striking Down Uzzah When the Ark of the Covenant was Mistreated

'Then the anger of the LORD was aroused against Uzza, and He struck him because he put his hand to the ark; and he died there before God. And David became angry because of the LORD's outbreak against Uzza; therefore that place is called

Perez Uzza to this day. David was afraid of God that day, saying, "How can I bring the ark of God to me?"' 1 Chron. 13:10-12.

Chapter 14

God Further Strengthens David's Kingdom with the Help of Hiram of Tyre, Giving him Victory Over the Philistines

'Then the fame of David went throughout all lands, and the LORD brought the fear of him upon all nations.' 1 Chron. 14:17.

Chapter 15

David Brings the Ark of the Covenant Properly into Jerusalem, and the Lord Establishes His House While Saul's House Continues to Diminish

'Then David said, "No one may carry the ark of God but the Levites, for the LORD has chosen them to carry the ark of God and to minister before Him forever."' 1 Chron. 15:2.

Chapter 16

David Places the Ark in the Tabernacle, and Sings Praise to God, Echoing 2 Samuel 22 and Psalm 105, and Appointing Levites to Lead in Worship Perpetually

'Sing to the LORD all the earth; Proclaim the good news of His salvation from day to day. Declare His glory among the nations, His wonders among all peoples. For the LORD is great and greatly to be praised; He is also to be feared above all gods. For all the gods of the peoples are idols, but the LORD made the heavens.' 1 Chron. 16:23-26.

Chapter 17

David Desires to Build a House for God, but God Builds His House Instead, Covenanting with him to Keep a Son on his Throne to Save His People, Mirroring 2 Samuel 7

'I will be his Father, and he shall be My son, and I will not take My mercy away from him, as I took it from him who was before you. And I will establish him in My house and in My kingdom forever; and his throne will be established forever.' 1 Chron. 17:13-14.

Chapter 18

God Remembers His Covenant, Giving David Victory Over his Enemies and Strengthening his Kingdom Further

'So David reigned over all Israel, and administered judgment and justice to all his people.' 1 Chron. 18:14.

Chapter 19
The King of Ammon Shames David's Servants, and God Gives David Victory Over the Ammonites and the Syrians

> 'And when the servants of Hadadezer saw that they were defeated by Israel, they made peace with David and became his servants. So the Syrians were not willing to help the people of Ammon anymore.' 1 Chron. 19:19.

Chapter 20
Joab Leads David's Armies to Victory Giving David the Glory, Omitting David's Sin with Bathsheba in Order to Highlight God's Covenant Faithfulness

> 'It happened in the spring of the year, at the time kings go out to battle, that Joab led out the armed forces and ravaged the country of the people of Ammon, and came and besieged Rabbah. But David stayed at Jerusalem. And Joab defeated Rabbah and overthrew it.' 1 Chron. 20:1.

Chapter 21
Satan Moves David to Number Israel, Tempting him to Trust in his Own Might, God Humbles him by Judging the People, David Takes Responsibility for his Sin, and Purchases Ornan's Threshing Floor Where Solomon Would Build the Temple

> 'Then King David said to Ornan, "No, but I will surely buy it for the full price, for I will not take what is yours for the LORD, nor offer burnt offerings with that which costs me nothing."' 1 Chron. 21:24.

Chapter 22
David Prepares to Build the Temple, Exhorting Solomon to Rest on God's Covenant Promises, Exhorting the People to Do the Same

> 'He shall build a house for My name, and he shall be My son, and I will be his Father; and I will establish the throne of his kingdom over Israel forever.' 1 Chron. 22:10.

Chapter 23
David Appoints Priests and Levites to Lead in Singing and Temple Worship

'For David said, "The LORD God of Israel has given rest to His people, that they may dwell in Jerusalem forever."' 1 Chron. 23:25.

Chapter 24
David Lists the Divisions of the Priests and Levites to Sustain God's Worship

'Now these are the divisions of the sons of Aaron. The sons of Aaron were Nadab, Abihu, Eleazar, and Ithamar. And Nadab and Abihu died before their father, and had no children; therefore Eleazar and Ithamar ministered as priests. Then David with Zadok of the sons of Eleazar, and Ahimelech of the sons of Ithamar, divided them according to the schedule of their service.' 1 Chron. 24:1-3.

Chapter 25
David Appoints the Sons of Asaph, Heman, and Jeduthun to Lead Worship with Instruments and Singing

'Moreover David and the captains of the army separated for the service some of the sons of Asaph, Heman, and Jeduthun, who should prophecy with harps, stringed instruments, and cymbals.' 1 Chron. 25:1.

Chapter 26
David Appoints Gatekeepers and Treasurers from Among the Levites

'Concerning the divisions of the gatekeepers: of the Korahites, Meshelemiah the son of Kore, of the sons of Asaph.' 1 Chron. 26:1.

Chapter 27
David Orders Military Divisions, Giving Precedence to Benaiah the Son of Jehoiada, Listing the Leaders of the Tribes and Other Officials

'The third captain of the army for the third month was Benaiah, the son of Jehoiada the priest, who was the chief; in his division were twenty-four thousand.' 1 Chron. 27:5.

Chapter 28
Echoing Chapter 22, David Exhorts Solomon a Second Time in Preparing to Build the Temple and Remaining Faithful to the Lord, Urging him to be Strong and of Good Courage in the Lord

'Now He said to me, "It is your son Solomon who shall build My house and My courts; for I have chosen him to be My son, and I will be his Father. Moreover I will establish his kingdom forever, if he is steadfast to observe My commandments and My judgments, as it is this day."' 1 Chron. 28:6-7.

Chapter **29**

David Praises God for His Faithfulness and Trusts in His Covenant Promises

'Yours, O LORD, is the greatness, the power and the glory, the victory and majesty; for all that is in the heaven and earth is Yours; Yours is the kingdom, O Lord, and You are exalted as head over all.' 1 Chron. 29:11.

2 Chronicles

God encourages His covenant people in exile to look to the future for the fulfillment of the Davidic covenant

Chapter **1**

Solomon Asks for Wisdom in Order to See God Fulfill His Covenant Promises

> 'And Solomon said to God, "You have shown great mercy to David my father, and have made me king in his place. Now, O LORD God, let your promise to David my father be established, for you have made me king over a people like the dust of the earth in multitude. Now give me wisdom and knowledge, that I may go out and come in before this people; for who can judge this great people of Yours?"' 2 Chron. 1:8-10.

Chapter **2**

Solomon Asks Hiram, king of Tyre, to Help him Build God's Temple

> 'But who is able to build Him a temple, since heaven and the heaven of heavens cannot contain Him? Who am I then, that I should build Him a temple, except to burn sacrifice before Him?' 2 Chron. 2:6.

Chapter **3**

Solomon Builds the Temple

> 'Now Solomon began to build the house of the LORD at Jerusalem on Mount Moriah, where the LORD had appeared to his father David, at the place that David had prepared on the threshing floor of Ornan the Jebusite.' 2 Chron. 3:1.

Chapter **4**

Solomon Builds the Furniture and Utensils of the Temple

'Thus Solomon had all the furnishings made for the house of God.' 2 Chron. 4:19a.

Chapter 5

Solomon Finishes the Temple and the Glory of the Lord Fills the House, Fulfilling His Covenant Promise to Dwell With His People

'The house of the LORD was filled with a cloud, so that the priests could not continue ministering because of the cloud; for the glory of the LORD filled the house of God.' 2 Chron. 5:13c-14.

Chapter 6

Solomon Blesses the People and Prays that God Would Remember His Covenant with David

'Therefore, LORD God of Israel, now keep what You promised Your servant David my father, saying, "You shall not fail to have a man sit before Me on the throne of Israel, only if your sons take heed to their way, that they walk in My law as you have walked before Me." And now, O LORD God of Israel, let Your word come true, which You have spoken to Your servant David. But will God indeed dwell with men on the earth? Behold, heaven and the heaven of heavens cannot contain You. How much less this temple which I have built!' 2 Chron. 6:16-18.

Chapter 7

God Answers Solomon's Prayer By Consuming the Sacrifices with Fire From Heaven, Promising to Hear the People's Prayers, Giving Warnings of Exile

'And as for this house, which is exalted, everyone who passes by it will be astonished and say, "Why has the LORD done thus to this land and this house?" Then they will answer, "Because they forsook the LORD God of their fathers, who brought them out of the land of Egypt, and embraced other gods, and worshiped them and served them; therefore He has brought all this calamity on them."' 2 Chron. 7:21-22.

Chapter 8

The Lord Establishes and Strengthens Solomon's Kingdom, and Dwells With His People

'Now Solomon brought the daughter of Pharaoh up from the City of David to the house he had built for her, for he said, "My wife shall not dwell in the house of David king of Israel, because the places to which the ark of the LORD has come are holy."' 2 Chron. 8:11.

Chapter 9
The Lord Fulfills His Promise to Solomon, Enriching him and Showing God's Glory to the Queen of Sheba Through Solomon's Wisdom

'Blessed be the LORD your God, who delighted in you, setting you on His throne to be king for the LORD your God! Because your God has loved Israel, to establish them forever, therefore He made you king over them, to do justice and righteousness.' 2 Chron. 9:8.

Chapter 10
Rehoboam Becomes King After Solomon, and the Lord Brings About Israel's Rebellion, Anticipating Division and Eventual Exile

'So the king did not listen to the people; for the turn of events was from God, that the LORD might fulfill His word, which He had spoken by the hand of Ahijah the Shilonite to Jeroboam the son of Nebat.' 2 Chron. 10:15.

Chapter 11
The Lord Strengthens David's Kingdom Under Rehoboam in Spite of Israel's Rebellion

'Thus says the LORD, "You shall not go up or fight against your brethren! Let every man return to his house, for this thing is from Me."' 2 Chron. 11:4.

Chapter 12
Rehoboam Forgets the Lord in his Prosperity, Serving as a Warning to Future Generations

'Now it came to pass, when Rehoboam had established the kingdom and had strengthened himself, that he forsook the law of the LORD, and all Israel along with him ... And he did evil, because he did not prepare his heart to seek the LORD.' 2 Chron. 12:1, 14.

Chapter 13
Abijah Reigns in Rehoboam's Place, Defending his Kingdom Against Jeroboam, and Encouraging Future Generations by Modelling Trust in the Lord

> 'Now look, God Himself is with us as our Head, and His priests with sounding trumpets to sound the alarm against you. O children of Israel, do not fight against the LORD God of your fathers, for you shall not prosper! … Thus the children of Israel were subdued at that time; and the children of Judah prevailed, because they relied on the LORD God of their fathers.' 2 Chron. 13:12, 18.

Chapter 14
Asa Reigns in Abijah's Place, Giving Hope to the Exiles as an Example of Trusting in the Lord's Covenant Promises

> 'And Asa cried out to the LORD his God, and said, "LORD, it is nothing for You to help, whether with many or with those who have no power; help us, O LORD our God, for we rest on You, and in your name we go up against this multitude. O LORD, You are our God; do not let man prevail against You!"' 2 Chron. 14:11.

Chapter 15
The Lord Gives Hope to the Exiles by Showing His Faithfulness to His Covenant Promises, Including People from the Northern Tribes Who Followed the Lord

> 'Then they entered into a covenant to seek the LORD God of their fathers with all their heart and with all their soul … And all Judah rejoiced at the oath, for they had sworn with all their heart and sought Him with all their soul; and He was found by them, and the LORD gave them rest all around.' 2 Chron. 15:12, 15.

Chapter 16
The Lord Warns the People Not to Trust in Anyone Besides Him, Promising to Help Those Remaining Loyal to Him, and Illustrating the Point When Asa's Life Does not End Well

> 'For the eyes of the LORD run to and fro throughout the whole earth, to show Himself strong on behalf of those whose heart is loyal to Him. In this you have done foolishly; therefore from now on you shall have wars.' 2 Chron. 16:9.

Chapter 17

Jehoshaphat Reigns in Asa's Place, Seeking the Lord with the Levites Teaching the People the Law, and Becoming an Example of the Lord's Blessing on Faithfulness to His Covenant

> 'And his heart took delight in the ways of the LORD; moreover he removed the high places and wooden images from Judah ... So Jehoshaphat became increasingly powerful, and he built fortresses and storage cities in Judah. He had much property in the cities of Judah; and the men of war, mighty men of valor, were in Jerusalem.' 2 Chron. 17:6, 12-13.

Chapter 18

Jehoshaphat Allies himself with the Wicked King of Israel, and Micaiah Tells the King that God Sent a Lying Spirit to Show the Consequences of Covenant Unfaithfulness

> 'But Jehoshaphat said, "Is there not still a prophet of the LORD here, that we may inquire of Him?" So the king of Israel said to Jehoshaphat, "There is still one man by whom we may inquire of the LORD; but I hate him, because he never prophesies good concerning me, but always evil. He is Micaiah the Son of Imla." And Jehoshaphat said, "Let not the king say such things!"' 2 Chron. 18:6-7

Chapter 19

The Lord Rebukes Jehoshaphat for his Alliance with the Wicked and Jehoshaphat Shows the Exiles a Model of Repentance, Bringing Some from the Northern Tribes Back to the Lord, Appointing Righteous Judges and Levites

> 'And Jehu the son of Hanani the seer went out to meet him, and said to King Jehoshaphat, "Should you help the wicked and love those who hate the LORD? Therefore the wrath of the LORD is upon you. Nevertheless good things are found in you, in that you have removed the wooden images from the land, and have prepared your heart to seek God" ... "Behave courageously and the LORD will be with the good."' 2 Chron. 19:2-3, 11b.

Chapter 20

The Lord Tests Jehoshaphat's Loyalty by Raising Amon, Moab, and Edom Against him, and Jehoshaphat Provides the Exiles with a Positive Example of Seeking the Lord by Pleading His Covenant Promises, With a Final Warning Against Defection

> 'And Jehoshaphat feared, and set himself to seek the LORD, and proclaimed a fast throughout all Judah ... Are you not our God, who drove out of the inhabitants of this land before Your people Israel, and gave it to the descendants of Abraham Your friend forever?' 2 Chron. 20:3, 7.

Chapter 21

Jehoram Reigns in Jehoshaphat's Place, and the Lord Remembers His Covenant With David in Spite of the Nation's Apostasy, Though Jehoram Dies 'to no one's sorrow.'

> 'Yet the LORD would not destroy the house of David, because of the covenant that He had made with David, and since He had promised to give a lamp to him and to his sons forever.' 2 Chron. 21:7.

Chapter 22

Ahaziah Reigns in Jehoram's Place and Walks in the Ways of the Kings of Israel, and Athaliah Seizes the Throne After her Son's Death

> 'So the house of Ahaziah had no one to assume power over the kingdom.' 2 Chron. 22:9c.

Chapter 23

God Preserves Joash, Athaliah is Overthrown, and the People Rejoice That God Remembered His Covenant with David

> 'Then all the assembly made a covenant with the king in the house of God. And he said to them, "Behold, the king's son shall reign, as the LORD said to the sons of David."' 2 Chron. 23:3.

Chapter 24

Joash Sets his Heart on Restoring the Lord's House, but his Later Apostasy, Forgetting the Kindness of Jehoiada the Priest, Serves as a Warning to the Exiles

> 'Then the Spirit of God came upon Zechariah the son of Jehoiada the priest, who stood above the people, and said to them, "Thus says God, Why do you transgress the commandments of the LORD, so that you cannot prosper? Because you have forsaken the LORD, He has also forsaken you."' 2 Chron. 24:20.

Chapter 25

Amaziah Reigns in Joash's Place, and Serves the Lord, but Not with a Loyal Heart, Resulting in Israel Defeating Judah

> 'And he did what was right in the sight of the LORD, but not with a loyal heart.' 2 Chron. 25:2.

Chapter 26

Uzziah Reigns in Amaziah's Place, God Strengthens him While he Serves the Lord, then Strikes him With Leprosy When he Usurps the Role of the Priests, Exiling him From Temple Worship

> 'And he did what was right in the sight of the LORD, according to all that his father Amaziah had done. He sought God in the days of Zechariah, who had understanding in the visions of God; and as long as he sought the LORD, God made him prosper.' 2 Chron. 26:4-5.

Chapter 27

Jotham Reigns in Uzziah's Place, Seeking the Lord and Becoming a Model to the Exiles of God's Blessing on Faith

> 'So Jotham became mighty, because he prepared his ways before the LORD his God.' 2 Chron. 27:6.

Chapter 28

Ahaz Reigns in Jotham's Place, Turning to Idols and Suffering Defeat by his Enemies, Israel Having Mercy on Judah, and Ahaz Strengthens himself in Idolatry and Dies in Shame

> 'For Pekah the son of Remaliah killed one hundred and twenty thousand in Judah in one day, all valiant men, because they had forsaken the LORD God of their fathers.' 2 Chron. 28:6.

Chapter 29

Hezekiah Reigns in Ahaz's Place and Instructs the Levites to Restore God's Worship, in Contrast to Uzziah and in Repentance of Ahaz's Idolatry

> 'Now it is in my heart to make a covenant with the LORD God of Israel, that His fierce wrath may turn away from us. My sons, do not be negligent now, for the LORD has chosen you to stand before Him, to serve Him, and that you should minister to Him and burn incense.' 2 Chron. 29:10-11.

Chapter 30

Hezekiah Restores the Passover After Long Neglect, Inviting the Northern Tribes to Participate in Restored Worship, Giving Hope to the Exiles if they Prepare their Hearts to Seek the Lord

> 'For if you return to the LORD, your brethren and your children will be treated with compassion by those who lead them captive, so that they may come back to this land; for the LORD your God is gracious and merciful, and will not turn His face from you if you return to Him.' 2 Chron. 30:9.

Chapter 31

Hezekiah's Reforms Spill into the Exiled Northern Kingdom, and he Promotes the Work of the Levities in Sustaining God's Worship

> 'Now when all this was finished, all Israel who were present went out to the cities of Judah and broke the sacred pillars in pieces, cut down the wooden images, and threw down the high places and altars – from all Judah, Benjamin, Ephraim, and Manasseh – until they had utterly destroyed them all. Then all the children of Israel returned to their own cities, every man to his possession.' 2 Chron. 31:1.

Chapter 32

Sennacherib of Assyria Boasts Against the Lord, the Lord Shows that He Alone is God, Hezekiah Turns to Pride and Then the Lord Delays the Exile Because he Humbles himself

> 'However, regarding the ambassadors of the princes of Babylon, whom they sent to him to inquire about the wonder that was done in the land, God withdrew from him, in order to test him, that He might know all that was in his heart.' 2 Chron. 32:31.

Chapter 33

Manasseh Reigns in Hezekiah's Place, Turns Israel to Idolatry, Repents on Humbling himself in Prison, and Amon Reigns in his Place and Reverts to his Father's Former Idolatry

> 'Now when he was in affliction, he implored the God of his fathers, and prayed to Him; and He received his entreaty, heard his supplication, and brought him back to Jerusalem into his kingdom. Then Manasseh knew that the LORD was God.' 2 Chron. 33:12-13.

CHAPTER **34**

Josiah Reigns in Manasseh's Place, Abolishing Idolatry in Both the Southern and Northern Kingdoms, and Finding the Book of the Law While Restoring Temple Worship he Humbles himself and Leads the People in Repentance

> 'Then the king stood in his place and made a covenant before the LORD, to keep His commandments and His testimonies and His statutes with all his heart and with all his soul, to perform the words of the covenant that were written in this book. And he made all who were present in Jerusalem and Benjamin take a stand. So the inhabitants of Jerusalem did according to the covenant of God, the God of their fathers.' 2 Chron. 34:31-32.

CHAPTER **35**

Josiah Restores the Passover in Restoring Covenant with God, but he Dies in Battle Against the King of Egypt

> 'There had been no Passover kept in Israel like that since the days of Samuel the prophet; and none of the kings of Israel had kept such a Passover as Josiah kept, with the priests and the Levites, all Judah and Israel who were present, and the inhabitants of Jerusalem.' 2 Chron. 35:18.

CHAPTER **36**

Jehoahaz, Jehoiakim, Jehoiachin, and Zedekiah are the Last Kings of Judah Before Nebuchadnezzar Takes Them into Exile for their Covenant Breaking, yet the Lord Gives the Exiles Hope in the Decree of Cyrus

> 'And the LORD God of their fathers sent warnings to them by His messengers, rising up early and sending them, because He had compassion on His people and on His dwelling place. But they mocked the messengers of God, despising His words, and scoffed at His prophets, until the wrath of the LORD arose against His people, till there was no remedy.' 2 Chron. 36:15-16.

Ezra

God restores the worship of His covenant people as the exiles return to the land and rebuild the temple

Chapter **1**
God Remembers His Covenant With Israel by Stirring Up Cyrus' Spirit to Send the Exiles Back to the Land to Rebuild the Temple, Stirring Up the Spirits of the Select Few to Go

> 'Then the heads of the father's houses of Judah and Benjamin, and the priests and the Levites, with all whose spirits God had moved, arose to go up and build the house of the LORD which is in Jerusalem.' Ezra 1:5.

Chapter **2**
The Lord Sends Back About Fifty Thousand People, in Contrast to the Millions of Israel, to Rebuild the Temple, but not All the People Could Trace their Genealogies, Hindering the Ability of the Priests to Lead the Work

> 'These sought their listing among those who were registered by genealogy, but they were not found; therefore they were excluded from the priesthood as defiled." Ezra 2:62.

Chapter **3**
Joshua the Priest and Zerubbabel the Governor Rebuild the Altar and Restore Worship, According to the Mosaic Covenant, But When the Temple Foundation is Laid, Many Rejoice in What they Have While Many Weep for What they Lost in Exile

> 'But many of the priests and Levites and heads of the fathers' houses, old men who had seen the first temple, wept with a loud voice when the foundation of this temple was laid before their eyes. Yet many shouted aloud for joy, so that the people

could not discern the noise of the shout of joy from the noise of the weeping of the people, for the people shouted with a loud shout, and the sound was heard afar off.' Ezra 3:12-13.

Chapter 4
God Raises Opposition Against the Rebuilding Efforts, Zerubbabel Resists Israel's Enemies, but Artaxerxes Prohibits the Rebuilding Effort Until the Time of Darius

'Thus the work of the house of God which is at Jerusalem ceased, and it was discontinued until the second year of the reign of Darius king of Persia.' Ezra 4:24.

Chapter 5
The Lord Raises up Haggai and Zechariah to Strengthen Israel, and the Governor Writes to Darius

'And thus they returned us an answer, saying, "We are the servants of the God of heaven and earth, and we are rebuilding the temple that was built many years ago, which a great king of Israel built and completed. But because our fathers provoked the God of heaven to wrath, He gave them into the hand of Nebuchadnezzar king of Babylon, the Chaldean, who destroyed this temple and carried the people away to Babylon."' Ezra 5:11-12.

Chapter 6
Darius Decrees that the Jews Continue Rebuilding the Temple at the King's Expense, the People Finish the Temple, and Celebrate the Passover

'So the elders of the Jews built, and they prospered through the prophesying of Haggai the prophet and Zechariah the son of Iddo. And they built and finished it, according to the commandment of the God of Israel, and according to the command of Cyrus, Darius, and Artaxerxes king of Persia.' Ezra 6:14.

Chapter 7
The Lord Sends Ezra to Implement the Law of Moses at the King's Command and he Praises God for His Covenant Faithfulness

'Blessed be the LORD God of our fathers, who has put such a thing as this in the king's heart, to beautify the house of the

LORD which is in Jerusalem, and has extended mercy to me before the king and his counselors, and before all the king's mighty princes. So I was encouraged, as the hand of the LORD my God was upon me; and I gathered the leading men of Israel to go up with me.' Ezra 7:27-28.

Chapter 8

Ezra Brings a Second Wave of Exiles Back to the Land, and the Good Hand of God Provides him With Levites and Guides him Safely to the Land

'For I was ashamed to request of the king an escort of soldiers and horsemen to help us against the enemy on the road, because we had spoken to the king, saying, "The hand of our God is upon all those for good who seek Him, but His power and His wrath are against all those who forsake Him." So we fasted and entreated our God for this, and He answered our prayer.' Ezra 8:22-23.

Chapter 9

The People Break Covenant With God by Intermarrying with the People of the Land, and Ezra Leads them in a Prayer of Confession

'O LORD God of Israel, You are righteous, for we are left as a remnant, as it is this day. Here we are before You, in our guilt, though no one can stand before You because of this!' Ezra 9:15.

Chapter 10

The People Renew Covenant With God by Putting Away their Foreign Wives, but Ezra Ends on an Ominous Note with the Covenant People and Priests Having Mixed and Had Children With the People of the Land

'Now therefore, let us make a covenant with our God to put away all these wives and those who have been born to them, according to the advice of my master and of those who tremble at the commandment of our God; and let it be done according to the law.' Ezra 10:3.

Nehemiah

God protects His covenant people, rebuilding the wall of Jerusalem, and exhorts them to repentance and directs them to covenant faithfulness

Chapter **1**
Nehemiah Prays that God Would Remember His Covenant and Strengthen the Returned Exiles by Rebuilding the Wall of Jerusalem

> 'And I said, "I pray, LORD God of heaven, O great and awesome God, You who keep Your covenant and mercy with those who love You and observe your commandment … Now these are Your servants and Your people, whom You have redeemed by Your great power, and by Your strong hand."' Neh. 1:5, 10.

Chapter **2**
The Good Hand of God is Upon Nehemiah, Granting him Favor in the King's Sight, as he Returns to Jerusalem and Surveys the Ruined Wall

> 'And I told them of the hand of my God which had been good upon me, and also of the king's words that he had spoken to me. So they said, "Let us rise up and build." Then they set their hands to this good work.' Neh. 2:18.

Chapter **3**
Every Family Rebuilds the Wall in Front of their Own Homes, with Some Hints of Troubles Resurfacing Later in the Book

> 'Next to him the Tekoites made repairs; but their nobles did not put their shoulders to the work of their LORD.' Neh. 3:5.

Chapter 4
Sanballat and Tobiah Lead Israel's Enemies in Mocking and Threatening them in their Work, While Nehemiah Leads Israel in Prayer, Defending themselves, and Giving God Glory for Preserving them

> 'Nevertheless we made our prayer to our God and because of them we set a watch against them day and night ... And I looked, and arose and said to the nobles, to the leaders, and to the rest of the people, "Do not be afraid of them. Remember the LORD, great and awesome, and fight for your brethren, your sons, your daughters, your wives, and your houses ... Wherever you hear the sound of the trumpet, rally to us there. Our God will fight for us."' Neh. 4:9, 14, 20.

Chapter 5
The Nobles of Israel Abuse the Poor People, Nehemiah Calls them to Repentance, and Leads them by his Own Example of Generosity

> 'Remember me, my God, for good, according to all that I have done for this people.' Neh. 5:19.

Chapter 6
Nehemiah Retains his Integrity as God's Enemies Plot Against him, Serving as a Model of Prayer and Faith as God Helps him Complete the Wall of Jerusalem

> 'So the wall was finished on the twenty-fifth day of Elul, in fifty-two days. And it happened, when all our enemies heard of it, and all the nations around us saw these things, that they were disheartened in their own eyes; for they perceived that this work was done by our God.' Neh. 6:15-16.

Chapter 7
Nehemiah Establishes Good Leadership and Worship, Recording a Fresh Genealogy of the People and Priests Under Zerubbabel and Joshua, Some of the Genealogical Lines Failing

> 'Now the city was large and spacious, but the people in it were few, and the houses were not rebuilt. Then my God put it into my heart to gather the nobles, the rulers, and the people, that they might be registered by genealogy.' Neh. 7:4-5a.

CHAPTER 8
Ezra and the Priests Teach the People the Law of Moses, Nehemiah Exhorts them to Rejoice Instead of Mourn, and the People Hear the Law as they Keep the Feast of Tabernacles, Following Deuteronomy 31:9-13

'And Nehemiah, who was the governor, Ezra the priest and scribe, and the Levites who taught the people said to all the people, "This day is holy to the LORD your God; do not mourn nor weep." For all the people wept, when they heard the words of the Law. Then he said to them, "God your way, eat the fat, drink the sweet, and send portions to those for whom nothing is prepared; for this day is holy to our LORD. Do not sorrow, for the joy of the LORD is your strength."' Neh. 8:9-10.

CHAPTER 9
After the Feast of Tabernacles, Nehemiah and the Priests Continue Reading the Law in Fasting and Mourning, While Nehemiah Renews Covenant with God Through a Prayer of Confession, Pleading the Terms of the Abrahamic and Mosaic Administrations of the Covenant of Grace

'Yet for many years You had patience with them, and testified against them by Your Spirit in Your prophets. Yet they would not listen; Therefore You gave them into the hand of the peoples of the lands. Nevertheless in Your great mercy You did not utterly consume them nor forsake them; For You are God, gracious and merciful.' Neh. 9:30-31.

CHAPTER 10
The Leaders of the People Respond by Renewing Covenant with God, giving Specific Examples of Pledged Obedience

'These joined with their brethren, their nobles, and entered into a curse and an oath to walk in God's Law, which was given by Moses the servant of God, and to observe and do all the commandments of the LORD our Lord, and His ordinances and His statutes.' Neh. 10:29.

CHAPTER 11
Nehemiah Lists the Families of Those who Willingly Dwelt in Jerusalem

> 'And the people blessed all the men who willingly offered themselves to dwell at Jerusalem.' Neh. 11:2.

Chapter 12
Nehemiah Ensures the Genealogies of the Priests in Order to Maintain the Covenant with God by Leading Temple Worship, According to God's Covenant with David

> 'Also that day they offered great sacrifices, and rejoiced, for God made them rejoice with great joy; the women and the children also rejoiced, so that the joy of Jerusalem was heard afar off.' Neh. 12:43.

Chapter 13
The People Break their Covenant with God at Every Point, in Spite of Nehemiah's Efforts at Continued Reform, Who Commits his Cause to God

> 'Remember me, O my God, concerning this, and do not wipe out my good deeds that I have done for the house of my God, and for its services! … Remember me, O my God, concerning this also, and spare me according to the greatness of Your mercy! … Remember them, O my God, because they have defiled the priesthood and the covenant of the priesthood and the Levites … Remember me, O my God, for good!' Neh. 13:14, 22b, 29, 31b.

Esther

God protects His covenant people under a foreign empire, even though His name never appears explicitly

Chapter **1**

God Sets the Stage for Preserving His Covenant People in Exile When Ahasuerus Deposes Queen Vashti[1]

> 'And the reply pleased the king and the princes, and the king did according to the word of Memucan. Then he sent letters to all the king's provinces, to each in its own script, and to every people in their own language, that each man should be master in his own house, and speak in the language of his own people.' Esther 1:21-22.

Chapter **2**

God Raises Esther to Become Queen in Vashti's Place, and Providentially Guides Mordecai to Prevent an Attempt on the King's Life

> 'And Mordecai brought up Hadassah, that is Esther, his uncle's daughter, for she had neither father nor mother. The young woman was lovely and beautiful. When her father and mother died, Mordecai took her as his own daughter.' Esther 2:7.

Chapter **3**

God Raises Up Haman an Agagite to Threaten the Jews, and Mordecai Refuses to Pay him Homage, Leading to a Plot to Kill the Jews

---

1. While God's names and titles do not appear in Esther, in line with the rest of Scripture, God is the primary actor behind these events of His providence regarding His covenant people.

> 'The couriers went out, hastened by the king's command; and the decree was proclaimed in Shushan the citadel. So the king and Haman sat down to drink, but the city of Shushan was perplexed.' Esther 3:15.

Chapter 4
Mordecai Exhorts Esther to Intervene for the People Before the King, Implicitly Trusting God to Deliver His Covenant People, and Esther Calls the People to Fast and Pray for her

> 'For if you remain completely silent at this time, relief and deliverance will arise for the Jews from another place, but you and your father's house will perish. Yet who knows whether you have come to the kingdom for such a time as this?' Esther 4:14.

Chapter 5
God Grants Esther Favor in the King's Sight and she Invites Haman to Two Banquets Before the King, While Haman Plots to Kill Mordecai

> 'Then his wife Zeresh and all his friends said to him, "Let a gallows be made, fifty cubits high, and in the morning suggest to the king that Mordecai be hanged on it; then go merrily with the king to the banquet." And the thing pleased Haman; so he had the gallows made.' Esther 5:14.

Chapter 6
God Directs Events so that the King Remembers Mordecai's Work in Saving his Life, Haman is Humbled While Seeking his Own Exaltation, and Haman's Family Concludes that None Can Stand Against the Jews

> 'When Haman told his wife Zeresh and all his friends everything that had happened to him, his wise men and his wife Zeresh said to him, "If Mordecai, before whom you have begun to fall, is of Jewish descent, you will not prevail against him but will surely fall before him."' Esther 6:13.

Chapter 7
Esther Reveals Haman's Plot to Destroy the Jews to the King, Haman Seals his Destruction, and the King Hangs him on the Gallows Prepared for Mordecai, God Showing that the Wicked Fall into their Own Nets

'Now Harbonah, one of the king's eunuchs, said to the king, "Look! The gallows, fifty cubits high, which Haman made for Mordecai, who spoke good on the king's behalf, is standing at the house of Haman." Then the king said, "Hang him on it!"' Esther 7:9.

CHAPTER **8**

God Saves the Jews Through Esther's Intervention with the King

'By these letters the king permitted the Jews who were in every city to gather together and protect their lives – to destroy, kill, and annihilate all the forces of any people or province that would assault them, both little children and women, and to plunder their possessions.' Esther 8:11.

CHAPTER **9**

Mordecai Establishes the Feast of Purim with the King's Authority in Order to Commemorate God's Protection of His Covenant People

'So they called these days Purim, after the name Pur...So the decree of Esther confirmed these matters of Purim, and it was written in the book.' Esther 9:26a, 32.

CHAPTER **10**

God Exalts Mordecai in Persia in Order to Secure His Covenant People in Peace

'For Mordecai the Jew was second to King Ahasuerus, and was great among the Jews and well received by the multitude of his brethren, seeking the good of his people and speaking peace to all his countrymen.' Esther 10:3.

Job

God displays His power, righteousness, and wisdom as the God of providence, directing Job and his friends to remember His character

CHAPTER **1**

Job is Righteous and Cares for the Righteousness of his Family, God Permits Satan to Test Job's Faith, and Job Trusts the Lord After Losing Everything

> 'And he said: "Naked I came from my mother's womb, and naked I shall return there. The LORD gave, and the LORD has taken away; blessed be the name of the LORD." In all this Job did not sin nor charge God with wrong.' Job 1:21-22.

CHAPTER **2**

God Next Permits Satan to Take Job's Health, Job Still Justifies God, and his Friends Come to Comfort him

> 'But he said to her, "You speak as one of the foolish women speaks. Shall we indeed accept good from God, and shall we not accept adversity?" In all this Job did not sin with his lips.' Job 2:10.

CHAPTER **3**

In Job's First Speech, he Curses the Day of his Conception and Birth

> 'For the thing I greatly feared has come upon me, and what I dreaded has happened to me. I am not at ease, nor am I quiet; I have no rest, for trouble comes.' Job 3:25-26.

CHAPTER **4**

Eliphaz Makes his First Speech, Reminding Job of his Past Integrity, but Tells him that no Innocent People Suffer, Implying that Job had Sinned, and Relating a Vision about the Terror of God

'Can a mortal be more righteous than God? Can a man be more pure than his Maker? If He puts no trust in His servants, if He charges His angels with error, how much more those who dwell in houses of clay, whose foundation is in the dust, who are crushed before a moth?' Job 4:17-19.

Chapter 5

Eliphaz Continues with Greater Boldness, Stating that God is Chastening Job for Hidden Sins, Encouraging him to Seek God

'He catches the wise in their own craftiness, and the counsel of the cunning comes quickly upon them ... Behold, happy is the man whom God corrects; therefore do not despise the chastening of the Almighty.' Job 5:13, 17.

Chapter 6

Job Makes his Second Speech, Defending his Complaints, Relating his Sorrows and Defending his Integrity

'To him who is afflicted, kindness should be shown by his friend, even though he forsakes the fear of the Almighty ... Yield now, let there be no injustice! Yes, concede, my righteousness still stands! Is there injustice on my tongue? Cannot my taste discern the unsavory?' Job 6:14, 29.

Chapter 7

Job Resolves to Continue his Complaint in Light of the Brevity of his Life, and Asks What God Has Against him

'My days are swifter than a weaver's shuttle, and are spent without hope. Oh, remember that my life is a breath! My eye will never again see good ... I loathe my life; I would not live forever. Let me alone, for my days are but a breath.' Job 7:6-7, 16.

Chapter 8

Bildad Gives his First Speech, Expressing Impatience at Job's Complaining, Pointing to God's Righteousness and Offering Job Hope if he Returns to God

'For we were born yesterday, and know nothing, because our days on earth are a shadow.' Job 8:9.

Chapter 9
Job's Third Speech Points to God's Irresistible Power, His Doing as He Pleases, and Job's Cry for a Mediator Between him and God

> 'Truly I know it is so, but how can a man be righteous before God? ... If I called and He answered me, I would not believe that He was listening to my voice ... The earth is given into the hand of the wicked. He covers the faces of its judges. If it is not He, who else could it be?' Job 9:2, 16, 24.

Chapter 10
Job Gives Free Course to his Complaint in Light of his Integrity Before God

> 'My soul loathes my life; I will give free course to my complaint, I will speak in the bitterness of my soul ... Although you know I am not wicked, and there is no one who can deliver from Your hand?' Job 10:1, 7.

Chapter 11
Zophar Makes his First Speech, Accusing Job of Empty Talk and Seeking to Vindicate God's Character, and Accusing Job of Wickedness

> 'Can you search out the deep things of God? Can you find out the limits of the Almighty? They are higher than heaven – what can you do? Deeper than Sheol – what can you know? Their measure is longer than the earth and broader than the sea ... For an empty-headed man will be wise, when a wild donkey's colt is born a man.' Job 11:7-9, 12.

Chapter 12
Job's Fourth Speech Acknowledges God's Control, Wisdom, and Irresistible Power

> 'With Him are wisdom and strength, He has counsel and understanding.' Job 12:13.

Chapter 13
Job Professes his Desire to Reason with God and Denounces his Friends as Worthless

> 'Though He slay me, yet will I trust Him. Even so, I will defend my own ways before Him.' Job 13:15.

Chapter 14

Job Reflects on the Troubles of Man's Short Life

> 'Oh, that You would hide me in the grave, that You would conceal me until Your wrath is past, that You would appoint for me a set time, and remember me! If a man dies, shall he live again? All the days of my hard service I will wait, till my change comes.' Job 14:13-14.

Chapter 15

In his Second Speech, Eliphaz Grows Bolder in Accusing Job of Sin

> 'Yes, you cast off fear, and restrain prayer before God ... If God puts no trust in His saints, and the heavens are not pure in His sight, how much less man, who is abominable and filthy, who drinks iniquity like water!' Job 15:4, 15-16.

Chapter 16

Job's Fifth Speech Rejects his Miserable Counsellors and Accuses God of Hating him

> 'I have heard such things; miserable comforters are you all! ... He tears me in His wrath, and hates me He gnashes at me with His teeth; my adversary sharpens His gaze on me ... Oh, that one might plead for a man with God, as a man pleads for his neighbor!' Job 16:2, 9, 21.

Chapter 17

Job Denounces his Friends and Maintains his Integrity, Even While Hope Escapes him

> 'Yet the righteous will hold to his way, and he who has clean hands will be stronger and stronger.' Job 17:9.

Chapter 18

Bildad's Second Speech Rebukes Job Openly, Telling Job that he Suffers as a Wicked Man

> 'Surely such are the dwellings of the wicked, and this is the place of him who does not know God.' Job 18:21.

Chapter 19

Job, in his Sixth Speech, Accuses God of Wronging him, but Expresses Trust in his Redeemer as Well

'Know then that God has wronged me, and has surrounded me with His net ... Why do you persecute me as God does, and are not satisfied with my flesh? ... For I know that my Redeemer lives, and He shall stand at last on the earth; and after my skin is destroyed, this I know, that in my flesh I shall see God, whom I shall see for myself, and my eyes shall behold, and not another. How my heart yearns within me!' Job 19:6, 22, 25-27.

Chapter **20**
Zophar's Second Speech Retaliates Against Job, Accusing him of Being the Wicked Man

'I have heard the rebuke that reproaches me, and the spirit of my understanding causes me to answer ... This is the portion from God for a wicked man, the heritage appointed to him by God.' Job 20:3, 29.

Chapter **21**
Job's Seventh Speech Notes that the Wicked Often Prosper, Though God Will Judge them in the End

'Why do the wicked live and become old, yes, become mighty in power? ... For the wicked are reserved for the day of doom; they shall be brought out on the day of wrath.' Job 21:7, 30.

Chapter **22**
Eliphaz, in his Third Speech, Argues that Job has Sinned, but there is Still Hope if he Returns to God

'Can a man be profitable to God, though he who is wise may be profitable to himself? Is it any pleasure to the Almighty that you are righteous? Or is it gain to Him that you make your ways blameless?' Job 22:2-3.

Chapter **23**
Job's Eighth Speech Complains that God is Hidden from him

'But He is unique, and who can make Him change? And whatever His soul desires, that He does. For He performs what is appointed for me, and many such things are with Him. Therefore I am terrified at His presence; when I consider this, I am afraid of Him. For God made my heart weak, and the Almighty terrifies me; because I was not cut off from the presence of darkness, and He did not hide deep darkness from my face.' Job 23:13-17.

Chapter 24

Job Laments the Prosperity of the Wicked in Spite of God's Sovereignty

'Since times are no hidden from the Almighty, why do those who know Him see not His days? … But God draws the mighty away with His power; He rises up, but no man is sure of life. He gives them security, and they rely on it; yet His eyes are on their ways.' Job 24:1, 22-23.

Chapter 25

Bildad's Third and Final Speech Briefly Extols the Loftiness of God and the Lowliness of Man

'How then can man be righteous before God? Or how can he be pure who is born of a woman?' Job 25:4.

Chapter 26

Job Begins his Ninth and Final Speech, Beginning with Man's Frailty and God's Majesty

'By His Spirit He adorned the heavens; His hand pierced the fleeing serpent. Indeed these are the mere edges of His ways, and how small a whisper we hear of Him! But the thunder of His power who can understand?' Job 26:13-14.

Chapter 27

Job Professes to Maintain his Integrity, Even While Charging the Almighty with Injustice

'As God lives, who has taken away my justice, and the Almighty, who has made my soul bitter, as long as my breath is in me, and the breath of God in my nostrils, my lips will not speak wickedness, nor my tongue utter deceit. Far be it from me, that I should say you are right; till I die I will not put away my integrity from me.' Job 27:2-5.

Chapter 28

Job Meditates on the Limitations of Man's Wisdom

'God understands its way, and He knows its place … And to man He said, "Behold, the fear of the Lord, that is wisdom, and to depart from evil is understanding."' Job 28:23, 28.

Chapter 29
Job Wishes that Things Were as they Once Had Been When he Prospered and Cared for Others

> 'Because I delivered the poor who cried out, the fatherless and the one who had no helper.' Job 29:12.

Chapter 30
Job Contrasts his Former Prosperity with his Current Distress, Blaming God for Cruelty to him

> 'But You have become cruel to me; with the strength of Your hand You oppose me.' Job 30:21.

Chapter 31
Job Reflects on the Integrity of his Life, Showing that his Suffering Was not for his Sins, and Proclaiming a Curse Against himself if he has Secretly Lived an Evil Life

> 'If I have covered my transgressions as Adam, by hiding my iniquity in my bosom ... Oh, that I had one to hear me! Here is my mark. Oh, that the Almighty would answer me, that my Prosecutor had written a book! Surely I would carry it on my shoulder, and bind it on me like a crown; I would declare to Him the number of my steps; like a prince I would approach Him.' Job 31:33, 35-37.

Chapter 32
Elihu is Angry Because Job Justified himself Rather than God, and Because Job's Friends Condemned Job Wrongly

> 'Then the wrath of Elihu, the son of Barachel the Buzite, of the family of Ram, was aroused against Job; his wrath was aroused because he justified himself rather than God. Also against his three friends his wrath was aroused, because they had found no answer, and yet had condemned Job ... Great men are not always wise, nor do the aged always understand justice.' Job 32:2-3, 9.

Chapter 33
Elihu Begins to Address Job in God's Place, Giving him Concrete Examples of Errors in his Speech, Followed by Encouragements to Repent

> 'The Spirit of God has made me, and the breath of the Almighty gives me life ... Truly I am as your spokesman before God;

I also have been formed out of clay ... Look, in this you are not righteous. I will answer you, for God is greater than man. Why do you contend with Him? For He does not give an account of any of His words. For God may speak in one way, or in another, yet man does not perceive it ... If you have anything to say, answer me; speak, for I desire to justify you.' Job 33:4, 6, 12-14, 32.

CHAPTER **34**

Elihu Defends God's Justice and Acknowledges Job's Affliction

'What man is like Job, who drinks scorn like water? ... Therefore listen to me, you men of understanding: far be it from God to do wickedness, and from the Almighty to commit iniquity. For He repays man according to his work, and makes man to find reward according to his way.' Job 34:7, 10-11.

CHAPTER **35**

Elihu Rebukes Job for Acting as Though he is More Righteous than God, Using Words that God will Take up Later in the Book

'If you sin, what do you accomplish against Him? Or, if your transgressions are multiplied, what do you do to Him? If you are righteous, what do you give Him? Or what does He receive from your hand? ... Therefore Job opens his mouth in vain; he multiplies words without knowledge.' Job 35:6-7, 16.

CHAPTER **36**

Elihu Justifies God, Urging Job to Trust Him

'Take heed, do not turn to iniquity, for you have chosen this rather than affliction. Behold, God is exalted by His power; who teaches like Him? Who has assigned Him His way, or who has said, "You have done wrong?"' Job 36:21-23.

CHAPTER **37**

Elihu Sets Forth God's Glory in the Excellence of His Works

'He comes from the north as golden splendor; with God is awesome majesty. As for the Almighty, we cannot find Him; He is excellent in power, in judgment and abundant justice; he does not oppress. Therefore men fear Him; He shows no partiality to any who are wise of heart.' Job 37:22-24.

Chapter 38
The Lord Begins to Speak to Job, Echoing Elihu's Speech, and Pointing to God's Might and Wisdom in Creation and Providence

'Who is this who darkens counsel by words without knowledge? Now prepare yourself like a man; I will question you, and you shall answer Me.' Job 38:2-3.

Chapter 39
God Shows that He Gives and Withholds Wisdom in the Creatures He Made, Illustrating Job's Need to Trust God's Wisdom

'Because God deprived her of wisdom, and did not endow her with understanding.' Job 39:17.

Chapter 40
Job Repents of his Speech Against God, God Warns him Against Justifying himself and Condemning God, and God Shows His Power in the Behemoth ('wild ox,' in NKJV)

'Then Job answered the LORD and said: "Behold, I am vile; what shall I answer you? I lay my hand over my mouth. Once I have spoken, but I will not answer; yes, twice, but I will proceed no further." Then the LORD answered Job out of the whirlwind, and said: "Now prepare yourself like a man; I will question you, and you shall answer Me: Would you indeed annul My judgment? Would you condemn Me that you may be justified?"' Job 40:3-8.

Chapter 41
The Lord Concludes the Mediations on His Power and Wisdom with the Leviathan

'No one is so fierce that he would dare stir him up. Who then is able to stand against Me? Who has preceded Me, that I should pay him? Everything under heaven is Mine.' Job 41:10-11.

Chapter 42
Job Confesses his Faith in God's Character, and Repents of his Sins, and God Accepts His Speech, Forgiving his Sins and Restoring his Wealth

'Then Job answered the LORD and said: "I know that You can do everything, and that no purpose of Yours can be withheld from You. You asked, Who is this who hides counsel without knowledge? Therefore I have uttered what I did not understand, things too wonderful for me, which I did not know. Listen, please, and let me speak; You said, I will question you, and you shall answer Me. I have heard of You by the hearing of the ear, but now my eye sees You. Therefore I abhor myself, and repent in dust and ashes." And so it was, after the LORD had spoken these words to Job, that the LORD said to Eliphaz the Temanite, "My wrath is aroused against you and your two friends, for you have not spoken of Me what is right, as My servant Job has."' Job 42:1-7.

Psalms

God sets forth application of His covenant promises to His people in various circumstances of life, looking to the past, the present, and the future

CHAPTER **1**

The Psalmist Contrast the Blessedness of the Godly, and the Curse on the Ungodly, Setting the Tone for the Psalter

> 'For the LORD knows the way of the righteous, but the way of the ungodly shall perish.' Ps. 1:6

CHAPTER **2**

The Lord will Send His Christ to Rule Over the Nations, Setting Forth Another Major Theme of the Psalter, and Focusing on the Covenant Promises to David and Abraham

> 'I will declare the decree: the LORD said to Me, "You are My Son, today I have begotten You. Ask of Me, and I will give You the nations for Your inheritance."' Ps. 2:7-8.

CHAPTER **3**

The Psalmist Cries to God in Distress Under Persecution, Taking Rest in the God of Salvation, and Appealing to the Terms of the Mosaic Covenant

> 'But You, O LORD, are a shield for me, my glory and the One who lifts up my head. I cried to the LORD with my voice, and He heard me from His holy hill ... Salvation belongs to the LORD. Your blessing is upon Your people.' Ps. 3:3-4, 8.

CHAPTER **4**

David Rests in the Midst of Distress through Prayer to the Lord and Faith in His Covenant Promises, Singling out the Aaronic Blessing in Numbers 6

'Be angry, and do not sin. Meditate within your heart on your bed and be still. Offer the sacrifices of righteousness, and put your trust in the LORD. There are many who say, "Who will show us any good?" LORD, lift up the light of your countenance upon us.' Ps. 4:4-6.

Chapter 5
David Looks to the Lord's Righteousness to Protect the Godly and to Overthrow the Wicked

'For You are not a God who takes pleasure in wickedness, nor shall evil dwell with You. The boastful shall not stand in Your sight; You hate all workers of iniquity ... But let all those rejoice who put their trust in You; let them ever shout for joy, because You defend them; let those also who love Your name be joyful in You. For You, O LORD, will bless the righteous; with favor You will surround him as with a shield.' Ps. 5:4-5, 11-12.

Chapter 6
David Prays that the Lord Would Extend his Life so that he Might Continue to Praise the Lord, and Trusts the Lord to Judge his Enemies

'For in death there is no remembrance of You; in the grave who will give You thanks?' Ps. 6:5.

Chapter 7
David Recalls his Prayer When Saul Persecuted him, Trusting in God's Justice

'Oh let the wickedness of the wicked come to an end, but establish the just; for the righteous God tests the hearts and minds. My defense is of God, who saves the upright in heart. God is a just judge, and God is angry with the wicked every day.' Ps. 7:9-11.

Chapter 8
David Praises God for His Excellence in the Creation of Man

'For You have made him a little lower than the angels, and You have crowned him with glory and honor. You have made him to have dominion over the works of Your hands; You have put all things under his feet.' Ps. 8:5-6.

Chapter 9

David Places his Faith in God's Covenant Presence with His People, Pleading that God Would not Let Man Prevail

> 'But the LORD shall endure forever; He has prepared His throne for judgment. He shall judge the world in righteousness, and He shall administer judgment for the peoples in uprightness. The LORD also will be a refuge for the oppressed, a refuge in times of trouble ... The LORD is known by the judgment He executes; the wicked is snared in the work of his own hands. Meditation.' Ps. 9:7-9, 16.

Chapter 10

The Psalmist Pleads with the Lord not to Forget His People in their Distress, Looking to the Lord's Covenant Mercies for Comfort

> 'The LORD is King forever and ever; the nations have perished out of His land. LORD, You have heard the desire of the humble; You will prepare their heart; You will cause Your ear to hear, to do justice to the fatherless and the oppressed, that the man of the earth may oppress no more.' Ps. 10:16-18.

Chapter 11

David Trusts in the Lord Instead of Fleeing from the Wicked, Looking to the Lord's Righteous Judgment

> 'For the LORD is righteous, He loves righteousness; His countenance beholds the upright.' Ps. 11:7.

Chapter 12

David Reflects on the Fact that Though Man's Words are Treacherous, God's Words are Trustworthy

> 'The words of the LORD are pure words, like silver tried in a furnace of earth, purified seven times. You shall keep them, O LORD, You shall preserve them from this generation forever.' Ps. 12:6-7.

Chapter 13

David Cries Out for God to Help him Before it is too Late, Relying on God's Covenant Mercy and Salvation

> 'But I have trusted in Your mercy; my heart shall rejoice in Your salvation. I will sing to the LORD, because He has dealt bountifully with me.' Ps. 13:5-6.

Chapter 14
David Reflects on the Folly of Those Ignoring God in their Hearts, Pleading with the Lord to Bring Salvation

> 'The fool has said in his heart, "There is no God." They are corrupt, they have done abominable works, there is none who does good. The LORD looks down from heaven upon the children of men, to see if there are any who understand, who seek God. They have all turned aside, they have together become corrupt; there is none who does good, no, not one.' Ps. 14:1-3.

Chapter 15
David Reflects on the Holiness of the People Approaching God in Worship

> 'LORD, who may abide in Your tabernacle? Who may dwell in Your holy hill? ... He who does these things shall never be moved.' Ps. 15:1, 5b.

Chapter 16
David Asks the Lord to Preserve him from Death in Light of David's Delight in the Lord

> 'For You will not leave my soul in Sheol, nor will You allow Your Holy One to see corruption. You will show me the path of life; in Your presence is fullness of joy; at Your right hand are pleasures forevermore.' Ps. 16:10-11.

Chapter 17
David Prays for God's Deliverance from the Wicked in Faithfulness to His Covenant, While Meditating on God as his Inheritance

> 'Show Your marvelous lovingkindness by Your right hand, O You who save those who trust in You from those who rise against them. Keep me as the apple of Your eye; hide me under the shadow of Your wings ... As for me, I will see Your face in righteousness; I shall be satisfied when I awake in Your likeness.' Ps. 17:7-8, 15.

Chapter 18
David Celebrates God's Covenant Faithfulness in Delivering him from All of his Enemies, Echoing 2 Samuel 22

> 'I will love You, O LORD, my strength. The LORD is my rock and my fortress and my deliverer; my God, my strength, in

whom I will trust; my shield and the horn of my salvation, my stronghold. I will call upon the LORD, who is worthy to be praised; so shall I be saved from my enemies.' Ps. 18:1-3.

Chapter 19
David Reflects on God's Revelation of His Glory, both in Nature and in Scripture

'Who can understand his errors? Cleanse me from secret faults. Keep back Your servant also from presumptuous sins; let them not have dominion over me. Then I shall be blameless, and I shall be innocent of great transgression. Let the words of my mouth and the meditation of my heart be acceptable in Your sight, O LORD, my strength and my Redeemer.' Ps. 19:12-14.

Chapter 20
David Depicts the People Praying for God's Covenant Blessings on the King for the Sake of the Nation

'Now I know that the LORD saves His anointed; He will answer him from His holy heaven with the saving strength of His right hand. Some trust in chariots, and some in horses; but we will remember the name of the LORD our God.' Ps. 20:6-7.

Chapter 21
David Reflects on the Lord Hearing the King and Saving His Covenant People

'For the king trusts in the LORD, and through the mercy of the Most High he shall not be moved ... Be exalted, O LORD, in Your own strength! We will sing and praise Your power.' Ps. 21:7, 13.

Chapter 22
David Cries Out to God from the Depths of Despair, Pointing to the Suffering, Death, and Resurrection of the Christ for the Salvation of His People

'My God, My God, why have You forsaken Me? Why are You so far from helping Me, and from the words of My groaning? ... They divide My garments among them, and for My clothing they cast lots ... A posterity shall serve Him. It will be recounted of the Lord to the next generation, they will come and declare His righteousness to a people who will be born, that He has done this.' Ps. 22:1, 18, 30-31.

Psalm 23

As the Shepherd of Israel, David Reflects on the Lord as his Shepherd

'Surely goodness and mercy shall follow me all the days of my life; and I will dwell in the house of the LORD forever.' Ps. 23:6.

Chapter 24

The Character of Those Who Can Approach the Lord

'He shall receive blessings from the LORD, and righteousness from the God of his salvation.' Ps. 24:5.

Chapter 25

David Lifts his Soul to the God of his Salvation, Who Remembers His Covenant with David

'Good and upright is the LORD; therefore He teaches sinners in the way. The humble He guides in justice, and the humble He teaches in His way. And the paths of the LORD are mercy and truth, to such as keep His covenant and His testimonies.' Ps. 25:8-10.

Chapter 26

David Prays for the Lord to Vindicate him, Remembering His Covenant

'But as for me, I will walk in my integrity; redeem me and be merciful to me. My foot stands in an even place; in the congregations I will bless the LORD.' Ps. 26:11-12.

Chapter 27

David Would Have Lost Heart Under Trial, if the Covenant Mercies of the Lord Were not his Light in the Land of the Living

'One thing I have desired of the LORD, that will I seek: that I may dwell in the house of the LORD all the days of my life, to behold the beauty of the LORD, and to inquire in His temple … I would have lost heart, unless I had believed that I would see the goodness of the LORD in the land of the living. Wait on the LORD; be of good courage, and He shall strengthen your heart; wait, I say, on the LORD!' Ps. 27:4, 13-14.

Chapter 28
David Cries to the Lord his Rock to Deliver him from Death

'The LORD is my strength and my shield; my heart trusted in Him, and I am helped; therefore my heart greatly rejoices, and with my song I will praise Him. The LORD is their strength, and He is the saving refuge of His anointed. Save Your people, and bless Your inheritance; shepherd them also, and bear them up forever.' Ps. 28:7-9.

Chapter 29
David Praises the God of the Thunder Storm as the God Who Gives Covenant Peace to His People

'Give unto the LORD, O you mighty ones, give unto the LORD glory and strength. Give unto the LORD the glory due to His name; worship the LORD in the beauty of holiness ... The LORD will give strength to His people; the LORD will bless His people with peace.' Ps. 29:1-2, 11.

Chapter 30
David's Prayer at the Dedication of his House, Recounting the Lord's Turning his Mourning into Dancing

'You have turned for me my mourning into dancing; You have put off my sackcloth and clothed me with gladness, to the end that my glory may sing praise to You and not be silent. O LORD my God, I will give thanks to You forever.' Ps. 30:11-12.

Chapter 31
David Prays God's Covenant Presence and Mercies in the Face of his Enemies

'Into Your hand I commit my spirit; You have redeemed me, O LORD God of truth ... But as for me, I trust in You, O LORD; I say, "You are my God." My times are in Your hand; deliver me from the hand of my enemies, and from those who persecute me. Make Your face shine upon Your servant; save me for Your mercies' sake.' Ps. 31:5, 14, 15.

Chapter 32
David Praises the Lord for Forgiven Sin

> 'Blessed is he whose transgression is forgiven, whose sin is covered. Blessed is the man to whom the LORD does not impute iniquity, and in whose spirit there is no deceit … Be glad in the LORD and rejoice, you righteous; and shout for joy, all you upright in heart!' Ps. 32:1-2, 11.

Chapter 33
The Psalmist Praises God for His Sovereignty in Creation and Providence

> 'By the word of the LORD the heavens were made, and all the host of them by the breath of His mouth. He gathers the waters of the sea together as a heap; He lays up the deep in storehouses.' Ps. 33:6-7.

Chapter 34
David Praises God for Delivering him from Abimelech

> 'The Angel of the LORD encamps all around those who fear Him, and delivers them … The young lions lack and suffer hunger; but those who seek the LORD shall not lack any good thing.' Ps. 34:7, 10.

Chapter 35
David Pleads God's Covenant Curses Against his Enemies

> 'Let them be like chaff before the wind, and let the Angel of the LORD chase them. Let their way be slippery, and let the Angel of the LORD pursue them.' Ps. 35:5.

Chapter 36
David Meditates on the Wickedness of the Wicked Directing them, Versus God's Covenant Mercies Directing him

> 'Your mercy, O LORD, is in the heavens; Your faithfulness reaches to the clouds. Your righteousness is like the great mountains; Your judgments are a great deep; O LORD, You preserve man and beast. How precious is Your lovingkindness, O God! Therefore the children of men put their trust under the shadow of Your wings. They are abundantly satisfied with the fulness of Your house, and You give them drink from the river of Your pleasures. For with You is the fountain of life; in Your light we see light.' Ps. 36:5-9.

CHAPTER 37
David Contrasts the Character of the Righteous and the Wicked

> 'Trust in the LORD, and do good; dwell in the land, and feed on His faithfulness. Delight yourself also in the LORD, and He shall give you the desires of your heart.' Ps. 37:3-4.

CHAPTER 38
David Prays that the Lord Would not Rebuke him in Wrath, Placing his Hope in the Lord to Deliver him from his Enemies

> 'For I will declare my iniquity; I will be in anguish over my sin ... Do not forsake me, O LORD; O my God, be not far from me! Make haste to help me, O Lord, my salvation!' Ps. 38:18, 21-22.

CHAPTER 39
David Kept Silent from Good and Evil, Considering the Brevity of his Life and Asking God to Remember his Tears

> 'LORD, make me to know my end, and what is the measure of my days, that I may know how frail I am. Indeed, You have made my days as handbreadths, and my age is as nothing before You; certainly every man at his best state is but a vapor.' Ps. 39:4-5.

CHAPTER 40
David Praises God for Raising him from the Miry Pit, Confessing his Sins, and Looking to the Messiah Who will do All of God's Will

> 'Many, O LORD, are Your wonderful works, which You have done; and Your thoughts toward us cannot be recounted to You in order; if I would declare and speak of them, they are more than can be numbered. Sacrifice and offering You did not desire; My ears You have opened. Burnt offering and sin offering You did not require. Then I said, "Behold, I come; in the scroll of the book it is written of Me. I delight to do Your will, O My God, and Your law is within My heart."' Ps. 40:5-8.

CHAPTER 41
David Closes the First Book of the Psalter by Recounting the Forgiveness of Sins, Deliverance from Enemies, and Pointing to the Betrayal of the Messiah

'All who hate Me whisper together against Me; against Me they devise My hurt. "An evil disease," they say, "clings to him. And now that he lies down, he will rise up no more." Even my own familiar friend in whom I trusted, who ate my bread, has lifted his heel against me.' Ps. 41:7-9.

Chapter 42

The Sons of Korah Long for God's Presence in Covenant Worship in the Midst of Distress, Resting in the Lord's Covenant Faithfulness

'As the deer pants for the water brooks, so pants my soul for You, O God. My soul thirsts for God, for the living God. When shall I come and appear before God?' Ps. 42:1-2.

Chapter 43

The Psalmist Continues with a Similar Theme, Looking to Appear Before God's Tabernacle in Worship

'Oh, send out Your light and Your truth! Let them lead me; let them bring me to Your holy hill and to Your tabernacle.' Ps. 43:3.

Chapter 44

The Sons of Korah Remember God's Past Covenant Faithfulness in Bringing Israel into the Land in Order to Plead for Deliverance from Present Distress

'All this has come upon us; but we have not forgotten You, nor have we dealt falsely with Your covenant … Yet for Your sake we are killed all day long; we are accounted as sheep for the slaughter.' Ps. 44:17, 22.

Chapter 45

The Sons of Korah Contemplate the Glory of the Divine Messiah and His Bride

'Your throne, O God, is forever and ever; a scepter of righteousness is the scepter of Your kingdom. You love righteousness and hate wickedness; therefore God, Your God, has anointed You will the oil of gladness more than Your companions.' Ps. 45:6-7.

Chapter 46

The Sons of Korah Trust in God as their Refuge and Strength, Looking to His Covenant Presence in the City of God, Even When the World Seems to be Turned Upside Down

'God is in the midst of her, she shall not be moved; God shall help her, just at the break of dawn ... Be still and know that I am God; I will be exalted among the nations, I will be exalted in the earth. The LORD of hosts is with us; the God of Jacob is our refuge.' Ps. 46:5, 10-11.

Chapter 47

The Sons of Korah Praise the Most High as King Over All the Earth, Who Remembers His Covenant with Abraham

'Oh, clap your hands, all you peoples! Shout to God with the voice of triumph! For the LORD Most High is awesome; He is a great King over all the earth. He will subdue the peoples under us, and the nations under our feet. He will choose our inheritance for us, the excellence of Jacob whom He loves.' Ps. 47:1-4.

Chapter 48

The Sons of Korah Celebrate God's Covenant Presence and Reign in Mount Zion and His Faithfulness in Delivering His People

'According to Your name, O God, so is Your praise to the ends of the earth; Your right hand is full of righteousness ... For this is God, our God forever and ever; He will be our guide even to death.' Ps. 48:10, 14.

Chapter 49

The Sons of Korah Meditate on God's Wisdom in Dealing with the Righteous and the Wicked

'None of them can by any means redeem his brother, nor give to God a ransom for him – for the redemption of their souls is costly, and it shall cease forever – that he should continue to live eternally, and not see the Pit.' Ps. 49:7-9.

Chapter 50

Asaph Contemplates God's Judgment of the Righteous and the Wicked, Calling Hypocrites in Israel to Repentance

'Now consider this, you who forget God, lest I tear you in pieces, and there be none to deliver: whoever offers praise glorifies Me; and to him who orders his conduct aright I will show the salvation of God.' Ps. 50:22-23.

Chapter 51

David Offers his Prayer of Repentance When he Sinned with Bathsheba, Coming to God with the True Sacrifices of a Broken and Contrite Spirit

> 'Against You, You only, have I sinned, and done this evil in Your sight – that You may be found just when You speak, and blameless when You judge. Behold, I was brought forth in iniquity, and in sin my mother conceived me ... Do not cast me away from Your presence, and do not take Your Holy Spirit from me. Restore to me the joy of Your salvation, and uphold me by Your generous Spirit.' Ps. 51:4-5, 11-12.

Chapter 52

David Prays Against the Betrayal of Doeg the Edomite, Trusting the Lord to Vindicate him, Looking Back to 1 Samuel 22

> 'But I am like a green olive tree in the house of God; I trust in the mercy of God forever and ever. I will praise You forever, because You have done it; and in the presence of Your saints I will wait on Your name, for it is good.' Ps. 52:8-9.

Chapter 53

Echoing Psalm 14, David Contemplates the Character of the Wicked Who Forget God, Pleading with God to Bring Salvation from Zion

> 'Oh, that the salvation of Israel would come out of Zion! When God brings back the captivity of His people, let Jacob rejoice and Israel be glad.' Ps. 53:6.

Chapter 54

David Trusts God's Covenant Faithfulness When the Ziphites Sought to Deliver him to Saul, Looking Back to 1 Samuel 23

> 'Behold, God is my helper; the Lord is with those who uphold my life. He will repay my enemies for their evil. Cut them off in Your truth.' Ps. 54:4-5.

Chapter 55

David Asks the Lord to Divide the Counsel of his Enemies, Reflecting on the Pain of Betrayal, and Exhorting Others to Trust in the Lord

> 'But it was you, a man my equal, my companion and my acquaintance. We took sweet counsel together, and walked

to the house of God in the throng … Cast your burden on the LORD, and He shall sustain you; He shall never permit the righteous to be moved.' Ps. 55:13-14, 22.

Chapter 56
David Resolves to Trust in God and Keep his Vows When he Fell into the Hands of the Philistines, Looking Back to 1 Samuel 21

'Whenever I am afraid, I will trust in You. In God (I will praise His word), in God I have put my trust; I will not fear. What can flesh do to me?' Ps. 56:3-4.

Chapter 57
David Praises God for Delivering him from Saul in the Cave, Looking Back to 1 Samuel 22

'For Your mercy reaches unto the heavens, and Your truth unto the clouds. Be exalted, O God, above the heavens; let Your glory be above all the earth.' Ps. 57:10-11.

Chapter 58
David Reflects on the Character of the Wicked, Pleading with God to Show His Just Judgment

'The wicked are estranged from the womb; they go astray as soon as they are born, speaking lies. Their poison is like the poison of a serpent; they are like the deaf cobra that stops its ear, which will not heed the voice of charmers, charming ever so skillfully … Surely He is a God who judges in the earth.' Ps. 58:3-5, 11b.

Chapter 59
David Praises God for His Covenant Faithfulness, Committing his Cause to God when Saul Sought to Kill him in his House, Looking Back to 1 Samuel 19

'But You, O LORD, shall laugh at them; You shall have all the nations in derision. I will wait for You, O You his Strength; for God is my defense. My God of mercy shall come to meet me; God shall let me see my desire on my enemies. Do not slay them, lest my people forget; scatter them by Your power, and bring them down, O Lord our shield.' Ps. 59:8-11.

Chapter 60
David Recounts his Victory in 2 Samuel 8, with Joab's Victory Over the Edomites, Trusting God to Strengthen him

'Give us help from trouble, for the help of man is useless. Through God we will do valiantly, for it is He who shall tread down our enemies.' Ps. 60:11-12.

Chapter 61

David Praises God for Prolonging his Life, Trusting His Covenant Faithfulness Wherever he is

'Hear my cry, O God; attend to my prayer. From the end of the earth I will cry to You, when my heart is overwhelmed; lead me to the rock that is higher than I. For You have been a shelter for me, a strong tower from the enemy. I will abide in Your tabernacle forever; I will trust in the shelter of Your wings.' Ps. 61:1-4.

Chapter 62

David Exhorts Others to Trust God's Covenant Faithfulness, which he Knows by Experience

'My soul, wait silently for God alone, for my expectation is from Him. He only is my rock and salvation; He is my defense; I shall not be moved. In God is my salvation and my glory; the rock of my strength, and my refuge, is in God. Trust in Him at all times, you people; pour out your heart before Him; God is a refuge for us.' Ps. 62:5-8.

Chapter 63

Looking Back to 1 Samuel 22, David Delights in God's Covenant Faithfulness More than Life

'O God, You are my God; early will I seek You; my soul thirsts for You; my flesh longs for You in a dry and thirsty land where there is no water. So I have looked for You in the sanctuary, to see Your power and Your glory. Because Your lovingkindness is better than life, my lips shall praise You.' Ps. 63:1-3.

Chapter 64

David Pleads to the Lord to Deliver him from the Plots of the Wicked, Trusting that the Lord Will Hear him

'All men shall fear, and shall declare the work of God for they shall wisely consider His doing. The righteous shall be glad in the LORD, and trust in Him. And all the upright in heart shall glory.' Ps. 64:9-10.

Chapter 65

David Praises God for Providing Atonement for Sin, and for Causing the Priests and King to Come Near to Him

'Praise is awaiting You, O God, in Zion; and to You the vow shall be performed. O You who hear prayer, to You all flesh will come. Iniquities prevail against me; as for our transgressions, You will provide atonement for them. Blessed is the man You choose, and cause to approach You, that he may dwell in Your courts. We shall be satisfied with the goodness of Your house, of Your holy temple.' Ps. 65:1-4.

Chapter 66

The Psalmist Calls All Nations to Praise the Lord for His Mighty Works in the Exodus, Trusting the Lord Through Affliction and Praying from a Sincere Heart

'Come and hear, all you who fear God, and I will declare what He has done for my soul. I cried to Him with my mouth, and He was extolled with my tongue. If I regard iniquity in my heart, the Lord will not hear. But certainly God has heard me; He has attended to the voice of my prayer. Blessed be God, who has not turned away my prayer, nor His mercy from me!' Ps. 66:16-20.

Chapter 67

The Psalmist Prays the Aaronic Blessing from Numbers 6, so that the Nations Might Come to Know and Praise the Lord

'God be merciful to us and bless us, and cause His face to shine upon us, that Your way may be known on earth, Your salvation among the nations. Let the peoples praise you, O God; let all the peoples praise You. Oh, let the nations be glad and sing for joy! For You shall judge the people righteously, and govern the nations on earth.' Ps. 67:1-4.

Chapter 68

David Prays the Terms of Numbers 10, Pleading with God to Arise and Scatter His Enemies, Praising God for His Triumphal Procession Among the Nations

'You have ascended on high, You have led captivity captive; You have received gifts among men, even from the rebellious, that the LORD God might dwell there. Blessed be the Lord, who daily loads us with benefits, the God of our salvation!' Ps. 68:18-19.

Chapter 69

David Praises God for His Covenant Faithfulness, Reflects on Betrayal, and Points to the Zeal and Suffering of the Messiah

'Because zeal for Your house has eaten me up, and the reproaches of those who reproach You have fallen on me ... They also gave me gall for my food, and for my thirst gave me vinegar to drink. Let their table become a snare before them, and their well-being a trap ... Let their dwelling place be desolate; let no one live in their tents.' Ps. 69:9, 21, 25.

Chapter 70

Echoing the End of Psalm 40, David Prays for Speedy Deliverance

'Let all those who seek You rejoice and be glad in You; and let those who love Your salvation say continually, "Let God be magnified!" But I am poor and needy; make haste to me, O God! You are my help and deliverer; O LORD, do not delay.' Ps. 70:4-5.

Chapter 71

David Praises God for His Covenant Faithfulness in his Youth, and Pleads for His Presence to Continue in his Old Age

'For You are my hope, O LORD God; You are my trust from my youth. By You I have been upheld from birth; You are He who took me out of my mother's womb. My praise shall be continually of You.' Ps. 71:5-6.

Chapter 72

Solomon Closes Book Two of the Psalter, Praising the Lord for the Terms of the Davidic Covenant, Exalting God for His Wondrous Works in the Kingdom of the Messiah

'In His days the righteous shall flourish, and abundance of peace, until the moon is no more. He shall have dominion also from sea to sea, and from the River to the ends of the earth.' Ps. 72:7-8.

Chapter 73

Asaph Opens Book Three of the Psalter, Relating his Sin of Envying the Wicked and then Looking to the Lord as his Portion When he Turned to Worship

'Nevertheless I am continually with You; You hold me by my right hand. You will guide me with Your counsel, and afterward receive me to glory. Whom have I in heaven but You? And there is none upon the earth that I desire besides You. My flesh and my heart fail; but God is the strength of my heart and my portion forever.' Ps. 73:23-26.

Chapter 74

Asaph Laments the Captivity of Israel, but Pleads God's Character and Covenant to Restore them

'For God is my King of old, working salvation in the midst of the earth … Have respect to the covenant; for the dark places of the earth are full of the haunts of cruelty.' Ps. 74:12, 20.

Chapter 75

Asaph Appeals to God as Judge to Judge his and Israel's Enemies

'We give thanks to You, O God, we give thanks! For Your wondrous works declare that Your name is near. When I choose the proper time, I will judge uprightly. The earth and all its inhabitants are dissolved; I set up its pillars firmly.' Ps. 75:1-3.

Chapter 76

Asaph Remembers the God Who Leads His People in Battle

'In Judah God is known; His name is great in Israel. In Salem also is His tabernacle, and His dwelling place in Zion. There He broke the arrows of the bow, the shield and sword of battle.' Ps. 76:1-3.

Chapter 77

Asaph Moves From Being Troubled by God and His Providence, to Comfort by Remembering God's Mighty Acts in Faithfulness to His Covenant

'Your way, O God, is in the sanctuary; who is so great a God as our God? You are the God who does wonders; Your have declared Your strength among the peoples. You have with Your arm redeemed Your people, the sons of Jacob and Joseph.' Ps. 77:13-15.

Chapter 78

Asaph Exhorts God's People to Teach their Children God's Works, Warning them with Examples of Those who Rejected the Covenant

> 'We will not hide them from their children, telling the generation to come the praises of the LORD, and His strength and His wonderful works that He has done ... Because they did not believe God, and did not trust in His salvation ... For their heart was not steadfast with Him, nor were they faithful to His covenant.' Ps. 78:4, 22, 37.

Chapter **79**

Asaph Laments the Suffering of the Covenant People for their Sins, Pleading with God for Forgiveness and Deliverance

> 'Help us, O God of our salvation, for the glory of Your name; and deliver us, and provide atonement for our sins, for Your name's sake!' Ps. 79:9.

Chapter **80**

Asaph Pleads with the Shepherd of Israel to Revive Israel, His Vine, by Causing His Face to Shine Upon them, Appealing to the Aaronic Blessing in Numbers 6 and the Promises of the Davidic Covenant

> 'Give ear, O Shepherd of Israel, You who lead Joseph like a flock; You who dwell between the cherubim, shine forth! Before Ephraim, Benjamin, and Manasseh, stir up Your strength, and come and save us! Restore us, O God; cause Your face to shine, and we shall be saved!' Ps. 80:1-3.

Chapter **81**

Asaph Recounts God's Covenant Promises and Faithfulness, Lamenting the Consequences of the People's Sins

> 'I am the LORD your God, who brought you out of the land of Egypt; open your mouth wide, and I will fill it. But My people would not heed My voice, and Israel would have none of Me.' Ps. 81:10-11.

Chapter **82**

Asaph Exhorts the 'gods' who Govern the People to Imitate God in Doing Justice

> 'I said, "You are gods, and all of you are children of the Most High. But you shall die like men, and fall like one of the princes." Arise, O God, judge the earth; for You shall inherit all nations.' Ps. 82:6-8.

Chapter 83

Asaph Pleads with God not to be Silent in the Face of the Noise of his Enemies, Remembering How God Delivered the People in the Book of Judges

> 'Fill their faces with shame, that they may seek Your name, O LORD. Let them be confounded and dismayed forever, yes, let them be put to shame and perish, that they may know that You, whose name alone is the LORD, are the Most High over all the earth.' Ps. 83:16-18.

Chapter 84

The Sons of Korah Long for God's Covenant Presence in Public Worship in the Temple, Pleading the Terms of the Davidic Covenant

> 'O God, behold our shield, and look upon the face of Your anointed. For a day in Your courts is better than a thousand. I would rather be a doorkeeper in the house of my God than dwell in the tents of wickedness. For the LORD God is a sun and shield; the LORD will give grace and glory; no good thing will He withhold from those who walk uprightly. O LORD of hosts, blessed is the man who trusts in You!' Ps. 84:9-12.

Chapter 85

The Sons of Korah Praise the Lord for Bringing the People Back from Captivity, but they Plead with God to Revive them in His Covenant Mercies

> 'LORD, You have been favorable to Your land; You have brought back the captivity of Jacob. You have forgiven the iniquity of Your people; You have covered all their sin … Will You not revive us again, that Your people may rejoice in You? … Mercy and truth have met together; righteousness and peace have kissed.' Ps. 85:1-2, 6, 10.

Chapter 86

David Praises God for the Revelation of His name in Exodus 34, Asking for God's Continued Covenant Presence

> 'For You, Lord, are good, and ready to forgive, and abundant in mercy to all those who call upon You … For You are great, and do wondrous things; You alone are God. Teach me Your way, O LORD; I will walk in Your truth; unite my heart to fear

Your name ... But You, O Lord, are a God full of compassion, and gracious, longsuffering and abundant in mercy and truth.' Ps. 86:5, 10-11, 15.

Chapter **87**

The Sons of Korah Meditate on the Lord's Love for the City of God

'His foundation is in the holy mountains. The LORD loves the gates of Zion more than all the dwellings of Jacob. Glorious things are spoken of you, O city of God!' Ps. 87:1-3.

Chapter **88**

Heman the Ezrahite Laments Before God, Asking Him to Extend his Life, Being the Only Lament in the Psalms Without Explicit Praise

'Will You work wonders for the dead? Shall the dead arise and praise You? Shall Your lovingkindness be declared in the grave? Or Your faithfulness in the place of destruction? Shall Your wonders be known in the dark? And Your righteousness in the land of forgetfulness?' Ps. 88:10-12.

Chapter **89**

Ethan the Ezrahite Remembers the Davidic Covenant in Order to Plead with the Lord to Restore the Exiles, Closing Book Three of the Psalter

'He shall cry to Me, "You are my Father, my God, and the rock of my salvation." Also I will make him My firstborn, the highest of the kings of the earth. My mercy I will keep for him forever, and My covenant shall stand firm with him ... Nevertheless My lovingkindness I will not utterly take from him, nor allow My faithfulness to fail. My covenant I will not break, nor alter the word that has gone out of My lips. Once I have sworn by My holiness; I will not lie to David: his seed shall endure forever, and his throne as the sun before Me.' Ps. 89:26-28, 33-36.

Chapter **90**

Moses Opens Book Four of the Psalter, Resting on God's Eternality in Contrast to the People Who Perished in the Wilderness, Giving Hope in God's Unchanging Character for Generations to Come

'Before the mountains were brought forth, or ever You had formed the earth and the world, even from everlasting to everlasting, You are God … Let Your work appear to Your servants, and Your glory to their children. And let the beauty of the LORD our God be upon us, and establish the work of our hands for us; yes, establish the work of our hands.' Ps. 90:2, 16-17.

Chapter 91

The Psalmist Encourages those who Trust in the Lord with Promises of His Covenant Presence and Protection

'Because you have made the LORD, who is my refuge, even the Most High, your dwelling place, no evil shall befall you, nor shall a plague come near your dwelling; for He shall give His angels charge over you, to keep you in all your ways. In their hands they shall bear you up, lest you dash your foot against a stone.' Ps. 91:9-11.

Chapter 92

The Psalmist Celebrates the Blessings of the Sabbath Day as the Time to Praise God for His Covenant Faithfulness in Judging the Wicked and Saving the Righteous

'The righteous shall flourish like a palm tree, he shall grow like a cedar in Lebanon. Those who are planted in the house of the LORD shall flourish in the courts of our God. They shall still bear fruit in old age; they shall be fresh and flourishing, to declare that the LORD is upright; He is my rock, and there is no unrighteousness in Him.' Ps. 92:12-15.

Chapter 93

The Psalmist Praises the Lord for His Might and Lordship Over Creation, Especially the Sea

'Your throne is established from of old; You are from everlasting. The floods have lifted up, O LORD, the floods have lifted up their voice; the floods lift up their waves. The LORD on high is mightier than the noise of many waters, than the mighty waves of the sea.' Ps. 93:2-4.

Chapter 94

The Psalmist Commits Vengeance to God as He Commanded in Deuteronomy 32, Contrasting the True God to Dumb Idols

'Unless the LORD had been my help, my soul would have soon settled in silence. If I say, "My foot slips," Your mercy,

> O LORD, will hold me up. In the multitude of my anxieties within me, Your comforts delight my soul.' Ps. 94:17-19.

Chapter **95**

The Psalmist Calls Israel to Worship the Lord for His Covenant Mercies as their Shepherd, Warning them Against the Generation that Died in the Wilderness in the Book of Numbers

> 'For He is our God, and we are the people of His pasture, and the sheep of His hand. Today, if you will hear His voice, do not harden your hearts, as in the rebellion, as in the day of trial in the wilderness ... So I swore in My wrath, they shall not enter My rest.' Ps. 95:7-8, 11.

Chapter **96**

The Psalmist Calls the Nations to Sing to the Lord, Calling Nature as Witness and Looking to Final Judgment

> 'Oh, sing to the LORD a new song! Sing to the LORD, all the earth. Sing to the LORD, bless His name; proclaim the good news of His salvation from day to day. Declare His glory among the nations, His wonders among all peoples. For the LORD is great and greatly to be praised; He is to be feared above all gods.' Ps. 96:1-4.

Chapter **97**

The Psalmist Reflects on the Lord's Presence in the Cloud and Fire, Scattering His Enemies, Calling all gods to Submit to Him, and Leading the Righteous to Rejoice in Him

> 'The LORD reigns; let the earth rejoice; let the multitude of isles be glad! Clouds and darkness surround Him; Righteousness and justice are the foundation of His throne. A fire goes before Him, and burns up His enemies round about.' Ps. 97:1-3.

Chapter **98**

The Psalmist Calls the Nations to Sing to the Lord, Reflecting on God's Covenant, Calling Nature as Witness, and Looking to the Final Judgment

> 'The LORD has made known His salvation; His righteousness He has revealed in the sight of the nations. He has remembered His mercy and His faithfulness to the house of Israel; all the ends of the earth have seen the salvation of our God.' Ps. 98:2-3.

Chapter 99

The Psalmist Praises God for His Holy Covenant Presence Among His People, Remembering His Covenant with Moses

> 'The LORD reigns; let the peoples tremble! He dwells between the cherubim; let the earth be moved! The LORD is great in Zion, and He is high above all the peoples. Let them praise Your great and awesome name – He is holy.' Ps. 99:1-3.

Chapter 100

The Psalmist Calls All Lands to Worship the Covenant Lord, Who is the Shepherd of His People

> 'Know that the LORD, He is God; it is He who made us, and not we ourselves; we are His people and the sheep of His pasture ... For the LORD is good; His mercy is everlasting, and His truth endures to all generations.' Ps. 100:3, 5.

Chapter 101

David Resolves to Rule in Righteousness, Reflecting the Lord's Covenant Reign

> 'My eyes shall be on the faithful of the land, that they may dwell with me; He who walks in a perfect way, He shall serve me.' Ps. 101:6.

Chapter 102

The Psalmist Presents a Complaint for the Afflicted, Expressing Anguish of Soul in Deep Distress, and Remembering the Lord's Unchanging Faithfulness to His Servants and their Children

> 'Of old You laid the foundation of the earth, and the heavens are the work of Your hands. They will perish, but You will endure; yes, they will all grow old like a garment; like a cloak You will change them, and they will be changed. But You are the same, and Your years will have no end. The children of Your servants will continue, and their descendants will be established before You.' Ps. 102:25-28.

Chapter 103

David Praises the Lord for Experiencing His Covenant Mercies, Praising God for Caring for him Like a Father and Forgiving his Sins, and Calling all Created Things to Worship Him

'But the mercy of the LORD is from everlasting on those who fear Him, and His righteousness to children's children, to such as keep His covenant, and to those who remember His commandments to do them.' Ps. 103:17-18.

Chapter 104

The Psalmist Reflects on God's Glory in Creation and Redemption, Focusing on His Providential Care for Creation, and Showing that the Wicked Do not Fit in God's World

'You send for Your Spirit, they are created; and You renew the face of the earth. May the glory of the LORD endure forever; may the LORD rejoice in His works.' Ps. 104:30-31.

Chapter 105

The Lord Reflects on God's Covenant with Abraham, Isaac, and Jacob, Encouraging a New Generation to Trust in God's Covenant Presence

'He remembers His covenant forever, the word which He commanded, for a thousand generations, the covenant which He made with Abraham, and His oath to Isaac, and confirmed it to Jacob for a statute, to Israel as an everlasting covenant … For He remembered His Holy promise, and Abraham His servant. He brought out His people with joy, His chosen ones with gladness. He gave them the lands of the Gentiles, and they inherited the labor of the nations, that they might observe His statutes and keep His laws. Praise the LORD!' Ps. 105:8-10, 42-45.

Chapter 106

The Psalmist Concludes Book Four of the Psalter, Resting in God's Covenant Mercies, Giving Examples of God's Readiness to Forgive His People When they Sin

'Remember me, O LORD, with the favor You have toward Your people. Oh, visit me with Your salvation, that I may see the benefit of Your chosen ones, that I may rejoice in the gladness of Your nation, that I may glory with Your inheritance.' Ps. 106:4-5.

Chapter 107

The Psalmist Opens Book Five of the Psalter by Urging People to Praise God for His Goodness and His Wondrous Works in Repeatedly Delivering His People from Affliction

'Oh, that men would give thanks to the LORD for His goodness, and for His wonderful works to the children of men! Let them exalt Him also in the assembly of the people, and praise Him in the company of the elders ... The righteous see it and rejoice, and all iniquity stops its mouth. Whoever is wise will observe these things, and they will understand the lovingkindness of the LORD.' Ps. 107:31-32, 42-43.

Chapter 108
David Takes Confidence in God to Gain Victory Over his Enemies, Stirring up his Heart to Praise the Lord

'O God, my heart is steadfast; I will sing and give praise, even with my glory. Awake lute and harp! I will awaken the dawn. I will praise You, O LORD, among the peoples, and I will sing praises to You among the nations. For Your mercy is great above the heavens, and Your truth reaches to the clouds. Be exalted, O God, above the heavens, and Your glory above all the earth.' Ps. 108:1-5.

Chapter 109
David Prays that God Would Speak Against the Speech of his Enemies, Urging God to Bring his Enemy Down and Put Another in his Place

'Set a wicked man over him, and let an accuser stand at his right hand. When he is judged, let him be found guilty, and let his prayer become sin. Let his days be few, and let another take his office ... But You, O GOD the Lord, deal with me for Your name's sake; because Your mercy is good, deliver me.' Ps. 109:6-8, 21.

Psalm 110
David Reflects on the Reign of the Messiah as King and as Priest after the Order of Melchizedek

'The LORD said to my Lord, "Sit at My right hand, till I make Your enemies Your footstool" ... The LORD has sworn and will not relent, "You are a priest forever, according to the order of Melchizedek."' Ps. 110:1, 4.

Chapter 111
The Psalmist Reflects in Acrostic on the Character of the Righteous Lord, Who Remembers His Covenant

'The works of the LORD are great, studied by all who have pleasure in them. His work is honorable and glorious, and His righteousness endures forever … He has sent redemption to His people; He has commanded His covenant forever; Holy and awesome is His name.' Ps. 111:2-3, 9.

Chapter **112**

The Psalmist Reflects in Acrostic on the Character of the Righteous Man, Who Imitates the Covenant Lord

'Wealth and riches will be in his house, and his righteousness endures forever … He has dispersed abroad, he has given to the poor; his righteousness endures forever; his horn will be exalted with honor.' Ps. 112:3, 9.

Chapter **113**

The Psalmist Praises God for His Incomprehensible Exaltation and for His Condescension to the Lowly

'Who is like the LORD our God, who dwells on high, who humbles Himself to behold the things that are in the heavens and the earth? He raises the poor out of the dust, and lifts the needy out of the ash heap, that He may seat him with princes – with the princes of His people.' Ps. 113:5-8.

Chapter **114**

The Psalmist Celebrates God's Covenant Presence with His People in Parting the Red Sea and the Jordan

'Judah became His sanctuary, and Israel His dominion … Tremble, O earth, at the presence of the Lord, at the presence of the God of Jacob.' Ps. 114:2, 7.

Chapter **115**

The Psalmist Gives Glory to God for His Covenant Mercy and Truth, Contrasting Him with the gods of the Nations, and Exhorting Israel to Trust in Him

'Not unto us, O LORD, not unto us, but to Your name give glory, because of Your mercy, because of Your truth. Why should the Gentiles say, "So where is their God?" But our God is in heaven; He does whatever He pleases.' Ps. 115:1-3.

Chapter 116
The Psalmist Loves the Lord for Hearing his Prayers, Speaking in Faith About the Lord's Covenant Faithfulness in Delivering him from Death

> 'I believed, therefore I spoke, "I am greatly afflicted." I said in my haste, "All men are liars." What shall I render to the LORD for all His benefits toward me? I will take the cup of salvation, and call upon the name of the LORD. I will pay my vows to the LORD now in the presence of all His people. Precious in the sight of the LORD is the death of His saints.' Ps. 116:10-15.

Chapter 117
In the Shortest Chapter in the Bible, the Psalmist Calls All Nations to Praise the Lord for His Covenant Faithfulness

> 'Praise the LORD, all you Gentiles! Laud Him, all you peoples! For His merciful kindness is great toward us, and the truth of the LORD endures forever. Praise the LORD!' Ps. 117:1-2.

Chapter 118
The Psalmist Praises the Lord for His Eternal Covenant Mercies, Preserving his Life in the Face of Overwhelming Odds, Showing that the Stone Which the Builders Reject Would Become the Chief Cornerstone, Looking to the Messiah's Triumphal Entry into Jerusalem

> 'The stone which the builders rejected has become the chief cornerstone. This was the LORD's doing; it is marvelous in our eyes. This is the day that the LORD has made; we will rejoice and be glad in it.' Ps. 118:22-24.

Chapter 119
In the Longest Chapter in the Bible, the Psalmist Uses an Acrostic to Show His Love for the Lord of the Law Through Loving the Law of the Lord

> 'Oh, how I love Your law! It is my meditation all the day ... Your word is a lamp to my feet and a light to my path.' Ps. 119:97, 105.

Chapter 120
The Songs of Ascents to the Temple Begin with the Psalmist Longing for Peace While his Enemies Seek War

'My soul has dwelt too long with one who hates peace. I am for peace; but when I speak, they are for war.' Ps. 120:6-7.

Chapter 121

A Song of Ascents Looking to the Lord's Vigilant Protection

'I will lift up my eyes to the hills – from whence comes my help? My help comes from the LORD, who made heaven and earth. He will not allow your foot to be moved; He who keeps you will not slumber. Behold, He who keeps Israel shall neither slumber nor sleep.' Ps. 121:1-4.

Chapter 122

A Song of Ascent by David, Rejoicing in God's Covenant Presence in Jerusalem in Public Worship

'For the sake of my brethren and companions, I will now say, "Peace be within you." Because of the house of the LORD our God I will seek your good.' Ps. 122:8-9.

Chapter 123

A Song of Ascents Looking to God for Help in the Face of the Contempt of Enemies

'Unto You I lift up my eyes, O You who dwell in the heavens. Behold, as the eyes of servants look to the hand of their masters, as the eyes of a maid to the hand of her mistress, so our eyes look to the LORD our God, until He has mercy on us.' Ps. 123:1-2.

Chapter 124

A Song of Ascents by David Reflecting on the Lord's Faithful Help in Overwhelming Distress

'If it had not been the LORD who was on our side, let Israel now say – if it had not been the LORD who was on our side, when men rose up against us, they would have swallowed us alive, when their wrath was kindled against us ... Our help is in the name of the LORD, who made heaven and earth.' Ps. 124:1-3, 8.

Chapter 125

A Song of Ascents in Which the Psalmist Celebrates the Security of God's People in His Covenant Presence

'Those who trust in the LORD are like Mount Zion, which cannot be moved, but abides forever. As the mountains surround Jerusalem, so the LORD surrounds His people from this time forth and forevermore.' Ps. 125:1-2.

Chapter 126

A Song of Ascents Celebrating the Return from Captivity, Asking the Lord to Further the Return

'When the LORD brought back the captivity of Zion, we were like those who dream. Then our mouth was filled with laughter, and our tongue with singing. Then they said among the nations, "The LORD has done great things for them." The LORD has done great things for us, and we are glad.' Ps. 126:1-3.

Chapter 127

A Song of Ascents Acknowledging that Only the Lord Can Build the Households of Believers

'Unless the LORD builds the house, they labor in vain who build it; unless the LORD guards the city, the watchman stays awake in vain. It is vain for you to rise up early, to sit up late, to eat the bread of sorrows; for so He gives His beloved sleep.' Ps. 127:1-2.

Chapter 128

A Song of Ascents Celebrating the Lord's Covenant Faithfulness to the Families of those who Fear Him

'Blessed is every one who fears the LORD, who walks in who walks in His ways ... The LORD bless you out of Zion, and may you see the good of Jerusalem all the days of your life. Yes, may you see your children's children. Peace be upon Israel!' Ps. 128:1, 5-6.

Chapter 129

A Song of Ascents Proclaiming Malediction on Those Afflicting God's People

'The LORD is righteous; He has cut in pieces the cords of the wicked.' Ps. 129:4.

Chapter 130

A Song of Ascents in Which the Psalmist Trusts in God's Covenant Mercies For the Forgiveness of Sins

'If You, LORD, should mark iniquities, O Lord, who could stand? But there is forgiveness with You, that You may be feared.' Ps. 130:3-4.

Chapter 131

A Song of Ascents Illustrating the Humility of Those Approaching God

'LORD, my heart is not haughty, nor my eyes lofty. Neither do I concern myself with great matters, nor with things too profound for me. Surely I have calmed and quieted my soul, like a weaned child with his mother; like a weaned child with his mother; like a weaned child is my soul within me. O Israel, hope in the LORD from this time forth and forever.' Ps. 131:1-3.

Chapter 132

A Song of Ascents Asking the Lord to Remember the Davidic and Mosaic Covenants, Appealing to Numbers 10 and 2 Samuel 7

'For Your servant David's sake, do not turn away the face of Your Anointed. The LORD has sworn in truth to David; He will not turn from it: "I will set upon your throne the fruit of your body. If your sons will keep My covenant and My testimony which I shall teach them, their sons also shall sit upon your throne forevermore."' Ps. 132:10-13.

Chapter 133

A Song of Ascents in which David Celebrates the Blessedness of the Unity of God's People

'Behold, how good and how pleasant it is for brethren to dwell together in unity! It is like the precious oil upon the head, running down on the beard, the beard of Aaron, running down on the edge of his garments. It is like the dew of Hermon, descending upon the mountains of Zion; for there the LORD commanded the blessing – life forevermore.' Ps. 133:1-3.

Chapter 134

A Song of Ascents Calling God's People to Evening Worship

'Behold, bless the LORD, all you servants of the LORD, who by night stand in the house of the LORD! Lift up your hands in the sanctuary, and bless the LORD. The LORD who made heaven and earth bless you from Zion!' Ps. 134:1-3.

Chapter 135
The Psalmist Calls Israel to Praise the Lord for His Covenant Faithfulness to them, and for His Works of Creation, Providence, and Redemption, Contrasting the True God with the Idols of the Nations

'Praise the LORD, for the LORD is good; sing praises to His name, for it is pleasant. For the LORD has chosen Jacob for Himself, Israel for His special treasure. For I know that the LORD is great, and our Lord is above all gods. Whatever the LORD pleases He does, in heaven and in earth, in the seas and in all deep places.' Ps. 135:3-6.

Chapter 136
The Psalmist Praises God for His Enduring Covenant Mercies in Creation, Providence, and Redemption

'Oh, give thanks to the LORD, for He is good! For His mercy endures forever. Oh, give thanks to the God of gods! For His mercy endures forever. Oh, give thanks to the Lord of lords! For His mercy endures forever. To Him who alone does great wonders, for His mercy endures forever.' Ps. 136:1-4.

Chapter 137
The Psalmist Weeps Over the Babylonian Captivity, Praying Imprecations Against Those who Mistreated Israel

'If I forget you, O Jerusalem, let my right hand forget its skill! If I do not remember you, let my tongue cling to the roof of my mouth – if I do not exalt Jerusalem above my chief joy.' Ps. 137:5-6.

Chapter 138
David Praises the Lord Before All Powers and Authority for the Lord's Covenant Faithfulness in Exalting the Lowly

'I will praise You with my whole heart; before the gods I will sing praises to You. I will worship toward Your holy temple, and praise Your name for Your lovingkindness and Your truth; for You have magnified Your word above Your name ... Though the LORD is on high, yet He regards the lowly; but the proud He knows from afar.' Ps. 138:1-2, 6.

Chapter 139

David Celebrates God's Omniscience and Omnipresence, Taking Comfort from God's Covenant with him, Hating Those who Hate God, and Hating What is Contrary to God in himself

> 'Where can I go from Your Spirit? Or where can I flee from Your presence? ... Search me, O God, and know my heart; try me, and know my anxieties; and see if there is any wicked way in me, and lead me in the way everlasting.' Ps. 139:7, 23-24.

Chapter 140

David Prays that the Lord Would Save him from Evil Men, Placing Confidence in God Who Brings His People into His Covenant Presence

> 'I said to the LORD, "You are my God; hear the voice of my supplications, O LORD. O GOD the Lord, the strength of my salvation, You have covered my head in the day of battle. Do not grant, O LORD, the desires of the wicked; do not further his wicked scheme, lest they be exalted. As for the head of those who surround me, let the evil of their lips cover them."' Ps. 140:6-9.

Chapter 141

David Cries to the Lord to Help him Quickly, Offering his Prayer to God as Incense, and Asking God to Enable him to Receive Rebukes from the Righteous Humbly

> 'Let the righteous strike me; it shall be a kindness. And let him rebuke me; it shall be as excellent oil; let my head not refuse it. For still my prayer is against the deeds of the wicked.' Ps. 141:5.

Chapter 142

David Prayed When he Hid in the Cave from Saul (1 Samuel 24), Placing his Hope in God Alone

> 'Attend to my cry, for I am brought very low; deliver me from my persecutors, for they are stronger than I.' Ps. 142:6.

Chapter 143

David Humbles himself in Light of his Sins, Meditating on God and His Works When Overwhelmed with Trials, and Asking God to Teach him Godliness

'Do not enter into judgment with Your servant, for in Your sight no one living is righteous ... Teach me to do Your will, for You are my God; Your Spirit is good. Lead me in the land of uprightness.' Ps. 143:2, 10.

Chapter 144

David Praises the Lord his Rock, for Training his Hands for War and Blessing His People with His Presence by Remembering His Covenant with them

'Blessed be the LORD my Rock, Who trains my hands for war, and my fingers for battle – my lovingkindness and my fortress, my high tower and my deliverer, my shield and the One in whom I take refuge, who subdues my people under me. LORD, what is man, that You take knowledge of him? Or the son of man, that You are mindful of him? Man is like a breath; his days are like a passing shadow.' Ps. 144:1-4.

Chapter 145

David Praises God for His Incomprehensible Greatness, Meditating on the Revelation of God's Name in Exodus 34, and His Common Grace to All and Special Grace to His People

'Great is the LORD, and greatly to be praised; and His greatness is unsearchable. One generation shall praise Your works to another, and declare Your mighty acts ... The LORD is gracious and full of compassion, slow to anger and great in mercy. The LORD is good to all, and His tender mercies are over all His works.' Ps. 145:3-4, 8-9.

Chapter 146

The Psalmist Praises the Lord, Who Alone Can Help His People in His Faithfulness to His Covenant with Jacob

'Do not put your trust in princes, nor in a son of man, in whom there is no help. His spirit departs, he returns to his earth; in that very day his plans perish. Happy is he who has the God of Jacob for his help, whose hope is in the LORD his God.' Ps. 146:3-5.

Chapter 147

The Psalmist Praises God for His Infinite Understanding and Might, Exalting Him for the Gift of His Word Above All His Other Blessings

> 'He declares His word to Jacob, His statutes and His judgments to Israel. He has not dealt thus with any nation; and as for His judgments, they have not known them. Praise the LORD!' Ps. 147:19-20.

Chapter **148**

The Psalmist Calls the Whole Earth to Praise the Lord in Light of His Covenant Faithfulness to His People

> 'Let them praise the name of the LORD, for His name alone is exalted; His glory is above the earth and heaven. And He has exalted the horn of His people, the praise of all His saints – of the children of Israel, a people near to Him. Praise the LORD!' Ps. 148:13-14.

Chapter **149**

The Psalmist Calls Israel to Praise the Lord in Every Activity of Life, Including Judgment

> 'For the LORD takes pleasure in His people; He will beautify the humble with salvation.' Ps. 149:4.

Chapter **150**

The Psalter Closes Calling Everything that Has Breath to Praise the Lord in Every Place

> 'Praise Him for His mighty acts; praise Him according to His excellent greatness!' Ps. 150:2.

Proverbs

God teaches His covenant people the nature and implications of the fear of the Lord as it applies to every area of life

Chapter 1
The Fruits of Walking in Knowledge and the Fear of the Lord

> 'The fear of the LORD is the beginning of knowledge, but fools despise wisdom and instruction.' Prov. 1:7.

Chapter 2
The Promise of Finding Wisdom When We Pursue Her

> 'Then you will understand the fear of the LORD, and find the knowledge of God. For the LORD gives wisdom; from His mouth come knowledge and understanding; He stores up sound wisdom for the upright; He is a shield to those who walk uprightly; He guards the paths of justice, and preserves the way of His saints.' Prov. 2:5-8.

Chapter 3
The Fruits of Wisdom for Those Who Listen to their Parents' Instruction

> 'My son, do not despise the chastening of the LORD, nor detest His correction; for whom the LORD loves He corrects, just as a father the son in whom he delights.' Prov. 3:11-12.

Chapter 4
The Writer Enforces the Exhortation to Pursue Wisdom by his Own Example

> 'But the path of the just is like the shining sun, that shines ever brighter unto the perfect day.' Prov. 4:18.

Chapter 5
Warnings Against the Adulterous Woman

> 'For the ways of man are before the eyes of the LORD, and He ponders all his paths.' Prov. 5:21.

Chapter 6
Encouragements to Flee What the Lord Hates and to Pursue What He Loves

> 'These six things the LORD hates, yes, seven are an abomination to Him: A proud look, a lying tongue, hands that shed innocent blood, a heart the devises wicked plans, feet that are swift in running to evil, a false witness who speaks lies, and one who sows discord among brethren.' Prov. 6:16-19.

Chapter 7
Exhortation to Keep the Commandments and Warnings Against the Harlot

> 'Do not let your heart turn aside to her ways, do not stray into her paths; for she has cast down many wounded, and all who were slain by her were strong men. Her house is the way to hell, descending to the chambers of death.' Prov. 7:25-27.

Chapter 8
Wisdom's Call and Invitation to All Who Will Hear Her

> 'The fear of the LORD is to hate evil; pride and arrogance and the evil way and the perverse mouth I hate ... For whoever finds me finds life, and obtains favor from the LORD; but he who sins against me wrongs his own soul; and those who hate me love death.' Prov. 8:13, 35-36.

Chapter 9
The Contrast Between the Call of Wisdom and the Call of Folly

> 'He who corrects a scoffer gets shame for himself, and he who rebukes a wicked man only harms himself. Do not correct a scoffer, lest he hate you; rebuke a wise man, and he will love you. Give instruction to a wise man, and he will be still wiser; teach a just man, and he will increase in learning. The fear of the LORD is the beginning of wisdom, and the knowledge of the Holy One is understanding.' Prov. 9:7-10.

CHAPTER **10**
The Proverbs of Solomon Begin

'The LORD will not allow the righteous to famish, but he casts away the desire of the wicked ... The blessing of the LORD makes one rich, and He adds no sorrow with it ... The fear of the LORD prolongs days, but the years of the wicked will be shortened.' Prov. 10:3, 22, 27.

CHAPTER **11**
Exhortations to Honesty and Expectations from the Lord

'Those who are of a perverse heart are an abomination to the LORD, but the blameless in their ways are His delight.' Prov. 11:20.

CHAPTER **12**
The Contrast Between the Character and Ends of the Righteous and the Wicked

'Whoever loves instruction loves knowledge, but he who hates correction is stupid. A good man obtains favor from the LORD, but a man of wicked intentions he will condemn.' Prov. 12:1-2.

CHAPTER **13**
The Blessings of Hard Work and Curses Upon Laziness

'The soul of the lazy man desires, and has nothing; but the soul of the diligent shall be made rich. A righteous man hates lying, but a wicked man is loathsome and comes to shame.' Prov. 13:4-5.

CHAPTER **14**
God's Blessings on the Upright, Who Fear Him

'In the fear of the LORD there is strong confidence, and His children will have a place of refuge. The fear of the LORD is a fountain of life, to turn one away from the snares of death ... He who oppresses the poor reproaches his Maker, but he who honors Him has mercy on the needy.' Prov. 14:26-27, 31.

CHAPTER **15**
Further Instructions About Wise Speech and the Fear of the Lord

'A soft answer turns away wrath, but a harsh word stirs up anger. The tongue of the wise uses knowledge rightly, but the mouth of fools pours forth foolishness. The eyes of the LORD are in every place, keeping watch on the evil and the good. A wholesome tongue is a tree of life, but perverseness in it breaks the spirit.' Prov. 15:1-4.

Chapter **16**
The Lord's Providential Direction of All Things

'The preparations of the heart belong to man, but the answer of the tongue is from the LORD. All the ways of a man are pure in his own eyes, but the LORD weighs the spirits. Commit your works to the LORD, and your thoughts will be established. The LORD has made all for Himself, yes, even the wicked for the day of doom. Everyone proud in heart is an abomination to the LORD; though they join forces, none will go unpunished.' Prov. 16:1-5.

Chapter **17**
The Importance of Doing Righteousness and Caring for the Poor

'The refining pot is for silver and the furnace for gold, but the LORD tests the hearts. An evildoer gives heed to false lips; a liar listens eagerly to a spiteful tongue. He who mocks the poor reproaches his Maker; he who is glad at calamity will not go unpunished.' Prov. 17:3-5.

Chapter **18**
The Importance of Listening, Speaking Cautiously, and Trusting in the Lord

'The name of the LORD is a strong tower; the righteous run to it and are safe.' Prov. 18:10.

Chapter **19**
Righteousness, Wealth, and Poverty

'The fear of the LORD leads to life, and he who has it will abide in satisfaction; he will not be visited with evil.' Prov. 19:23.

Chapter **20**
Wait on the Lord, Work Hard, and Mind Your Own Business

'Do not say, "I will recompense evil;" wait for the LORD, and He will save you. Diverse weights are an abomination to the LORD, and dishonest scales are not good. A man's steps are of the LORD; how then can a man understand his own way?' Prov. 20:22-24.

Chapter 21
The Lord's Sovereignty Over the Righteous and the Unrighteous, and the Rich and the Poor

'The king's heart is in the hand of the LORD, like the rivers of water He turns it wherever He wishes. Every way of a man is right in his own eyes, but the LORD weighs the hearts. To do justice and righteousness is more acceptable to the LORD than sacrifice ... There is no wisdom or understanding or counsel against the LORD. The horse is prepared for the day of battle, but deliverance is of the LORD.' Prov. 21:1-4, 30-31.

Chapter 22
Live in God's Sight and Be More Concerned with Wisdom than with Your Circumstances

'By humility and the fear of the LORD are riches and honor and life.' Prov. 22:4.

Chapter 23
Beware of Appetite and Drunkenness

'Do not let your heart envy sinners, but be zealous for the fear of the LORD all the day; for surely there is a hereafter, and your hope will not be cut off.' Prov. 23:17.

Chapter 24
Do not Fret Because of Evil Men and Learn to Work Hard

'My son, fear the LORD and the king; do not associate with those given to change; for their calamity will rise suddenly, and who knows the ruin those two can bring.' Prov. 24:21-22.

Chapter 25
Hezekiah's Collection of Solomon's Proverbs Begins by Stressing the Need to be Faithful and Dependable

'Do not exalt yourself in the presence of the king, and do not stand in the place of the great; for it is better that he say to you, "Come up here," than that you should be put lower in the presence of the prince, whom your eyes have seen.' Prov. 25:6-7.

Chapter 26

Warnings Against Foolishness, Laziness, and Wickedness

'The great God who formed everything, gives the fool his hire and the transgressor his wages.' Prov. 26:10.

Chapter 27

Rebuke, Friendship, and the Value of Hard Work and Wise Planning

'Do not boast about tomorrow, for you do not know what a day may bring forth. Let another man praise you, and not your own mouth; a stranger, and not your own lips.' Prov. 27:1-2.

Chapter 28

Godliness is More Important than Circumstances

'Those who forsake the law praise the wicked, but such as keep the law content with them. Evil men do not understand justice, but those who seek the LORD understand all. Better is the poor who walks in his integrity than one perverse in his ways, though he be rich.' Prov. 28:4-6.

Chapter 29

The Fear of the Lord Versus the Fear of Man

'The fear of man brings a snare, but whoever trust in the LORD shall be safe. Many seek the ruler's favor, but justice comes for man from the LORD.' Prov. 29:25-26.

Chapter 30

The Wisdom of Agur

'Surely I am more stupid than any man, and do not have the understanding of a man. I neither learned wisdom nor have knowledge of the Holy One. Who has ascended into heaven, or descended? Who has gathered the wind in His fists? Who has bound the waters in a garment? Who has established all the ends of the earth? What is His name, and what is His Son's name, if you know? Every word of God is pure; He is a shield to those who put their trust in Him. Do not add to His words, lest

He rebuke you, and you be found a liar. Two things I request of You (deprive me not before I die): remove falsehood and lies from me; give me neither poverty nor riches – feed me with the food allotted to me; lest I be full and deny You, and say, "Who is the LORD?" Or lest I be poor and steal, and profane the name of my God.' Prov. 30:2-9.

Chapter 31

Advice from King Lemuel's Mother About Kings and Wives

'Charm is deceitful and beauty is passing, but a woman who fears the LORD, she shall be praised.' Prov. 31:30.

Ecclesiastes

God shows the futility of life without respect to Him, and the value of all things when people fear Him and keep His commandments

Chapter 1

Life Under the Sun is Vain and There is Nothing New

'I, the Preacher, was king over Israel in Jerusalem. And I set my heart to seek and search out by wisdom concerning all that is done under heaven; the burdensome task that God has given to the sons of man, by which they may be exercised. I have seen all the works that are done under the sun; and indeed, all is vanity and grasping for the wind.' Eccles. 1:12-14.

Chapter 2

Wisdom and Folly are Vain in Themselves, but We Find Meaning in Enjoying Work for God's Glory

'Nothing is better for a man than that he should eat and drink, and that his soul should enjoy good in all his labor. This also, I saw, was from the hand of God. For who can eat, or who can have enjoyment, more than I? For God gives wisdom and knowledge and joy to a man who is good in His sight; but to the sinner He gives the work of gathering and collecting that he may give to him who is good before God. This also is vanity and grasping for the wind.' Eccles. 2:24-26.

Chapter 3

There is a Right Time for All Things and God Will Call Every Work into Account

'I know that nothing is better for them than to rejoice, and to do good in their lives, and also that every man should eat and drink and enjoy the good of all of his labor – it is the gift of God.' Eccles. 3:12-13.

Chapter 4
Self-Centered Work is Vain, and Friendship is Better than Popularity

'Two are better than one, because they have a good reward for their labor. For if they fall, one will lift up his companion. But woe to him who is alone when he falls, for he has no one to help him up. Again, if two lie down together, they will keep warm; but how can one be warm alone? Though one may be overpowered by another, two can withstand him. And a threefold cord is not quickly broken.' Eccles. 4:9-12.

Chapter 5
Learning to Fear God in Vows, Worship, and Labor

'Here is what I have seen: It is good and fitting for one to eat and drink, and to enjoy the good of all his labor in which he toils under the sun all the days of his life which God gives him; for it is his heritage. As for every man to whom God has given riches and wealth, and given him power to eat of it, to receive his heritage and rejoice in his labor – this is the gift of God. For he will not dwell unduly on the days of his life, because God keeps him busy with the joy of his heart.' Eccles. 5:18-20.

Chapter 6
The Vanity of Having the Good Things of this Life and Not Enjoying Them, and the Need to Look to God for Meaning in All Things

'There is an evil which I have seen under the sun, and it is common among men: A man to whom God has given riches and wealth and honor, so that he lacks nothing for himself of all he desires; yet God does not give him power to eat of it, but a foreigner consumes it. This is vanity, and it is an evil affliction.' Eccles. 6:1-2.

Chapter 7
The Wisdom Found Through Mourning and Humility

'Consider the work of God; for who can make straight what he has made crooked? In the day of prosperity be joyful, but in the day of adversity consider: surely God has appointed the one as well as the other, so that man can find out nothing that will come after him.' Eccles. 7:13-14.

Chapter 8
Remember that None Have Power of the Time of Life and Death and Gain Wisdom from this Fact

'Because the sentence against an evil work is not executed speedily, therefore the heart of the sons of men is fully set in them to do evil. Though a sinner does evil a hundred times, and his days are prolonged, yet I surely know that it will be well with those who fear God, who fear before Him. But it will not be well with the wicked; nor will he prolong his days, which are as a shadow, because he does not fear before God.' Eccles. 8:11-13.

Chapter 9
Live Wisely in Light of Death, Working While there is Time to Work

'Go, eat your bread with joy, and drink your wine with a merry heart; for God has already accepted your works. Let your garments always be white, and your head lack no oil. Live joyfully with the wife whom you love all the days of your vain life which He has given you under the sun. Whatever your hand finds to do, do it with your might; for there is no work or device or knowledge or wisdom in the grave where you are going.' Eccles. 9:7-10.

Chapter 10
Work Wisely and Live Before God Sincerely

'Do not curse the king, even in your thought; do not curse the rich, even in your bedroom; for a bird of the air may carry your voice, and a bird in flight may tell the matter.' Eccles. 10:20.

Chapter 11
Diversify Your Labor and Remember God in All Things and in Every Stage of Life

'Rejoice, O young man, in your youth, and let your heart cheer you in the days of your youth; walk in the ways of your heart, and in the sight of your eyes; but know that for all these God will bring you into judgment. Therefore remove sorrow from your heart, and put away evil from your flesh, for childhood and youth are vanity.' Eccles. 11:9-10.

Chapter 12
Remembering the Creator and Walking in the Fear of God is the Bottom Line of the Meaning of Life

'Let us hear the conclusion of the whole matter: Fear God and keep His commandments, for this is man's all. For God will bring every work into judgment, including every secret thing, whether good or evil.' Eccles. 12:13-14.

Song of Solomon

God displays the intimacy of the union between a man and his bride, illustrating His closeness to His covenant people

CHAPTER **1**

The Delight of the Shulamite and her Beloved in Each Other

'Behold, you are fair, my love! Behold, you are fair! You have dove's eyes. Behold, you are handsome, my beloved! Yes, pleasant! Also our bed is green. The beams of our houses are cedar, and our rafters of fir.' Song 1:15-17.

CHAPTER **2**

The Time for Love Draws Near

'I charge you, O daughters of Jerusalem, by the gazelles or by the does of the field, do not stir up or awaken love until it pleases.' Song 2:7.

CHAPTER **3**

The Shulamite Seeks Earnestly for her Love

'I charge you, O daughters of Jerusalem, by the gazelles or by the does of the field, do not stir up nor awaken love until it pleases.' Song 3:5.

CHAPTER **4**

The Beloved Praises the Shulamite

'You are all fair, my love, and there is no spot in you.' Song 4:7.

CHAPTER **5**

The Shulamite Misses the Opportunity to Meet With her Beloved

'I charge you, O daughters of Jerusalem, if you find my beloved, that you tell him I am lovesick!' Song 5:8.

Chapter 6
The Beloved Praises the Shulamite Again

'Who is she who looks forth as the morning, fair as the moon, clear as the sun, awesome as an army with banners?' Song 6:10.

Chapter 7
The Beloved and the Shulamite Express their Most Intimate Delight in One Another

'I am my beloved's, and his desire is toward me.' Song 7:10.

Chapter 8
The Value of Love Established in Final Meditations

'Set me as a seal upon your heart, as a seal upon your arm; for love is as strong as death, jealousy as cruel as the grave; its flames are flames of fire, a most vehement flame. Many waters cannot quench love, nor can the floods drown it. If a man would give for love all the wealth of his house, it would be utterly despised.' Song 8:6-7.

Isaiah

God upholds His holiness, warning His rebellious people against covenant breaking, threatening exile, and promising redemption through His Servant

Chapter 1

The Lord Brings an Indictment Against His Children, Who have Become Like Sodom and out of Whom God Saves a Remnant by Calling them to Repentance

> 'Wash yourselves, make yourselves clean; put away the evil of your doings from before My eyes. Cease to do evil, learn to do good; seek justice, rebuke the oppressor; defend the fatherless, plead for the widow. "Come now, and let us reason together," says the LORD, "Though your sins are like scarlet, they shall be as white as snow; though they are red like crimson, they shall be as wool."' Isa. 1:16-18.

Chapter 2

In Spite of Israel's Sins, the Lord Will Bless All the Nations of the Earth Through His Covenant with The Remnant, Causing His Enemies to Flee from His Glory and Majesty

> 'Now it shall come to pass in the latter days that the mountain of the LORD's house shall be established on the top of the mountains, and shall be exalted above the hills; and all nations shall flow to it. Many people shall come and say, "Come, and let us go up to the mountain of the LORD to the house of the God of Jacob; He will teach us His ways, and we shall walk in His paths." For out of Zion shall go forth the law, and the word of the LORD from Jerusalem. He shall judge between the nations, and rebuke many people; they shall beat their swords

> into plowshares, and their spears into pruning hooks; nation shall not lift up sword against nation, neither shall they learn war anymore.' Isa. 2:2-4.

Chapter 3
The Lord Punishes Wicked Leaders and Wicked People by Giving them Those Incapable of Leadership, Condemning the Women for their Luxury

> 'Say to the righteous that it shall be well with them, for they shall eat the fruit of their doings. Woe to the wicked! It shall be ill with him, for the reward of his hands shall be given him. As for My people, children are their oppressors, and women rule over them. O My people! Those who lead you cause you to err, and destroy the way of your paths.' Isa. 3:10-12.

Chapter 4
After Humbling the People for their Sins, the Lord Will Exalt them by Restoring His Covenant Presence through His Servant the Branch

> 'In that day the Branch of the LORD shall be beautiful and glorious; and the fruit of the earth shall be excellent and appealing for those of Israel who have escaped.' Isa. 4:2.

Chapter 5
God Likens Israel to a Vine He Cared for, yet which Brought forth Wild Grapes, Hallowing His Own Name by Beginning to Pronounce Woes on Israel

> 'What more could have been done to My vineyard that I have not done in it? Why then, when I expected it to bring forth good grapes, did it bring forth wild grapes?' Isa. 5:4.

Chapter 6
The Lord Reveals Himself to Isaiah as the True King Seated on His Throne, Stressing His Holiness, Forgiveness, Judgment, and Salvation of a Remnant

> 'I saw the Lord sitting on a throne, high and lifted up, and the train of His robe filled the temple … .And one cried to another and said: "Holy, holy, holy is the LORD of hosts; the whole earth is full of His glory!" … And he touched my mouth with it, and said: "Behold this has touched your lips; your iniquity is taken away, and your sin purged." Also I heard the voice of

the Lord saying: "Whom shall I send, and who will go for Us?" Then I said, "Here am I! Send me."' Isa. 6:1, 3, 7-8.

Chapter 7
The Lord Will Preserve His Covenant with David, Removing the Immediate Threat Against Ahaz, and Promising the Virgin Conception of Immanuel

'But Ahaz said, "I will not ask, nor will I test the LORD!" Then he said, "Hear now, O house of David! Is it a small thing for you to weary men, but will you weary my God also? Therefore the Lord Himself will give you a sign: Behold, the virgin shall conceive and bear a Son, and shall call His name Immanuel."' Isa. 7:12-14.

Chapter 8
In the Meantime, the Lord Warns About the Coming of the King of Assyria, Exhorting the People to Turn to the Law Rather than to Attempts to Predict the Future

'Here am I and the children whom the LORD has given me! We are for signs and wonders in Israel from the LORD of hosts, who dwells in Mount Zion. And when they say to you, "Seek those who are mediums and wizards, who whisper and mutter," should not a people seek their God? Should they seek the dead on behalf of the living? To the law and to the testimony! If they do not speak according this word, it is because there is no light in them.' Isa. 8:18-20.

Chapter 9
The Darkness and Gloom on the People Will be Temporary, Because the Lord Will Fulfill His Covenant Through Immanuel, While the Lord's Anger Remains on the People Due to their Wicked Rulers

'For unto us a Child is born, unto us a Son is given; and the government will be upon His shoulder. And His name will be called Wonderful, Counsellor, Mighty God, Everlasting Father, Prince of Peace. Of the increase of His government and peace there will be no end, upon the throne of David and over His kingdom, to order it and establish it with judgment and justice from that time forward, even forever. The zeal of the LORD of hosts will perform this.' Isa. 9:6-7.

CHAPTER **10**

God Knows How to Judge the Assyrians, Whom He Will Use to Judge His People

'Shall the ax boast itself against Him who chops with it? Or shall the saw exalt itself against Him who saws with it? As if a rod could wield itself against those who lift it up, or as if a staff could lift up, as if it were not wood! … And it shall come to pass in that day that the remnant of Israel, and such as have escaped from the house of Jacob, will never again depend on him who defeated them, but will depend on the LORD, the Holy One of Israel, in truth. The remnant will return, the remnant of Jacob, to the Mighty God. For though your people, O Israel, be as the sand of the sea, a remnant of them will return; the destruction decreed will overflow with righteousness.' Isa. 10:15, 20-22.

CHAPTER **11**

The Lord will Send the Branch to Fulfill His Covenant Promises to His People and to Spread His Blessings to the Nations Through the Holy Spirit

'There shall come forth a Rod from the stem of Jesse, and a Branch shall grow out of his roots. The Spirit of the LORD shall rest upon Him, the Spirit of wisdom and understanding, the Spirit of counsel and might, the Spirit of knowledge and of the fear of the LORD. His delight is in the fear of the LORD, and He shall not judge by the sight of His eyes, nor decide by the hearing of His ears; but with righteousness He shall judge the poor, and decide with equity for the meek of the earth; He shall strike the earth with the rod of His mouth, and with the breath of His lips He shall slay the wicked. Righteousness shall be the belt of His loins, and faithfulness the belt of His waist.' Isa. 11:1-5.

CHAPTER **12**

God's People Praise the Lord for Fulfilling His Covenant and Dwelling Among Them

'Behold, God is my salvation, I will trust and not be afraid; "For YAH, the LORD, is my strength and my song; He also has become my salvation." Therefore with joy you will draw water from the wells of salvation.' Isa. 12:2-3.

Chapter 13
God's Coming Judgment Against Babylon Represents His Judgment Against All of His Enemies

> 'Behold, the day of the LORD comes, cruel, with both wrath and fierce anger, to lay the land desolate; and He will destroy its sinners from it.' Isa. 13:9.

Chapter 14
The Lord Encourages His People With Salvation and Denounces Babylon and Philistia

> 'For the LORD will have mercy on Jacob, and will still choose Israel, and settle them in their own land. The strangers will be joined with them, and they will cling to the house of Jacob. Then people will take them and bring them to their place, and the house of Israel will possess them for servants and maids in the land of the LORD; they will take them captive whose captives they were, and rule over their oppressors.' Isa. 14:1-2.

Chapter 15
God's Judgment Against Moab and the Prophet's Grief Over Moab

> 'My heart will cry out for Moab; his fugitives shall flee to Zoar, like a three-year-old heifer. For by the ascent of Luhith they will go up with weeping; for in the way of Horonaim they will raise up a cry of destruction.' Isa. 15:5-6.

Chapter 16
God Will Humble Moab's Pride Within Three Years, While He Remembers His Covenant with His People Through David

> 'In mercy the throne will be established; and One will sit on it in truth, in the tabernacle of David, judging and seeking justice and hastening righteousness.' Isa. 16:5.

Chapter 17
God's Universal Judgment of the Nations Moves Next to Syria and Israel

> 'In that day a man will look to his Maker, and his eyes will have respect for the Holy One of Israel. He will not look to the altars, the work of his hands; he will not respect what his fingers have made, nor the wooden images nor the incense altars.' Isa. 17:7-8.

Chapter 18

God Pronounces Judgment Against Ethiopia, Showing that His Salvation Will Eventually Encompass the Nations

> 'In that time a present will be brought to the LORD of hosts from a people tall and smooth of skin, and from a people terrible from their beginning onward, a nation powerful and treading down, whose land the rivers divide – to the place of the name of the LORD of hosts, to Mount Zion.' Isa. 18:7.

Chapter 19

God Will Ride on a Swift Cloud to Judge the Idols of Egypt, but He will Include them in His Covenant Promises of Salvation

> 'In that day there will be an altar to the LORD in the midst of the land of Egypt, and a pillar to the LORD at its border. And it will be for a sign and for a witness to the LORD of hosts in the land of Egypt; for they will cry to the LORD because of the oppressors and, and He will send them a Savior and a Mighty One, and He will deliver them. Then the LORD will be known to Egypt, and the Egyptians will know the LORD in that day, and will make a sacrifice and offering; yes, they will make a vow to the LORD and perform it. And the LORD will strike Egypt, He will strike and heal it; they will return to the LORD, and He will be entreated by them and heal them. In that day there will be a highway from Egypt to Assyria, and the Assyrian will come into Egypt and the Egyptians into Assyria, and the Egyptians will serve with the Assyrians. In that day Israel will be one of three with Egypt and Assyria – a blessing in the midst of the land, whom the LORD of hosts shall bless, saying, "Blessed is Egypt My people, and Assyria the work of My hands, and Israel My inheritance."' Isa. 19:19-25.

Chapter 20

Isaiah Becomes a Personal Sign of God's Judgment Against Egypt and Ethiopia in Order to Shame Israel for Trusting in Anything Other than the Lord

> 'Then they shall be afraid and ashamed of Ethiopia their expectation and Egypt their glory.' Isa. 20:5.

Chapter 21

The Lord Pronounces Judgment on Babylon, Edom, and Arabia

'And look, here comes a chariot of men with a pair of horsemen! Then he answered and said, Babylon is fallen, is fallen! And all the carved images of her gods He has broken to the ground.' Isa. 21:9.

Chapter 22

The Lord Ironically Denounces Jerusalem as the Valley of Vision, When their Idolatry and Living for This Life Only Has Made them Blind

'The key of the house of David I will lay on his shoulder; so he shall open, and no one shall shut; and he shall shut, and no one shall open.' Isa. 22:22.

Chapter 23

The Lord Singles Out Tyre as a Pattern of His Judgment of the Nations and Indicates Seventy Years of Exile

'The LORD has purposed it, to bring dishonor to the pride of all glory, to bring contempt to all the honorable of the earth.' Isa. 23:9

Chapter 24

The Lord Summarizes His Judgments on the Nations of the Earth, Bringing this Section to a Conclusion in Relation to His Covenant People

'The earth is also defiled under its inhabitants, because they have transgressed the laws, changed the ordinance, broken the everlasting covenant.' Isa. 24:5.

Chapter 25

After Completing the Judgment of All Nations, Isaiah Praises the Lord for Future Salvation

'And He will destroy on this mountain the surface of the covering cast over all people, and the veil that is spread over all nations. He will swallow up death forever, and the LORD God will wipe away tears from all faces; the rebuke of His people He will take away from all the earth; for the LORD has spoken." Isa. 25:7-8

Chapter 26

The Lord Predicts that His People Will Sing of His Salvation

'You will keep him in perfect peace, whose mind is stayed on You, because he trusts in You. Trust in the LORD forever, for in YAH, the LORD, is everlasting strength.' Isa. 26:3-4.

Chapter 27
The Lord will Punish the Enemies of His People When He Restores them in Faithfulness to His Covenant

> 'Has He struck Israel as He struck those who struck him? Or has He been slain according to the slaughter of those who were slain by Him?' Isa. 27:7.

Chapter 28
In the Meantime, Ephraim and Judah Must Repent in Light of Coming Judgment

> 'Therefore thus says the LORD GOD: "Behold, I lay in Zion a stone for a foundation, a tried stone, a precious cornerstone, a sure foundation; whoever believes will not act hastily."' Isa. 28:16.

Chapter 29
The Lord Will Punish Jerusalem, Removing the Prophets Whom they Would not Hear, in Order to Humble them and Remember His Covenant With Abraham for the Remnant

> 'Therefore the LORD said, "Inasmuch as these people draw near to me with their mouths and honor Me with their lips, but have removed their hearts far from Me, and their fear toward Me is taught by the commandment of men … Surely you have things turned around! Shall the potter be esteemed as the clay; for shall the thing made say to him who made it, 'He did not make me?' Or shall the thing formed say of him who formed it, 'He has no understanding?'"' Isa. 29:13, 16.

Chapter 30
The Covenant Curses Shall Fall on Israel for a Time Because they Trusted in Egypt Instead of God's Spirit and they Shut the Mouths of the Prophets

> 'Woe to the rebellious children, says the LORD, who take counsel, but not of Me, and who devise plans, but not of My Spirit, that they may add sin to sin.' Isa. 30:1.

Chapter 31
The Lord Reminds Israel that the Egyptians are Flesh and not Spirit, Calling them to Repent and Trust in His Covenant Promises

> 'Now the Egyptians are men, and not God; and their horses are flesh, and not spirit. When the LORD stretches out His

hand, both he who helps will fall, and he who is helped will fall down; they all will perish together.' Isa. 31:3.

Chapter 32

The Lord will Restore Righteousness Through His King and by His Spirit, Turning Covenant Curses into Covenant Blessings

'Until the Spirit is poured out from on high, and the wilderness becomes a fruitful field, and the fruitful field is counted a forest.' Isa. 32:15.

Chapter 33

Isaiah Prays for Deliverance in Light of Impending Doom, and the Lord Promises to Save the People Through a Davidic King

'Your eyes will see the King in His beauty; they will see the land that is very far off. Your heart will meditate on terror: "Where is the scribe? Where is he who weighs? Where is he who counts the towers?"' Isa. 33:17-18.

Chapter 34

The Lord Answers Isaiah's Prayer by Promising to Judge by Exile the Nations that Stand Against them

'All the host of heaven shall be dissolved, and the heavens shall be rolled up like a scroll; all their host shall fall down as the leaf falls from the vine, and as fruit falling from a fig tree.' Isa. 34:4.

Chapter 35

The Lord Promises Future Glory to Zion as He Returns the Exiles, Directing them to Future Salvation

'It shall blossom abundantly and rejoice, even with joy and singing. The glory of Lebanon shall be given to it, the excellence of Carmel and Sharon. They shall see the glory of the LORD, the excellency of our God. Strengthen the weak hands, and make firm the feeble knees. Say to those who are fearful-hearted, "Be strong, do not fear! Behold, your God will come with vengeance, with the recompense of God; He will come and save you."' Isa. 35:2-4.

Chapter 36

Sennacherib, King of Assyria Boasts Against the Lord, Tempting the People to Submit to His Rule and Repeating Material from 2 Kings and 2 Chronicles for Emphasis

'Look! You are trusting in the staff of this broken reed, Egypt, on which if a man leans, it will go into his hand and pierce it. So is Pharaoh king of Egypt to all who trust in him. But if you say to me, "We trust in the LORD our God," is it not He whose high places and whose altars Hezekiah has taken away, and said to Judah and Jerusalem, "You shall worship before this altar?"' Isa. 36:6-7.

Chapter 37
Sennacherib Boasts Against the Lord, Hezekiah Prays, and the Lord Promises Deliverance for His Covenant with David

'Thus you shall speak to Hezekiah king of Judah, saying: "Do not let your God in whom you trust deceive you, saying, Jerusalem shall not be given into the hand of the king of Assyria" ... Whom have you reproached and blasphemed? Against whom have you raised your voice, and lifted your eyes on high? Against the Holy One of Israel.' Isa. 37:10, 23.

Chapter 38
Hezekiah Shows His Faith in the Lord by Praying for the Lord to Extend His Life and Praising the Lord for His Mercies

'Indeed it was for my own peace that I had great bitterness; but you have lovingly delivered my soul from the pit of corruption, for you have cast all my sins behind your back.' Isa. 38:17.

Chapter 39
God Tests Hezekiah's Faith by Sending Envoys from Babylon, Hezekiah Fails the Test in his Pride, but Resigns himself to Praise the Lord for His Mercies, all of which Depicts What God Will Do with Israel

'So Hezekiah said to Isaiah, "The word of the LORD which you have spoken is good!" For he said, "At least there will be peace and truth in my days."' Isa. 39:8.

Chapter 40
The Lord Shifts Emphasis by Proclaiming His Glory for the Comfort of the Exiles When they Would Return to the Land After Exile

'O Zion, you who bring good tidings, get up into the high mountain; O Jerusalem, you who bring good tidings, lift up your voice with strength, lift it up, be not afraid; say to the cities of Judah, "Behold your God!" … He gives power to the weak, and to those who have no might He increases strength. Even the youths shall faint and be weary, and the young men shall utterly fail, but those who wait on the LORD shall renew their strength; they shall mount up with wings like eagles, they shall run and not be weary, they shall walk and not faint.' Isa. 40:9, 29-31.

Chapter 41

God Will Help His People as their Redeemer Who Fulfills His Covenant with Abraham, Showing the Futility of Idolatry

'Fear not, for I am with you; be not dismayed, for I am your God. I will strengthen you, yes, I will help you, I will uphold you with My righteous right hand.' Isa. 41:10.

Chapter 42

Remembering His Covenant, God Promises in the First Servant Song to Save His People Through His Spirit-Filled Servant, as His People Respond with their Own Song

'Behold! My Servant whom I uphold, My Elect One in whom My soul delights! I have put My Spirit upon Him; He will bring forth justice to the Gentiles. He will not cry out, nor raise His voice, nor cause His voice to be heard in the street. A bruised reed He will not break, and smoking flax He will not quench; He will bring forth justice for truth. He will not fail nor be discouraged, till He has established justice in the earth; and the coastlands shall wait for His law. Thus says God the LORD, who created the heavens and stretched them out, who spread forth the earth and that which comes from it, who gives breath to the people on it, and spirit to those who walk on it: "I, the LORD, have called You in righteousness, and will hold Your hand; I will keep You and give You as a covenant to the people, as a light to the Gentiles, to open blind eyes, to bring out the prisoners from prison, those who sit in darkness from the prison house. I am the LORD, that is My name; and My glory I will not give to another, nor My praise to carved images. Behold, the former things have come to pass, and new things I declare; before they spring forth I tell you of them."' Isa. 42:1-9.

Chapter 43

The Lord, Who is Israel's Creator and King, Becomes their Redeemer Who Blots Out Their Sins

> 'I, even I, am He who blots out your transgressions for My own sake; and I will not remember your sins.' Isa. 43:25.

Chapter 44

The Creator, Redeemer, and King of Israel is their God Who Blots Out their Transgressions, Showing the Futility of Idolatry by Mocking the Idols and Those Who Make Them

> 'For I will pour water on him who is thirsty, and floods on the dry ground; I will pour My Spirit on your descendants, and My blessing on your offspring ... Thus says the LORD, the King of Israel, and his Redeemer, the LORD of hosts; "I am the First and I am the Last; besides Me there is no God."' Isa. 44:3, 6.

Chapter 45

The Lord Predicts that He Will Raise Cyrus of Persia to Bring His People Back from Exile, Calling All the Ends of the Earth to Look to Him and Be Saved

> 'I form the light and create darkness, I make peace and create calamity. I, the LORD, do all these things ... Look to Me, and be saved, all you ends of the earth! For I am God, and there is no other. I have sworn by Myself; the word has gone out of My mouth in righteousness, and shall not return, to Me every knee shall bow, every tongue shall take an oath. He shall say, "Surely in the LORD I have righteousness and strength. To Him men shall come, and all shall be ashamed who are incensed against Him. In the LORD, all the descendants of Israel shall be justified, and shall glory."' Isa. 45:7, 22-25.

Chapter 46

The People Bear their Idols, but the Lord Promises to Bear them Instead

> 'Even to your old age, I am He, and even to gray hairs I will carry you! I have made, and I will bear; even I will carry and deliver you. To whom will you liken Me, and make Me equal and compare Me, that we should be alike?' Isa. 46:4-5.

Chapter 47

God Will Humble Babylon Who Likens herself to the Self-Existent God

'Therefore hear this now, you who are given to pleasures, who dwell securely, who say in your heart, "I am, and there is no one else besides me; I shall not sit as a widow, nor shall I know the loss of children."' Isa. 47:8.

Chapter 48

God Confronts and Removes Israel's Hypocrisy, Promising to Redeem them from Babylon for His Name's Sake

'For My name's sake I will defer My anger, and for My praise I will restrain it from you, so that I do not cut you off. Behold, I have refined you, but not as silver; I have tested you in the furnace of affliction. For My own sake, for My own sake, I will do it; for how should My name be profaned? And I will not give My glory to another. Listen to Me, O Jacob, and Israel, My called: I am He, I am the First, I am also the Last. Indeed My hand has laid the foundations of the earth, and My right hand has stretched out the heavens; when I call to them, they stand up together.' Isa. 48:9-13.

Chapter 49

Isaiah's Second Servant Song Presents the Servant as a Covenant for the Nations, Bringing Salvation to the Returned Exiles and the Whole Earth

'Then I said, "I have labored in vain, I have spent my strength for nothing and in vain; yet surely My just reward is with the LORD, and my work with my God." And now the LORD says, Who formed Me from the womb to be His Servant, to bring Jacob back to Him, so that Israel is gathered to Him (for I shall be glorious in the eyes of the LORD, and My God shall be My strength), indeed He says, "It is too small a thing that You should be My Servant to raise up the tribes of Jacob, and to restore the preserved ones of Israel; I will also give You as a light to the Gentiles, that You should be My salvation to the ends of the earth." … Thus says the LORD, "In an acceptable time I have heard You, and in the day of salvation I have helped You; I will preserve you and give You as a covenant to the people, to restore the earth, to cause them to inherit the desolate heritages."' Isa. 49:4-6, 8.

CHAPTER **50**

Isaiah's Third Servant Song Shows that God has not Divorced Israel, but that the Servant Will Suffer with the Lord's Help

> 'The LORD God has given Me the tongue of the learned, that I should know how to speak a word in season to him who is weary. He awakens me morning by morning, he awakens My ear to hear as the learned. The LORD God has opened My ear; and I was not rebellious, nor did I turn away. I gave My back to those who struck Me, and My cheeks to those who plucked out the beard; I did not hide My face from shame and spitting. For the LORD God will help Me; therefore I will not be disgraced; therefore I have set My face like a flint, and I know that I will not be ashamed. He is near who justifies Me; who will contend with Me? Let us stand together. Who is my adversary? Let him come near Me. Surely the LORD God will help Me; who is he who will condemn Me? Indeed they will grow old like a garment; the moth will eat them up. Who among you fears the LORD? Who obeys the voice of His Servant? Who walks in darkness and has no light? Let him trust in the name of the LORD and rely upon his God.' Isa. 50:4-10.

CHAPTER **51**

The Lord Comforts Zion by Remembering His Covenant with Abraham and Moses, Promising to Restore the Blessings of Eden and Overthrowing their Enemies

> 'Lift up your eyes to the heavens, and look on the earth beneath. For the heavens will vanish away like smoke, the earth will grow old like a garment, and those who dwell in it will die in like manner; but My salvation will be forever, and My righteousness will not be abolished. Listen to Me, you who know righteousness, you people in whose heart is My law: do not fear the reproach of men, nor be afraid of their insults. For the moth will eat them up like a garment, and the worm will eat them like wool; but My righteousness will be forever, and My salvation from generation to generation.' Isa. 51:6-8.

Chapter 52

The Lord Proclaims Good News, Announcing Salvation to the Nations, and Introducing the Fourth Servant Song as the Means by Which These Blessings Come

> 'How beautiful upon the mountains are the feet of him who brings good news, who proclaims peace, who brings glad tidings of good things, who proclaims salvation, who says to Zion, "Your God reigns!" … The LORD made bare His holy arm in the eyes of all nations; and the ends of the earth shall see the salvation of our God.' Isa. 52:7, 10.

Chapter 53

The Final Servant Song Concludes the Previous Three, Showing that Salvation Shall Come Through the Servant Bearing the Sins of the People, Suffering in their Place, and Interceding for their Salvation

> 'He is despised and rejected by men, a Man of sorrows and acquainted with grief. And we hid, as it were, our faces from Him; He was despised, and we did not esteem Him. Surely He has born our griefs and carried our sorrows; yet we esteemed Him stricken, smitten by God, and afflicted. But He was wounded for our transgressions, He was bruised for our iniquities; the chastisement for our peace was upon Him, and by His stripes we are healed. All we like sheep have gone astray; we have turned, every one to his own way; and the LORD has laid on Him the iniquity of us all … Yet it pleased the LORD to bruise Him; He has put Him to grief. When you make His soul an offering for sin, He shall see His seed, He shall prolong His days, and the pleasure of the LORD shall prosper in His hand. He shall see the labor of His soul, and be satisfied. By His knowledge, My righteous Servant shall justify many, for He shall bear their iniquities.' Isa. 53:3-6, 10-11.

Chapter 54

The Lord Calls the Exiles to Sing and Rejoice Because He Will Make a Perpetual Covenant of Peace With them that Shall be Like the Waters of Noah

> 'Sin, O barren, you who have not borne! Break forth into singing, and cry aloud, you who have not labored with child! For more are the children of the desolate than the children of

the married woman, says the LORD … All your children shall be taught by the LORD, and great shall be the peace of your children.' Isa. 54:1, 13.

Chapter 55

God Freely Calls All Who Hear to Look to Him and Live Because of His Covenant with David

'Incline your ear, and come to Me. Hear, and your soul shall live; and I will make an everlasting covenant with you – the sure mercies of David. Indeed I have given him as a witness to the people, a leader and commander for the peoples.' Isa. 55:3-4.

Chapter 56

God Will Bring His Righteousness and Justice to a Righteous and Just People, Who Show their Sincerity by Sabbath Keeping, Including Even Those Who Were Previously Excluded from Worship

'For thus says the LORD: "To the eunuchs who keep My Sabbaths, and choose what pleases Me, and hold fast My covenant, even to them I will give in My house and within My walls a place and a name better than that of sons and daughters; I will give them an everlasting name that shall not be cut off. Also the sons of the foreigner who join themselves to the LORD, to serve Him, and to love the name of the LORD, to be His servants – everyone who keeps from defiling the Sabbath, and holds fast to My covenant – even them I will bring to My holy mountain, and make them joyful in My house of prayer. Their burnt offerings and sacrifices will be accepted on My altar, for My house shall be called a house of prayer for all nations."' Isa. 56:4-7.

Chapter 57

The Lord Mercifully Takes the Righteous from Evil and Calls Idolaters to Repentance, Promising to Dwell with the Humble

'For thus says the High and Lofty One, Who inhabits eternity, whose name is Holy: "I dwell in the high and holy place, with him who has a contrite and humble spirit, to revive the spirit of the humble, and to revive the heart of the contrite ones" … "I create the fruit of the lips: Peace, peace to him who is far off and to him who is near," says the LORD, "and I will heal him."' Isa. 57:15, 19.

CHAPTER 58

The People Pretend to Honor the Lord, but the Lord Exposes their Hypocrisy by their Fasting, and Calls them to Sincere Repentance Through Sabbath Keeping

'If you turn away your foot from the Sabbath, from doing your pleasure on My holy day, and call the Sabbath a delight, the holy day of the LORD honorable, and shall honor Him, not doing your own ways, nor finding your own pleasure, nor speaking your own words, then you shall delight yourself in the LORD; and I will cause you to ride on the high hills of the earth, and feed you with the heritage of Jacob your father. The mouth of the LORD has spoken.' Isa. 58:13-14.

CHAPTER 59

The People's Sins Separate them from God Though His Hand is not Shortened that it Cannot Save, and the Lord Promises to Send the Redeemer to Zion and Put His Word and Spirit in their Mouths and that of their Descendants, in His New Covenant

'The Redeemer will come to Zion, and to those who turn from transgression in Jacob, says the LORD. "As for Me," says the LORD, "this is my covenant with them: My Spirit who is upon you, and My words which I have put in your mouth, shall not depart from your mouth, nor from the mouth of your descendants' descendants," says the LORD, "from this time forth and forevermore."' Isa. 59:20-21.

CHAPTER 60

God Will Cause Zion's Light to Shine, Drawing the Gentiles to Come to them With their Wealth, for God Will be their Light

'The sun shall no longer be your light by day, nor for brightness shall the moon give light to you; but the LORD God will be to you an everlasting light, and your God your glory. Your sun shall no longer go down, nor shall your moon withdraw itself; for the LORD will be your everlasting light, and the days of your mourning shall be ended. Also your people shall all be righteous; they shall inherit the land forever, the branch of My planting, the work of My hands, that I may be glorified. A little one shall become a thousand, and a small one a strong nation. I, the LORD, will hasten it in its time.' Isa. 60:19-22.

Chapter 61

The Spirit of the Lord Will Anoint the Christ to Proclaim Liberty and Vengeance, Saving the People Through an Everlasting Covenant

'The Spirit of the LORD GOD is upon Me, because the LORD has anointed Me to preach good tidings to the poor; He has sent Me to heal the brokenhearted, to proclaim liberty to the captives, and the opening of the prison to those who are bound; to proclaim the acceptable year of the LORD, and the day of the vengeance of our God; to comfort all who mourn, to console those who mourn in Zion, to give them beauty for ashes, the oil of joy for mourning, the garment of praise for the spirit of heaviness; that they may be called the trees of righteousness, the planting of the LORD, that He may be glorified.' Isa. 61:1-3.

Chapter 62

The Lord Will Fulfill His Covenant by Restoring the Forsaken People

'Indeed the LORD has proclaimed to the end of the world: "Say to the daughter of Zion, surely your salvation is coming; behold, His reward is with Him, and His work is before Him." And they shall call them The Holy People, the Redeemed of the LORD; and you shall be called Sought Out, and A City Not Forsaken.' Isa. 62:11-12.

Chapter 63

As the Father of His People, the Lord Pities them in Affliction, Saving them Through the Angel of the Covenant and by His Holy Spirit, Even Though their Fathers Grieved the Holy Spirit under the Covenant with Moses

'For He said, "Surely they are My people, children who will not lie." So He became their Savior. In all their affliction He was afflicted, and the Angel of His Presence saved them; in His love and in His pity He redeemed them; and He bore them and carried them all the days of old. But they rebelled and grieved His Holy Spirit; so He turned Himself against them as an enemy, and He fought against them. Then He remembered the days of old, Moses and His people, saying: "Where is He who brought them up out of the sea with the shepherd of His flock? Where is He who put His Holy Spirit within them?"' Isa. 63:8-10.

Chapter 64

Isaiah Responds to God's Faithfulness with Fervent Prayer that God Would Act to Save His People

'But we are all like an unclean thing, and all our righteousnesses are like filthy rags; we all fade as a leaf, and our iniquities, like the wind, have taken us away. And there is no one who calls on Your name, who stirs himself to take hold of You; for You have hidden Your face from us, and have consumed us because of our iniquities. But now, O LORD, You are our Father; we are the clay, and You our potter; and all we are the work of Your hand.' Isa. 64:6-8.

Chapter 65

The Lord Responds to Isaiah by Showing that He is More Eager to Hear than People are to Seek Him, and the Lord Distinguishes True and False Believers Within Israel

'I was sought by those who did not ask for Me; I was found by those who did not seek Me. I said, "Here I am, here I am," to a nation that was not called by My name. I have stretched out My hands all day long to a rebellious people, who walk in a way that is not good, according to their own thoughts ... It shall come to pass that before they call, I will answer; and while they are still speaking, I will hear. The wolf and the lamb shall feed together, the lion shall eat straw like the ox, and dust shall be the serpent's food. They shall not hurt or destroy in all My holy mountain, says the LORD.' Isa. 65:1-2, 24-25.

Chapter 66

The Lord Gives a Final Warning Against Hypocrisy in Worship, Promising to Vindicate His Persecuted Remnant in a New Heavens and New Earth, and Warning His Enemies of Coming Final Judgment

'Thus says the LORD: "Heaven is My throne, and the earth is My footstool. Where is the house that you will build Me? And where is the place of My rest? For all those things My hand has made, and all those things exist," says the LORD. "But on this one will I look: on him who is poor and contrite in spirit, and who trembles at My word."' Isa. 66:1-2.

Jeremiah

God threatens to tear down Israel for their covenant breaking, promising to build and to plant them again as they look forward to the new covenant in the Redeemer

Chapter 1

The Lord Calls Jeremiah to be His Prophet Against Israel and the Nations, Giving him Six Key Terms that Introduce the Judgment and Salvation Characterizing the Book

> 'See, I have this day set you over the nations and over the kingdoms, to root out and to pull down, to destroy and to throw down, to build and to plant.' Jer. 1:10.

Chapter 2

Israel Committed Idolatry Like an Unfaithful Wife to the Lord, and the Lord Calls them and their Prophets, Priests, and Kings to Humble Repentance

> 'Has a nation changed its gods, which are not gods? But My people have changed their Glory for what does not profit. Be astonished, O heavens, at this, and be horribly afraid; be very desolate,' says the LORD. 'For My people have committed two evils: they have forsaken Me, the fountain of living waters, and hewn themselves cisterns – broken cisterns that can hold no water.' Jer. 2:11-13.

Chapter 3

The Lord Calls Backsliding Israel to Return to Him as their Husband and Father, by Comparing Judah to Israel, and Promising to Give them Better Shepherds

> '"Return, O backsliding children," says the LORD; "for I am married to you. I will take you, one from a city and two from

a family, and I will bring you to Zion. And I will give you shepherds according to My heart, who will feed you with knowledge and understanding. Then it shall come to pass, when you are multiplied and increased in the land in those days," says the LORD, "that they will say no more, 'The ark of the covenant of the LORD.'" It shall not come to mind, nor shall they remember it, nor shall they visit it, nor shall it be made anymore. At that time Jerusalem shall be called The Throne of the LORD, and all the nations shall be gathered to it, to the name of the LORD, to Jerusalem. No more shall they follow the dictates of their evil hearts.' Jer. 3:14-17.

Chapter 4

The Lord Calls the People to Return to Him with Circumcised Hearts, Even though He Will Bring Disaster from the North Country, and Jeremiah Accuses the Lord of Deceiving Them

'Circumcise yourselves to the LORD, and take away the foreskins of your hearts, you men of Judah and inhabitants of Jerusalem, lest My fury come forth like fire, and burn so that no one can quench it.' Jer. 4:4.

Chapter 5

The People Call on God's Name Hypocritically in Insincerity, they Lie About God's Sovereign Providence, and they Love the Lies of the Prophets and the Priests

'"Shall I not punish them for these things?" says the LORD. "Shall I not avenge Myself on a nation such as this?" An astonishing and horrible thing has been committed in the land: the prophets prophecy falsely, and the priests rule by their own power; and My people love to have it so. But what will you do in the end?"' Jer. 5:29-31.

Chapter 6

The Lord Will Bring Impending Judgment from the North Because the Prophets and Priests Declare Peace When There is no Peace

'Because from the least of them even to the greatest of them, everyone is given to covetousness; and from the prophet even to the priest, everyone deals falsely. They have also healed the hurt of My people slightly, saying, "Peace, peace!" When there is no peace.' Jer. 6:13-14.

Chapter 7

The Lord Calls the People to Repent, Trusting in the Presence of the Lord Instead of the Temple of the Lord, Urging Jeremiah not to Pray for the People so Long as they Do not Repent

> 'Behold, you trust in lying words that cannot profit. Will you steal, murder, commit adultery, swear falsely, burn incense to Baal, and walk after other gods whom you do not know, and then come and stand before Me in this house which is called by My name, and say, "We are delivered to do all these abominations?" "Has this house, which is called by My name, become a den of thieves in your eyes? Behold I, even I, have seen it," says the LORD.' Jer. 7:8-11.

Chapter 8

The Lord Pronounces Judgment on the Princes, Priests, and Prophets for Preaching Peace Instead of Repentance, and Jeremiah Laments that there is no Balm in Gilead

> 'The wise men are ashamed, they are dismayed and taken. Behold, they have rejected the word of the LORD; so what wisdom do they have? ... For they have healed the hurt of the daughter of My people slightly, saying, "Peace, peace!" when there is no peace.' Jer. 8:9, 11.

Chapter 9

Jeremiah Laments the People Because they are not Valiant for Truth, Exhorting them that True Circumcision is in the Heart and True Boasting is in Knowing the Lord

> 'Thus says the LORD: "Let not the wise man glory in his wisdom, let not the mighty man glory in his might, nor let the rich man glory in his riches; but let him who glories glory in this, that he understands and knows Me, that I am the LORD, exercising lovingkindness, judgment, and righteousness in the earth. For in these I delight," says the LORD. "Behold, the days are coming," says the LORD, "that I will punish all who are circumcised with the uncircumcised – Egypt, Judah, Edom, the people of Ammon, Moab, and all who are in the farthest corners, who dwell in the wilderness. For all these nations are uncircumcised, and the house of Israel are uncircumcised in the heart."' Jer. 9:23-26.

Chapter 10

The Living God Ridicules the Dead Idols of the Nations, Pronouncing Judgment on Israel for their Bad Shepherds

> 'But the LORD is the true God; He is the living God and the everlasting King. At His wrath the earth will tremble, and the nations will not be able to endure His indignation. Thus you shall say to them: "The gods that have not made the heavens and the earth shall perish from the earth and from under these heavens."' Jer. 10:10-11.

Chapter 11

The Lord Rebukes Israel for Breaking the Covenant, Promising to Protect Jeremiah from the Men of Anathoth

> 'For according to the number of your cities were your gods, O Judah; and according to the number of the streets of Jerusalem you have set up altars to that shameful thing, altars to burn incense to Baal. So do not pray for this people, or lift up a cry or prayer for them; for I will not hear them in the time that they cry out to Me because of their trouble.' Jer. 11:13-14.

Chapter 12

Jeremiah Asks the Lord for Understanding Regarding His Judgments, the Lord Exhorts him to Persevere, and Promises a Remnant from All Nations

> 'Thus says the LORD: "Against all My evil neighbors who touch the inheritance which I have caused My people Israel to inherit – behold, I will pluck them out of their land and pluck out the house of Judah from among them. Then it shall be, after I have plucked them out, that I will return and have compassion on them and bring them back, everyone to his heritage and to his land. And it shall be, if they will learn carefully the ways of My people, to swear by My name, "As the LORD lives," as they taught My people to swear by Baal, then they shall be established in the midst of My people. But if they do not obey, I will utterly pluck up and destroy that nation," says the LORD.' Jer. 12:14-17.

Chapter 13

The Lord Illustrates Israel's Covenant Unfaithfulness with the Linen Sash and the Bottles of Wine, Calling them to Repent in Spite of their Stubborn Rebellion

'"For as the sash clings to the waist of a man, so I have caused the whole house of Israel and the whole house of Judah to cling to Me," says the Lord, "that they may become My people, for renown, for praise, and for glory; but they would not hear." … "Can the Ethiopian change his skin or the leopard its spots? Then may you also do good who are accustomed to do evil."' Jer. 13:11, 23.

Chapter 14
Jeremiah Prays for the People According to God's Covenant, but God Urges him Not to Pray for them, Relegating them to Sword, Famine, and Pestilence

'We acknowledge, O LORD, our wickedness and the iniquity of our fathers, for we have sinned against You. Do not abhor us, for Your name's sake; do not disgrace the throne of Your glory. Remember, do not break Your covenant with us.' Jer. 14:20-21.

Chapter 15
The Lord Will Assuredly Bring Judgment, not Accepting Intercession for them, and Strengthening Jeremiah Against them

'Then the LORD said to me, "Even if Moses and Samuel stood before Me, My mind would not be favorable towards this people. Cast them out of My sight, and let them go forth. And it shall be, if they say to you, Where should we go? Then you shall tell them, Such as are for death, to death; and such as are for the sword, to the sword; and such as are for famine, to the famine; and such as are for captivity, to the captivity."' Jer. 15:1-2.

Chapter 16
The Lord's Prohibition Against Jeremiah Taking a Wife Depicts How the Lord will Deal with the Exiles

'"Therefore behold, the days are coming," says the LORD, "that it shall not more be said, The LORD lives who brought up the children of Israel from the land of Egypt, but, The LORD lives who brought up the children of Israel from the land of the north and from all lands where He had driven them. For I will bring them back into their land which I gave to their fathers."' Jer. 16:14-15.

Chapter 17
Mirroring Psalm 1, the Lord Curses Those Trusting in Man and Blesses Those Trusting the Lord, Directing Israel to Restore the Sabbath as a Mark of Sincere Repentance

> 'I, the LORD, search the heart, I test the mind, even to give every man according to his ways, according to the fruit of his doings … "And it shall be, if you heed Me carefully," says the LORD, "to bring no burden through the gates of this city on the Sabbath day, to do no work in it, then shall enter the gates of this city kings and princes sitting on the throne of David, riding in chariots and on horses, they and their princes, accompanied by the men of Judah and the inhabitants of Jerusalem; and this city shall remain forever."' Jer. 17:10, 24-25.

Chapter 18
The Lord Uses the Potter and the Clay to Illustrate His Power to Destroy Nations that Refuse to Hear, and to Build Up Nations that Repent

> 'Then the word of the LORD came to me, saying: "O house of Israel, can I not do with you as this potter?" says the LORD. "Look, as the clay is in the potter's hand, so are you in My hand, O house of Israel! The instant I speak concerning a nation and concerning a kingdom, to pluck up, to pull down, and to destroy it, if that nation against whom I have spoken turns from its evil, I will relent of the disaster that I thought to bring upon it. And the instant that I speak concerning a nation and concerning a kingdom, to build and to plant it, if it does evil in My sight so that it does not obey My voice, then I will relent concerning the good with which I said I would benefit it."' Jer. 18:5-10.

Chapter 19
The Lord Uses the Sign of the Broken Flask to Illustrate the Transformation of the Valley of the Son of Hinnom into the Valley of Slaughter Because Israel Sacrificed their Children to Baal There

> 'Then you shall break the flask in the sight of the men who go with you, and say to them, "Thus says the LORD of hosts: Even so I will break this people and this city, as one breaks a potter's vessel, which cannot be made whole again; and they shall bury them in Tophet till there is no place to bury."' Jer. 19:10-11.

Chapter 20
Pashhur the False Prophet Strikes and Imprisons Jeremiah, who Pronounces Curses Against Pashhur, and Resigns himself to his Role as the Lord's Prophet

'Then I said, "I will not make mention of Him, nor speak anymore in His name." But His word was in my heart like a burning fire shut up in my bones; I was weary of holding it back, and I could not.' Jer. 20:9.

Chapter 21
King Zedekiah Sends the Prophets and Priests to Seek the Lord's Word from Jeremiah, Who Urges them to Defect to the Chaldeans

'Now you shall say to this people, "Thus says the LORD: Behold, I set before you the way of life and the way of death. He who remains in this city shall die by the sword, by famine, and by pestilence; but he who goes out and defects to the Chaldeans who besiege you, he shall live, and his life shall be as a prize to him. For I have set My face against this city for adversity and not for good," says the LORD. "It shall be given into the hand of the king of Babylon, and he shall burn it with fire."' Jer. 21:8-10.

Chapter 22
The Lord Pronounces Judgment Against David's House, Calls them to Repent and Act Like Josiah, and Threatens to End Coniah's Line Among the Davidic Kings

'O earth, earth, earth, hear the word of the LORD! Thus says the LORD: "Write this man down as childless, a man who shall not prosper in his days; for none of his descendants shall prosper, sitting on the throne of David, and ruling anymore in Judah."' Jer. 22:29-30.

Chapter 23
The Lord Rebukes the False Shepherds, Promises a Righteous Branch from David, and Shows that the False Prophets are a Burden to the People Rather than Bringing a Burden from the Lord

'Behold, the days are coming,' says the LORD, 'That I will raise to David a Branch of righteousness; a King shall reign and prosper, and execute judgment and righteousness in the earth. In His days Judah will be saved, and will dwell safely; now this is His name by which He will be called: THE LORD OUR RIGHTEOUSNESS. Therefore, behold, the days are coming,' says the LORD, 'that they shall no longer say, "As the LORD lives who brought up the children of Israel from the land of

Egypt," but, "As the LORD lives who brought up and led the descendants of the house of Israel from the north country and from all the countries where I had driven them." And they shall dwell in their own land.' Jer. 23:5-8.

Chapter 24
The Lord Likens the Exiles to Good Figs Who Will Return to the Land, and Those Staying in the Land to Rotten Figs that Cannot be Eaten

'Thus says the LORD, the God of Israel: "Like these good figs, so will I acknowledge those who are carried away captive from Judah, whom I have sent out of this place for their own good, into the land of the Chaldeans. For I will set my eyes on them for good, and I will bring them back to this land; I will build them and not pull them down, and I will plant them and not pluck them up. Then I will give them a heart to know Me, that I am the LORD; and they shall be My people, and I will be their God, for they shall return to Me with their whole heart."' Jer. 24:5-7.

Chapter 25
The Lord Promises Seventy Years of Exile Due to their Persistent Refusal to Hear the Lord's Prophets

'Moreover I will take from them the voice of mirth and the voice of gladness, the voice of the bridegroom and the voice of the bride, the sound of the millstones and the light of the lamp. And this whole land shall be a desolation and an astonishment, and these nations shall serve the king of Babylon seventy years.' Jer. 25:10-11.

Chapter 26
The Priests and the Prophets Call for Jeremiah to Die While the Princes Defend him, Appealing to the Example of Hezekiah Who Listened to Micah

'Micah of Moresheth prophesied in the days of Hezekiah king of Judah, and spoke to all the people of Judah, saying, "Thus says the LORD of hosts: Zion shall be plowed like a field, Jerusalem shall become a heap of ruins, and the mountain of the temple like the bare hills of the forest."' Jer. 26:18.

Chapter 27

Jeremiah Makes Symbols of Yokes and Bonds to Urge the People to Submit to Nebuchadnezzar, King of Babylon

> '"And it shall be, that the nation and kingdom which will not serve Nebuchadnezzar the king of Babylon, and which will not put its neck under the yoke of the king of Babylon, that nation I will punish," says the LORD, "with the sword, the famine, and pestilence, until I have consumed them by his hand."' Jer. 27:8.

Chapter 28

Hananiah the False Prophet Seeks to Deceive the People and Jeremiah Pronounces Doom Upon him

> 'The prophets who have been before me and before you of old prophesied against many countries and great kingdoms – of war and disaster and pestilence. As for the prophet who prophecies of peace, when the word of the prophet comes to pass, the prophet will be known as one whom the LORD has truly sent.' Jer. 28:8-9.

Chapter 29

The Lord Promises a Future and a Hope to the Exiles in Babylon, Summarizing His Message and Urging them to Repent and Trust in the Lord

> 'Therefore thus says the LORD concerning the king who sits on the throne of David, concerning all the people who dwell in this city, and concerning your brethren who have not gone out with you into captivity – thus says the LORD of hosts: Behold, I will send on them the sword, the famine, and the pestilence, and will make them like rotten figs that cannot be eaten, they are so bad. And I will pursue them with the sword, with famine, and with pestilence; and I will deliver them to trouble among all the kingdoms of the earth – to be a curse, an astonishment, a hissing, and a reproach among all the nations where I have driven them, because they have not heeded My words, says the LORD, which I sent to them by My servants the prophets, rising up early and sending them; neither would you heed, says the LORD.' Jer. 29:16-19.

Chapter 30

The Lord Promises to Restore the Exiles After the Captivity, According to the Abrahamic and Davidic Covenants

> 'But they shall serve the LORD their God, and David their king, whom I will raise up for them … You shall be My people, and I will be your God.' Jer. 30:9, 22.

Chapter 31
As Israel's Father, the Lord Will Save His People, Making a New Covenant with them in Which He Will Write the Law in their Hearts and Forgive their Sins

> 'Behold, the days are coming, says the LORD, when I will make a new covenant with the house of Israel and the house of Judah – not according to the covenant that I made with their fathers in the day that I took them by the hand to lead them out of the land of Egypt, My covenant which they broke, though I was a husband to them, says the LORD. But this is the covenant that I will make with the house of Israel after those days, says the LORD: I will put My law in their minds, and write it on their hearts; and I will be their God, and they shall be My people. No more shall every man teach his neighbor, and every man his brother, saying, "Know the LORD," for they shall all know Me, from the least of them to the greatest of them, says the LORD. For I will forgive their iniquity, and their sin I will remember no more.' Jer. 31:31-34.

Chapter 32
Jeremiah Buys a Field at the Lord's Instruction as a Pledge that the People Will Return from Exile, Reiterating the Promises of the New Covenant

> 'Behold, I will gather them out of all countries where I have driven them in My anger, in My fury, and in great wrath; I will bring them back to this place, and I will cause them to dwell safely. They shall be My people, and I will be their God; then I will give them one heart and one way, that they may fear Me forever, for the good of them and their children after them. And I will make an everlasting covenant with them, that I will not turn away from doing them good; but I will put My fear in their hearts so that they will not depart from Me. Yes, I will rejoice over them to do them good, and I will assuredly plant them in this land, with all My heart and with all My soul.' Jer. 32:37-41.

Chapter 33
The Lord Promises that this New Covenant Will Come by Remembering His Covenant with David, the Righteous Son of

David Will Create a Righteous People, and His Covenant Will be as Sure as Day and Night

> 'In those days and at that time I will cause to grow up to David a Branch of righteousness; He shall execute judgment and righteousness in the earth. In those days Judah will be saved, and Jerusalem will dwell safely. And this is the name by which she will be called: THE LORD OUR RIGHTEOUSNESS. For thus says the LORD, "David shall never lack a man to sit on the throne of the house of Israel; nor shall the priests, the Levites, lack a man to offer burnt offerings before Me, to kindle grain offerings, and to make sacrifices continually."' Jer. 33:15-18.

Chapter **34**

Jeremiah Warns King Zedekiah to Trust the Lord, but he and the People Break Covenant with God by Taking Israelites as Slaves, and the Lord Assures them of Exile

> 'Therefore thus says the LORD, "You have not obeyed Me in proclaiming liberty, every one to his brother and every one to his neighbor. Behold, I proclaim liberty to you," says the LORD – "to the sword, to pestilence, and to famine! And I will deliver you to trouble among all the kingdoms of the earth. And I will give the men who have transgressed My covenant, who have not performed the words of the covenant which they made before Me, when they cut the calf in two and passed between the parts of it … "' Jer. 34:17-18.

Chapter **35**

The Lord Appeals to the Rechabites' Obedience to their Father in Order to Shame Israel for their Disobedience to their God

> 'I have also sent to you all My servants the prophets, rising up early and sending them, saying, "Turn now everyone from his evil way, amend your doings, and do not go after other gods to serve them; then you will dwell in the land which I have given you and your fathers." But you have not inclined your ear, nor obeyed Me. Surely the sons of Jonadab the son of Rechab have performed the commandment of their father, which he commanded them, but this people has not obeyed Me.' Jer. 35:15-16.

Chapter **36**

Jeremiah has Baruch Read the Scroll of his Prophecy Before King Jehoiakim at the Insistence of the Leaders, the King Destroys the

Scroll, Jeremiah Rewrites the Prophecy with Added Threats, and the Lord Protects Jeremiah and Baruch

> 'Therefore thus says the LORD concerning Jehoiakim king of Judah: "He shall have no one to sit on the throne of David, and his dead body shall be cast out to the heat of the day and the frost of the night."' Jer. 36:30.

Chapter **37**

The Lord Assures King Zedekiah of the Certainty of the Exile, Jeremiah is Put in Prison for Claiming the Field that he Bought at the Lord's Instructions, and Zedekiah Secretly Seeks the Word of the Lord from him, Giving Jeremiah Some Protection

> 'For though you had defeated the whole army of the Chaldeans who fight against you, and there remained only wounded men among them, they would rise up, every man in his tent, and burn the city with fire.' Jer. 37:10,

Chapter **38**

Jeremiah is Put in Prison for Treason for Calling the People to Defect to the Chaldeans, Ebed-Melech Saves his Life, and Jeremiah Pleads with Zedekiah to Listen to the Word of the Lord

> 'Thus says the LORD: "He who remains in this city shall die by the sword, by famine, and by pestilence; but he who goes over to the Chaldeans shall live; his life shall be as a prize to him, and he shall live."' Jer. 38:2.

Chapter **39**

Echoing 2 Kings 25, Nebuchadnezzar Takes Jerusalem, Killing Zedekiah's Sons and Putting Out his Eyes, Taking Jeremiah Out of Prison While the Lord Promises to Bless Ebed-Melech

> '"For I will surely deliver you, and you shall not fall by the sword; but your life shall be as a prize to you, because you have put your trust in Me," says the LORD.' Jer. 39:18.

Chapter **40**

Nebuzaradan Recognizes the Lord Sent Israel into Captivity for their Sins, he Sends Jeremiah to Live with Gedaliah the Governor Who Promises the Lord's Protection to those Submitting to the Chaldeans, and Ishmael Plots to Kill Gedaliah

> 'Now the LORD has brought it, and has done just as He said. Because you people have sinned against the LORD, and

not obeyed His voice, therefore this thing has come upon you.' Jer. 40:3.

CHAPTER 41

Ishmael Kills Gedaliah and Some of the Chaldeans with him, Carrying Some of the People Away Captive, Johanan Rescues them, and the People Head to Egypt, Fearing the Wrath of the Chaldeans

'Now the pit into which Ishmael had cast all the dead bodies of the men whom he had slain, because of Gedaliah, was the same one Asa the king made for fear of Baasha king of Israel. Ishmael the son of Nethaniah filled it with the slain.' Jer. 41:9.

CHAPTER 42

All the People from the Least to the Greatest Seek God's Will Through Jeremiah Regarding Whether to go to Egypt, but they do so Hypocritically

'For you were hypocrites in your hearts when you sent me to the LORD your God, saying, "Pray for us to the LORD our God, and according to all that the LORD your God says, so declare to us and we will do it." And I have this day declared it to you, but you have not obeyed the voice of the LORD your God, or anything which He has sent you by me. Now therefore, know certainly that you shall die by the sword, by famine, and by pestilence in the place where you desire to go to dwell.' Jer. 42:20-22.

CHAPTER 43

The People Blame Baruch for Inciting Jeremiah to Prophesy Falsely, and the Lord Instructs Jeremiah to Set up Memorial Stones in Egypt as a Sign that Nebuchadnezzar, the Lord's Servant, Will Establish his Rule in Egypt

'So they went to the land of Egypt, for they did not obey the voice of the LORD. And they went as far as Tahpanhes … When he comes, he shall strike the land of Egypt and deliver to death those appointed for death, and to captivity those appointed for captivity, and to the sword those appointed for the sword.' Jer. 43:7, 11.

CHAPTER 44

The Lord Threatens to Overthrow Egypt and the Remnant of Judah with them, According to the Terms of Jeremiah's Call in

Chapter 1, Rebuking them for their Idolatry While the People Refuse to Give it up

> 'Therefore hear the word of the LORD, all Judah who dwell in the land of Egypt: "Behold, I have sworn by My great name," says the LORD, "that My name shall no more be named in the mouth of any man of Judah in all the land of Egypt, saying, The LORD God lives. Behold, I will watch over them for adversity and not for good. And all the men of Judah who are in the land of Egypt shall be consumed by the sword and by famine, until there is an end to them."' Jer. 44:26-27.

Chapter **45**

Baruch Complains About the Lord's Judgments, and the Lord Promises to Give him his Life as a Prize, Appealing to the Terms of Jeremiah's Call from Chapter 1

> 'Thus you shall say to him, "Thus says the LORD: Behold, what I have built I will break down, and what I have planted I will pluck up, that is, this whole land. And do you seek great things for yourself? Do not seek them; for behold, I will bring adversity on all flesh," says the LORD. "But I will give your life to you as a prize in all places, wherever you go."' Jer. 45:4-5.

Chapter **46**

The Lord Pronounces Judgment Against Egypt, but He Promises to Save the Remnant of Israel

> '"But do not fear, O My servant Jacob, and do not be dismayed, O Israel! For behold, I will save you from afar, and your offspring from the land of their captivity; Jacob shall return, have rest and be at ease; no one shall make him afraid. Do not fear, O Jacob My servant," says the LORD, "For I am with you; for I will make a complete end of all the nations to which I have driven you, but I will not make a complete end of you. I will rightly correct you, for I will not leave you wholly unpunished."' Jer. 46:27-28.

Chapter **47**

The Lord Begins to Pronounce Judgment Against the Nations, Beginning with Philistia, the Traditional Enemies of Israel

> 'O you sword of the LORD, how long until you are quiet? Put yourself up into your scabbard and be still! How can

it be quiet, seeing the LORD has given it a charge against Ashkelon and against the seashore? There He has appointed it." Jer. 47:6-7.

CHAPTER 48

The Lord Pronounces Judgment Against the Moabites, the Children of Lot, Judging them and their Gods

'And Moab shall be destroyed as a people, because he exalted himself against the LORD … Yet I will bring back the captives of Moab in the latter days, says the LORD. Thus far is the judgment of Moab.' Jer. 48:42, 47.

CHAPTER 49

The Lord Pronounces Judgment Against Ammon, Edom, Damascus, Kedar, and Elam, Preserving a Remnant in His Grace

'"But afterward I will bring back the captives of the people of Ammon," says the LORD … "For who is like Me? Who will arraign Me? And who is that shepherd who will withstand Me?" … "But it shall come to pass in the latter days: I will bring back the captives of Elam, says the LORD."' Jer. 49:6, 19b, 39.

CHAPTER 50

The Lord Begins His Final Proclamation Against Babylon and their gods, Summarizing His Judgments Against Israel and Promising to Save a Remnant of His People, Who Will Renew their Covenant with God

'They shall ask the way to Zion, with their faces toward it, saying, "Come and let us join ourselves to the LORD in a perpetual covenant that will not be forgotten." … But I will bring back Israel to his home, and he shall feed on Carmel and Bashan; his soul shall be satisfied on Mount Ephraim and Gilead. In those days and at that time, says the LORD, the iniquity of Israel shall be sought, but there shall be none; and the sins of Judah, but they shall not be found; for I will pardon those whom I preserve … Their Redeemer is strong; the LORD of hosts is His name. He will thoroughly plead their case, that He may give rest to the land, and disquiet the inhabitants of Babylon … For who is like Me? Who will arraign Me? And who is that shepherd who will withstand Me?" Jer. 50:5, 19-20, 34, 44b.

Chapter 51

The Lord Completes the Judgment Against Babylon Through the Medes and Persians, Calling His People to Flee from her Midst, Showing the Uniqueness of Israel's God, and Sealing up Jeremiah's Prophecy

> 'For Israel is not forsaken, nor Judah, by his God, the LORD of hosts, though their land was filled with sin against the Holy One of Israel ... The LORD has revealed our righteousness. Come and let us declare in Zion the work of the LORD our God ... The Portion of Jacob is not like them, for He is the Maker of all things; and Israel is the tribe of His inheritance. The LORD of Hosts is his name.' Jer. 50:5, 10, 19.

Chapter 52

The Lord Reviews the Fall and Captivity of Jerusalem to Babylon, but Gives Hope by Releasing Jehoiachin from Prison, Echoing 2 Kings 25

> 'For because of the anger of the LORD this happened in Jerusalem and Judah, till He finally cast them out from His presence. Then Zedekiah rebelled against the king of Babylon ... So Jehoiachin changed from his prison garments, and he ate bread regularly before the king all the days of his life.' Jer. 52:3, 33.

Lamentations

Lamenting the destruction of Jerusalem in exile, the prophet looks to God's covenant mercies, which are new every morning

Chapter 1

Jeremiah Takes the Lament of Jerusalem on his Lips and Mourns the Exile on their Behalf

> 'The LORD is righteous, for I rebelled against His commandment. Hear now, all peoples, and behold my sorrow; my virgins and my young men have gone into captivity.' Lam. 1:18.

Chapter 2

Jeremiah Laments the Lord's Destruction of Jerusalem and Temple Worship Due to the Sins of the People

> 'Her gates have sunk into the ground; He has destroyed and broken her bars. Her king and her princes are among the nations; the Law is no more, and her prophets find no vision from the LORD.' Lam. 2:9.

Chapter 3

Jeremiah Stresses the Lord's Action Behind his Suffering and that of Jerusalem, and he Confesses the Lord's Mercies and Sovereignty, Laying the Blame on the Sins of the People

> 'Through the LORD's mercies we are not consumed, because His compassions fail not. They are new every morning; great is Your faithfulness. "The LORD is my portion," says my soul, "therefore I hope in Him!" The LORD is good to those who wait for Him, to the soul who seeks Him ... Who is he who speaks and it comes to pass, when the LORD has not commanded it? Is it not from the mouth of the Most High that woe and

well-being proceed? Why should a living man complain, a man for the punishment of his sins?' Lam. 3:22-25, 37-39.

Chapter 4
Jeremiah Laments the Sins of the People, Laying the Blame on their Prophets and Priests, Resulting in the Removal of their King

'Because of the sins of her prophets and the iniquities of her priests, who shed in her midst the blood of the just … The breath of our nostrils, the anointed of the LORD, was caught in their pits, of whom we said, "Under his shadow we shall live among the nations."' Lam. 4:13, 20.

Chapter 5
Jeremiah Calls on the Lord to Remember their Afflictions Before it is too Late and to Judge their Enemies

'You, O LORD, remain forever; Your throne from generation to generation. Why do You forget us forever, and forsake us for so long a time? Turn us back to You, O LORD, and we will be restored; renew our days as of old, unless You have utterly rejected us, and are very angry with us!' Lam. 5:19-22.

Ezekiel

God removes His covenant presence from His people, dwelling with the exiles instead, and promises to restore His presence permanently by sending the Spirit under the new covenant

Chapter 1

Ezekiel Sees God on His Chariot, Introducing the Main Themes of his Vision

> 'And above the firmament over their heads was the likeness of a throne, in appearance like a sapphire stone; on the likeness of the throne was a likeness with the appearance of a man high above it. Also from the appearance of His waist upward I saw, as it were, the color of amber with the appearance of fire all around within it; and from the appearance of His waist and downward I saw, as it were, the appearance of fire with brightness all around. Like the appearance of a rainbow in a cloud on a rainy day, so was the appearance of the brightness all around it. This was the appearance of the likeness of the glory of the LORD. So when I saw it, I fell on my face, and heard a voice of One speaking.' Ezek. 1:26-28.

Chapter 2

The Lord Sends Ezekiel to Prophesy Whether the People Hear or Refuse, Commanding Ezekiel to Eat the Scroll as a Symbol of Assimilating God's Word into his Life and Ministry

> 'You shall speak My words to them, whether they hear or whether they refuse, for they are rebellious. But you, son of man, hear what I say to you. Do not be rebellious like that rebellious house; open your mouth and eat what I give you. Now when

I looked, there was a hand stretched out to me; and behold, a scroll of a book was in it. Then He spread it before me; and there was writing on the inside and on the outside, and written on it were lamentations and mourning and woe.' Ezek. 2:7-10.

Chapter 3
The Spirit of God Shows Ezekiel the Glory of the Lord in the Temple, Giving him the Terms of his Prophetic Ministry

'Nevertheless if you warn the righteous man that the righteous should not sin, and he does not sin, he shall surely live because he took warning; also you will have delivered your soul.' Ezek. 3:21.

Chapter 4
Ezekiel Portrays the Siege of Jerusalem Personally, Cooking his Bread Over Cow Dung

'Then the LORD said, "So shall the children of Israel eat their defiled bread among the Gentiles, where I will drive them."' Ezek. 4:13.

Chapter 5
Ezekiel Shaves his Head, Sending his Hair in Thirds to the Sword, Famine, and Pestilence, Saving a Few Hairs in his Belt to Symbolize the Remnant that God Will Save

'Thus shall My anger be spent, and I will cause My fury to rest upon them, and I will be avenged; and they shall know that I, the LORD, have spoken it in My zeal, when I have spent My fury upon them.' Ezek. 5:13.

Chapter 6
God Will Leave the Slain of Israel with their Dead Idols, and the Remnant Will Seek Him in Exile

'Yet I will leave a remnant, so that you may have some who escape the sword among the nations, when you are scattered throughout the countries. Then those of you who escape will remember Me among the nations where they are carried captive, because I was crushed by their adulterous heart which has departed from Me, and by their eyes which play the harlot after their idols; they will loathe themselves for the evils which they committed in all their abominations. And they shall know that I am the LORD; I have not said in vain that I would bring this calamity upon them.' Ezek. 6:8-10.

Chapter 7

They Shall Know that God is the Lord When His Eye Does not Spare or Pity them, and He Punishes their Prophets, Priests, and Kings

> 'Disaster will come upon disaster, and rumor will be upon rumor. Then they will seek a vision from a prophet; but the law will perish from the priest, and counsel from the elders. The king will mourn, the prince will be clothed with desolation, and the hands of the common people will tremble. I will do to them according to their way, and according to what they deserve I will judge them; then they shall know that I am the LORD.' Ezek. 7:26-27.

Chapter 8

The Lord's Presence Reappears from Chapter 1, Introducing the Next Key Section in the Book by Showing Ezekiel that the Further the People Go into the Temple, the Further from God's Presence they Go

> 'Furthermore He said to me, "Son of man, do you see what they are doing, the great abominations that the house of Israel commits here, to make Me go far away from My sanctuary? Now turn again, you will see greater abominations."' Ezek. 8:6.

Chapter 9

The Lord Sends Six Men to Destroy the City in a Vision, One of Whom Marks the Elect Remnant on their Foreheads, While the Men Defile the Temple with the Slain and the Lord's Presence Prepares to Leave the Temple

> 'Now the glory of the God of Israel had gone up from the cherub, where it had been, to the threshold of the temple. And He called to the man clothed with linen, who had the writer's inkhorn at his side, and the LORD said to him, "Go through the midst of the city, through the midst of Jerusalem, and put a mark on the foreheads of the men who sigh and cry over all the abominations that are done within it."' Ezek. 9:3-4.

Chapter 10

The Lord's Glory Prepares to Depart from the Temple as the Man Casts Fire on the Rebellious City

'Then the glory of the LORD departed from the threshold of the temple and stood over the cherubim. And the cherubim lifted their wings and mounted up from the earth in my sight. When they went out, the wheels were beside them; and they stood at the door of the east gate of the LORD's house, and the glory of the God of Israel was above them.' Ezek. 10:18-19.

Chapter 11

The Glory of the Lord Leaves the Temple, Concluding this Section, and the Lord Encourages the Elect Remnant by Promising His Presence Among them in Exile, Placing His Law in their Hearts by Giving them New Hearts Through the Holy Spirit

'Therefore say, "thus says the LORD God: Although I have cast them far off among the Gentiles, and though I have scattered them among the countries, yet I shall be a little sanctuary for them in the countries where they have gone … Then I will give them one heart, and I will put a new Spirit within them, and take the stony heart out of their flesh, and give them a heart of flesh, that they may walk in My statutes and keep My judgments and do them; and they shall be My people, and I will be their God."' Ezek. 11:16, 19-20.

Chapter 12

Ezekiel Acts out Judah's Captivity by Digging Through the Wall While Carrying his Possessions, While the People Respond that the Vision is Far Off

'Therefore say to them, "Thus says the LORD God: None of My words will be postponed any more, but the word which I speak will be done, says the LORD God."' Ezek. 12:28.

Chapter 13

The Lord Rebukes the Foolish Prophets for Misleading the People and Killing those Who Should Live and Sparing those Who Should Die

'Because with lies you have made the heart of the righteous sad, whom I have not made sad; and you have strengthened the hands of the wicked, so that he does not turn from his wicked way to save his life. Therefore you shall no longer envision futility nor practice divination; for I will deliver My people out of your hand, and you shall know that I am the LORD.' Ezek. 13:22-23.

Chapter 14

The Lord Rejects the Elders of Israel for Stealing the People's Hearts from God, the Lord will Remove the False Prophets Who Deceive them, and the Exile is Certain, Even if Noah, Daniel, and Job Were to Intercede for them

'Even if these three men, Noah, Daniel, and Job, were in it, they would deliver only themselves by their righteousness, says the LORD God.' Ezek. 14:14.

Chapter 15

Israel is Like an Outcast Vine that is Useful for Nothing Because of their Persistent Unfaithfulness

'Thus I will make the land desolate, because they have persisted in unfaithfulness, says the LORD God.' Ezek. 15:8.

Chapter 16

The Lord Tells a Shocking Parable to Illustrate Israel's Unfaithfulness, Showing that they Would be Most Ashamed of their Sins When He Makes Atonement for them

'Nevertheless I will remember My covenant with you in the days of your youth, and I will establish an everlasting covenant with you. Then you will remember your ways and be ashamed, when you receive your older and your younger sisters; for I will give them to you for daughters, but not because of My covenant with you. And I will establish My covenant with you. Then you shall know that I am the LORD, that you may remember and be ashamed, and never open your mouth anymore because of your shame, when I provide you an atonement for all you have done, says the LORD God.' Ezek. 16:60-63.

Chapter 17

The Lord Uses a Parable of Two Eagles to Show that Israel Sinned by Going to Egypt and not Submitting to the Chaldeans, Nevertheless Promising to Plant a Remnant

'On the mountain height of Israel I will plant it; and it will bring forth boughs, and bear fruit, and be a majestic cedar.

Under it will dwell birds of every sort; in the shadow of its branches they will dwell.' Ezek. 17:23.

Chapter 18

The Lord Refutes the People Who Say that the Way of the Lord is not Fair, since the Children Face Exile for the Sins of the Fathers, Calling the Wicked to Repentance and Hope

'The soul who sins shall die. The son shall not bear the guilt of the father, nor the father bear the guilt of the son. The righteousness of the righteous shall be upon himself, and the wickedness of the wicked shall be upon himself… Do I have any pleasure at all that the wicked should die? Says the LORD God, and not that he should turn from his ways and live? … Yet you say, "The way of the LORD is not fair." Hear now, O house of Israel, is it not My way which is fair, and your ways which are not fair?' Ezek. 18:20, 23, 25.

Chapter 19

Israel is Like a Vine Transplanted into the Wilderness, though her Rulers were Like Lions, Pushing them to Lament their Sad Condition

'And now she is planted in the wilderness, in a dry and thirsty land. Fire has come out from a rod of her branches and devoured her fruit, so that she has no strong branch – a scepter for ruling. This is a lamentation, and has become a lamentation.' Ezek. 19:13-14.

Chapter 20

The Lord Reminds Israel of His Kindness in Redeeming them from Egypt, Appealing to their Sabbath Breaking as the Example of Despising Him and Turning to Idols, and Applying the Mosaic Covenant Blessings and Curses

'I will make you pass under the rod, and bring you into the bond of the covenant … As for you, O house of Israel, says the LORD God: Go serve every one of you his idols – and hereafter – if you will not obey Me; but profane My holy name no more with your gifts and your idols … And there you shall remember your ways and all your doings with which you were defiled; and you shall loathe yourselves in your own sight because of all the evils that you have committed. Then you shall know that I am the LORD, when I have dealt with you for My name's sake, not according to your wicked ways nor according to your corrupt doings, O house of Israel, says the LORD.' Ezek. 20:37, 39, 43-44.

Chapter 21

Babylon is God's Sword to Punish Israel's Sins and those of the Nations, Beginning with Ammon

'Overthrown, overthrown, I will make it overthrown! It shall be no longer, until He comes whose right it is, and I will give it to Him.' Ezek. 21:27.

Chapter 22

God Rebukes Israel for Despising the Holy Things and Profaning the Sabbath, He Will Refine them Like Silver in a Furnace, and He Reproves their Prophets and Priests for not Interceding

'So I sought for a man among them who would make a wall, and stand in the gap before Me on behalf of the land, that I should not destroy it; but I found no one.' Ezek. 22:30.

Chapter 23

Israel and Judah are Likened to Two Harlot Sisters Rebelling Against the Lord, Singling out Jerusalem for Judgment, and Making Judgment Certain

'Moreover they have done this to Me: They have defiled My sanctuary on the same day and profaned My Sabbaths. For after they had slain their children for their idols, on the same day they came into My sanctuary to profane it; and indeed thus they have done in the midst of My house.' Ezek. 23:38-39.

Chapter 24

Jerusalem Will be Like a Cooking Pot in the Babylonian Siege, and Ezekiel Becomes a Sign to them When his Wife Dies and he Cannot Mourn Properly

'I, the LORD, have spoken it; it shall come to pass, and I will do it; I will not hold back, nor will I spare, nor will I relent; according to your ways and according to your deeds they will judge you, says the LORD God.' Ezek. 24:14.

Chapter 25

The Lord Pronounces Judgment on the Ammonites, the Moabites, the Edomites, and the Philistines, Judgment Beginning with Israel's Traditional Enemies

> 'Thus says the LORD God: "Because the Philistines dealt vengefully and took vengeance with a spiteful heart, to destroy because of the old hatred."' Ezek. 25:15.

Chapter 26
The Lord Proclaims Judgment Against Tyre as a Paradigm for His Judgments Against All Nations

> 'Son of man, because Tyre has said against Jerusalem, "Aha! She is broken who was the gateway of the peoples; now she is turned over to me; I shall be filled; she is laid waste."' Ezek. 26:2.

Chapter 27
The Prophet Takes Up a Lamentation for Tyre, Showing the Desolation of the Nations

> 'All the inhabitants of the isles will be astonished at you; their kings will be greatly afraid, and their countenance will be troubled. The merchants among the peoples will hiss at you; You will become a horror, and be no more forever.' Ezek. 27:35-36.

Chapter 28
The King of Tyre, Who Exalted himself as a god, Will Die the Death of the Uncircumcised, Sidon Will Share in her Judgment, and God Will Restore Israel

> 'Thus says the LORD God: "When I have gathered the house of Israel from the peoples among whom they are scattered, and I am hallowed in them in the sight of the Gentiles, then they will dwell in their own land which I gave to My servant Jacob. And they will dwell safely there, build houses, and plant vineyards; yes, they will dwell securely, when I execute judgments on all those around them who despise them. Then they shall know that I am the LORD their God."' Ezek. 28:25-26.

Chapter 29
The Lord Will Judge Egypt as a Paradigm for Removing Israel's Hope in Anyone Except the Lord

> 'No longer shall it be the confidence of the house of Israel, but will remind them of their iniquity when they turned to follow them. Then they shall know that I am the LORD God.' Ezek. 29:16.

Chapter 30
The Lord Shall Strengthen Babylon Against Egypt and Pharaoh

> "Then they shall know that I am the LORD, when I have set a fire in Egypt and all her helpers are destroyed.' Ezek. 30:8.

Chapter 31
God Will Cut Down Egypt Like a Great Tree

> 'To which of the trees in Eden will you then be likened in glory and greatness? Yet you shall be brought down with the trees of Eden to the depths of the earth; you shall lie in the midst of the uncircumcised, with those slain by the sword. This is Pharaoh and all his multitude, says the LORD.' Ezek. 31:18.

Chapter 32
The Prophets Takes Up a Concluding Lamentation for Egypt, Summarizing His Judgments Against Israel's Enemies and Israel's Helpers

> 'Pharaoh will see them and be comforted over all his multitude, Pharaoh and all his army, slain by the sword, says the LORD God. For I have caused My terror in the land of the living; and he shall be placed in the midst of the uncircumcised with those slain by the sword, Pharaoh and all his multitude, says the LORD God.' Ezek. 32:31-32.

Chapter 33
Ezekiel's Call is Reviewed, With Reference to Chapters 3, 11, and 18, Preparing for Ezekiel's Final Rebuke and Consolation to Israel, While the People Love Ezekiel's Preaching, Though Failing to Hear his Message

> 'Say to them: "As I live," says the LORD God, "I have no pleasure in the death of the wicked, but that the wicked turn from his way and live. Turn, turn from your evil ways! For why should you die, O house of Israel?"' Ezek. 33:11.

Chapter 34
The Lord Rebukes Israel's Shepherds Who Feed themselves Instead of the Flock, Promising to Search Out His Flock Himself by Establishing the Messiah as One Shepherd Over Them, Fulfilling the Davidic Covenant

> 'And I will establish one shepherd over them, and he shall feed them – My servant David. He shall feed them and be their shepherd. And I, the LORD, will be their God, and My servant David a prince among them; I, the LORD, have spoken.' Ezek. 34:23-24.

Chapter 35

The Lord Will Remember His Covenant with Israel by Judging Mount Seir of the Edomites for their Envy

> 'Because you have said, "These two nations and these two countries shall be mine, and we will possess them," although the LORD was there, therefore, as I live, says the LORD God, I will do according to your anger and according to the envy which you showed in your hatred against them; and I will make Myself known among them when I judge you.' Ezek. 35:10-11.

Chapter 36

The Lord Takes an Oath to Restore Israel According to His Covenant with them, Removing the Causes of Judgment by Promising to Forgive their Sins and Renew their Hearts in the New Covenant

> 'Then I will sprinkle clean water on you, and you shall be clean; I will cleanse you from all your filthiness and from all your idols. I will give you a new heart and put a new spirit within you; I will take the heart of stone out of your flesh and give you a heart of flesh. I will put My Spirit within you and cause you to walk in My statutes, and you will keep My judgments and do them. Then you shall dwell in the land that I gave to your fathers; you shall be My people, and I will be your God.' Ezek. 36:25-28.

Chapter 37

The Lord Illustrates the Promises of Chapter 36 Through a Vision of Putting the Spirit into an Army Built from Dry Bones, Establishing the Davidic Messiah as their Shepherd, Building on Chapter 34 and the Promises of the New Covenant

> 'David My servant shall be king over them, and they shall all have one shepherd; they shall also walk in My judgments and observe My statutes, and do them. Then they shall dwell in the land that I have given to Jacob My servant, where your

fathers dwelt; and they shall dwell there, they, their children, and their children's children, forever; and My servant David shall be their prince forever. Moreover I will make a covenant of peace with them, and it shall be an everlasting covenant with them; I will establish them and multiply them, and I will set My sanctuary in their midst forevermore.' Ezek. 37:24-26.

Chapter **38**

God Raises Up Gog and Magog as a Paradigm for His Victory Over all the Enemies of His People

'Thus I will magnify Myself and sanctify Myself, and I will be known in the eyes of many nations. Then they shall know that I am the LORD.' Ezek. 38:23.

Chapter **39**

Israel Will Cleanse the Land for Seven Months After God Fights for them as they Celebrate God's Covenant Faithfulness

'Then they shall know that I am the LORD their God, who sent them into captivity among the nations, but also brought them back to their land, and left none of them captive any longer. And I will not hide My face from them anymore; for I shall have poured out My Spirit on the house of Israel, says the LORD God.' Ezek. 39:28.

Chapter **40**

Ezekiel Begins His Final Vision of the Lord Restoring His Presence in Covenant with His People Through the Image of an Idyllic Enormous Temple

'The chamber which faces north is for the priests who have charge of the altar; these are the sons of Zadok, from the sons of Levi, who come near the LORD to minister to Him.' Ezek. 40:46.

Chapter **41**

The Angel Measures the Holy Place and the Area for the Temple

'He measured the length, twenty cubits; and the width, twenty cubits, beyond the sanctuary; and he said to me, "This is the Most Holy Place."' Ezek. 41:4.

Chapter **42**

The Lord Shows the Chambers for the Priests to Lead in Worship

'When the priests enter them, they shall not go out of the holy chamber into the outer court; but there they shall leave their garments in which they minister, for they are holy. They shall put on other garments; then they may approach that which is for the people.' Ezek. 42:14.

Chapter 43

The Glory of the Lord from Ezekiel's First Vision Comes to Dwell in the Idyllic Temple, Signifying His Restored Covenant Presence

'And He said to me, "Son of man, this is the place of My throne and the place of the soles of My feet, where I dwell in the midst of the children of Israel forever. No more shall the house of Israel defile My holy name, they nor their kings, by their harlotry or with the carcasses of their kings on their high places."' Ezek. 43:7.

Chapter 44

The Prince May Feast in God's Presence, Fulfilling the Davidic Covenant, While no one Uncircumcised in Heart or in Flesh May Enter the Temple, and God Regulates the Priesthood

'And the LORD said to me, "This gate shall be shut; it shall not be opened, and no man shall enter by it, because the LORD God of Israel has entered by it; therefore it shall be shut. As for the prince, because he is the prince, he may sit in it to eat bread before the LORD; he shall enter by way of the vestibule of the gateway, and go out by the same way."' Ezek. 44:2-3.

Chapter 45

The Lord Sections Off the Holy District Around the Sanctuary, Makes Provisions for the Prince, and Directs Israel to the Day of Atonement

'The land shall be his possession in Israel; and My princes shall no more oppress My people, but they shall give the rest of the land to the house of Israel, according to their tribes.' Ezek. 45:8.

Chapter 46

The Lord Restores Sabbath Worship, Orders the Prince to Respect Inheritance Laws, and Regulates the Offerings

'Thus says the LORD God, "The gateway of the inner court that faces toward the east shall be shut six working days; but on the Sabbath it shall be opened, and on the day of the New Moon it shall be opened.'" Ezek. 46:1.

CHAPTER 47

The Lord Signifies the Blessings of the New Covenant by Sending Healing Waters from the Temple to Heal the Nations, Incorporating Strangers into Israel

'Along the bank of the river, on this side and that, will grow all kinds of trees used for food; their leaves will not wither, and their fruit will not fail. They will bear fruit every month, because their water flows from the sanctuary. Their fruit will be for food, and their leaves for medicine.' Ezek. 47:12.

CHAPTER 48

The Lord Appoints New Divisions of the Tribes in the Land, Revolving Around the Holy District, and the Lord Fulfills His Covenant by Dwelling with His People

'All the way around shall be eighteen thousand cubits; and the name of the city from that day shall be: THE LORD IS THERE.' Ezek. 48:35.

Daniel

God reigns over the nations even when His covenant people are in exile, promising to subdue the nations under the Son of Man in His eternal kingdom

Chapter 1

God Establishes Daniel and his Friends in Faithfulness While in Exile in Babylon

> 'Now God had brought Daniel into the favor and goodwill of the chief of the eunuchs … As for these young men, God gave them knowledge and skill in all literature and wisdom; and Daniel had understanding in all visions and dreams.' Dan. 1:9, 17.

Chapter 2

Nebuchadnezzar's First Dream Sets the Tone for the Rest of the Book, Showing that God's Kingdom Will Swallow up Four Great Empires and Spread Throughout the Earth, Nebuchadnezzar Acknowledging that Daniel's God is Superior to Other gods

> 'Daniel answered and said: "Blessed be the name of God forever and ever, for wisdom and might are His. And He changes the times and the seasons; He removes kings and raises up kings; He gives wisdom to the wise and knowledge to those who have understanding. He reveals deep and secret things; He knows what is in the darkness, and light dwells with Him … And in the days of these kings the God of heaven will set up a kingdom which shall never be destroyed; and the kingdom shall not be left to other people; it shall break in pieces and consume all these kingdoms, and it shall stand forever."' Dan. 2:20-22, 44.

Chapter 3
Nebuchadnezzar Sets Up an Image of God in his Honor, Daniel's Friends are Thrown in the Fire for not Worshiping it, the Angel of the Lord Preserves them, and Nebuchadnezzar Further Recognizes the Supremacy of the True God

> 'Then Nebuchadnezzar was astonished; and he rose in haste and spoke, saying to his counsellors, "Did we not cast three men bound into the midst of the fire?" They answered and said to the king, "True, O king." "Look! he answered, "I see four men loose, walking in the midst of the fire; and they are not hurt, and the form of the fourth is like the Son of God" … Nebuchadnezzar spoke saying, "Blessed be the God of Shadrach, Meshach, and Abed-Nego, who sent His Angel and delivered His servants who trusted in Him, and they have yielded their bodies, that they should not serve nor worship any god except their own God! Therefore I make a decree that any people, nation, or language which speaks anything amiss against the God of Shadrach, Meshach, and Abed-Nego shall be cut in pieces, and their houses made an ash heap; because there is no God who can deliver like this."' Dan. 3:24-25, 28-29.

Chapter 4
Nebuchadnezzar Relates his Second Vision, Recognizing the Dominion of the True God as the Only God, After Losing his Kingdom and Being Restored

> 'This decision is by the decree of the watchers, and the sentence is by the word of the holy ones, in order that the living may know that the Most High rules in the kingdom of men, gives it to whomever He will, and sets over it the lowest of men. "This dream, I, King Nebuchadnezzar, have seen. Now you, Belteshazzar, declare its interpretation, since all the wise men of my kingdom are not able to make known to me the interpretation; but you are able, for the Spirit of the Holy God is in you … Now I, Nebuchadnezzar, praise and extol and honor the King of heaven, all of whose works are truth, and His ways justice. And those who walk in pride He is able to put down."' Dan. 4:17-18, 37.

Chapter 5
Belshazzar Forgets God's Works With Nebuchadnezzar and Uses the Items from the Temple to Worship the gods of Silver and

Gold, and the Spirit of God Warns him Through Daniel that his Kingdom Will Fall to the Medes and Persians

> 'I have heard of you, that the Spirit of God is in you, and that light and understanding and excellent wisdom are found in you … O king, the Most High gave Nebuchadnezzar your father a kingdom and majesty, glory and honor … But you his son, Belshazzar, have not humbled your heart, although you knew all this.' Dan. 5:14, 18, 22.

Chapter 6

The Other Rulers Envy Daniel and Plot to Destroy them, but God Preserves them in the Lions' Den and Darius Honors the True God, Acknowledging His Dominion Over All

> 'My God sent His angel and shut the lions' mouths, so that they have not hurt me, because I was found innocent before Him; and also, O king, I have done no wrong before you … I make a decree that in every dominion of my kingdom men must tremble and fear before the God of Daniel. For He is the living God, and steadfast forever; His kingdom is the one which shall not be destroyed, and His dominion shall endure to the end. He delivers and rescues, and He works signs and wonders in heaven and on earth, who has delivered Daniel from the power of the lions.' Dan. 6:22, 26-27.

Chapter 7

Daniel Sees a Summary Vision of Four Beasts Representing Four Kingdoms, While the Ancient of Days Gives an Everlasting Kingdom to the Son of Man, Echoing the Vision of Chapter 2

> 'I was watching in the night visions, and behold, One like the Son of Man, coming with the clouds of heaven! He came to the Ancient of Days, and they brought Him near before Him. Then to Him was given dominion and glory and a kingdom, that all peoples, nations, and languages should serve Him. His dominion is an everlasting dominion, which shall not pass away, and His kingdom the one which shall not be destroyed … Then the kingdom and dominion, and the greatness of the kingdoms under the whole of heaven, shall be given to the people, the saints of the Most High. His kingdom is an everlasting kingdom, and all dominions shall serve and obey Him.' Dan. 7:13-14, 27.

Chapter 8

Daniel Sees a Vision from Gabriel of a Ram and a Goat, Signifying the Kingdoms of Medo-Persian and Greece, Extending God's Dominion into the Future and Looking to the Coming of the Everlasting Kingdom

> 'The ram which you saw, have the two horns – they are the kings of Media and Persia. And the male goat is the kingdom of Greece. The large horn that is between his eyes is the first king. As for the broken horn and the four that stood up in its place, four kingdoms shall arise out of that nation, but not with its power.' Dan. 8:20-22.

Chapter 9

Daniel Fasts and Prays While Reading Jeremiah Because the Time of the Seventy Years of Exile Was Drawing to a Close, and through Gabriel, God Promises Seventy Weeks of Years Until the Coming of the Messiah and His Kingdom

> 'Seventy weeks are determined for your people and for your holy city, to finish the transgression, to make an end of sins, to make reconciliation for iniquity, to bring in everlasting righteousness, to seal up vision and prophecy, and to anoint the Most Holy. Know therefore and understand, that from the going forth of the command to restore and build Jerusalem until Messiah the Prince, there shall be seven weeks and sixty-two weeks; the street shall be built again, and the wall, even in troublesome times. And after the sixty-two weeks, Messiah shall be cut off, but not for Himself; and the people of the prince who is to come shall destroy the city and the sanctuary. The end of it shall be with a flood, and till the end of the war desolations are determined. Then he shall confirm a covenant with many for one week; but in the middle of the week he shall bring an end to sacrifice and offering. And on the wing of abominations shall be one who makes desolate, even until the consummation, which is determined, is poured out on the desolate.' Dan. 9:24-27.

Chapter 10

Daniel is Deeply Troubled by his Next Vision, which the Angel Strengthens him to Hear as a Prelude to Chapter 11

'Then he said, "Do you know why I have come to you? And now I must return to fight with the prince of Persia; and when I have gone forth, indeed the prince of Greece will come. But I will tell you what is noted in the Scripture of Truth. (No one upholds me against these, except Michael your prince)."' Dan. 10:20-21.

Chapter 11
The Angel Expands Part of the Vision from Chapter Eight, Showing the Conflict Between the Greek Kings of the North and the South, with God's People Suffering in the Middle of the Conflict

'So he shall return and show regard for those who forsake the holy covenant. And forces shall be mustered by him, and they shall defile the sanctuary fortress; then they shall take away the daily sacrifices, and place there the abomination of desolation. Those who do wickedly against the covenant he shall corrupt with flattery; but the people who know their God shall be strong, and carry out great exploits.' Dan. 11:30b-32.

Chapter 12
The Angel Concludes with Promises of Judgment Against Israel's Enemies, and the Final Judgment of the World, Ordering Daniel to Seal up the Prophecy Until the Time of the End

'And many of those who sleep in the dust of the earth shall awake, some to everlasting life, some to shame and everlasting contempt. Those who are wise shall shine like the brightness of the firmament, and those who turn many to righteousness like the stars forever and ever.' Dan. 12:2-3.

Hosea

God remembers His covenant faithfulness with Israel, His unfaithful wife, promising to restore her and spread her blessings to the nations

Chapter 1

Hosea Addresses the Same Kings as Isaiah, Plus the King of Israel, his Family Represents Israel's Harlotry Against the Lord, and the Lord Promises to Extend the Abrahamic Covenant to the Ends of the Earth

> 'Yet the number of the children of Israel shall be as the sand of the sea, which cannot be numbered. And it shall come to pass in the place where it was said to them, "You are not My people," there it shall be said to them, "You are sons of the living God." Then the children of Judah and the children of Israel shall be gathered together, and appoint for themselves one Head; and they shall come up out of the land, for great will be the day of Jezreel.' Hosea 1:10-11.

Chapter 2

The Lord Brings Charges Against Judah and Israel for Baal Worship, Removes the Names of the Baals from them, and Restores His Marriage Covenant with them

> 'And it shall be in that day, says the LORD, that you will call Me "My Husband," and no longer call me "My Master," for I will take from her mouth the names of the Baals, and they shall be remembered by their name no more ... Then I will sow her for Myself in the earth, and I will have mercy on her who had not obtained mercy; then I will say to those who were not My people, "You are My people!" and they shall say, "You are my God!"' Hosea 2:16, 23.

Chapter 3
Hosea's Marriage to an Adulterous Woman Signifies the Lord's Marriage Covenant with Israel, the Lord Promising to Humble them and Bring them Back for the Sake of the Davidic Covenant

> 'Afterward the children of Israel shall return and seek the LORD their God and David their king. They shall fear the LORD and His goodness in the latter days.' Hosea 3:5.

Chapter 4
The Lord Brings Charges Against Israel for Covenant Breaking, Blaming the Priests for Depriving them of Knowledge, Rebuking the People for Idolatry Through Jeroboam's Golden Calves

> 'For Israel is stubborn like a stubborn calf; now the LORD will let them forage like a lamb in an open country. Ephraim is joined to idols, let him alone.' Hosea 4:16-17.

Chapter 5
Judgment is Certain Against Ephraim Because they Will not Listen to the Lord

> 'Ephraim is oppressed and broken in judgment, because he willingly walked by human precept.' Hosea 5:11.

Chapter 6
God Encourages Israel to Look to His Covenant Faithfulness, and to Cease from their Covenant Unfaithfulness

> 'O Ephraim, what shall I do to you? O Judah, what shall I do to you? For your faithfulness is like a morning cloud, and like the early dew it goes away. Therefore I have hewn them by the prophets, I have slain them by the words of My mouth; and your judgments are like light that goes forth. For I desire mercy and not sacrifice, and the knowledge of God more than burnt offerings. But like Adam[1] they transgressed the covenant; there they dealt treacherously with Me.' Hosea 6:4-7.

---

1. I have replaced the NKJV, 'like men,' with, 'like Adam.' As Hosea appeals consistently to earlier examples of covenant keeping and covenant breaking, the reference to Adam fits better here than a generic reference to mankind, or to a city called Adam.

Chapter 7

Ephraim is Like a Half-Baked Cake and a Silly Dove, Refusing to Hear the Lord Through His Prophets

> 'And the pride of Israel testifies to his face, but they do not return to the LORD their God, nor seek Him for all of this.' Hosea 7:10.

Chapter 8

Israel Has Rejected God's Covenant by Worshiping Golden Calves in Samaria, Making Altars for Sin and for Sinning

> 'Because Ephraim has made many altars for sin, they have become for him altars for sinning. I have written for him the great things of My law, but they were considered a strange thing.' Hosea 8:11-12.

Chapter 9

God Threatens to Reverse the Terms of the Covenant, Undoing the Exodus and Creating a New Wilderness Wandering

> 'My God will cast them away, because they did not obey Him, and they shall be wanderers among the nations.' Hosea 9:17.

Chapter 10

Israel Made a Covenant Falsely, Turning the House of God (Bethel) into the House of Idolatry (Beth Aven), and the Lord Calls them to Return to Him in Righteousness

> 'Sow for yourselves righteousness; reap in mercy; break up your fallow ground, for it is time to seek the LORD, till He comes and rains righteousness on you.' Hosea 10:12.

Chapter 11

God Recounts His Kindness to Israel, Calling them out of Egypt as His Son and Raising him, and God Continues to Remember His Covenant with them Even if they Will not

> 'When Israel was a child, I loved him, and out of Egypt I called My son … I will not execute the fierceness of My anger; I will not again destroy Ephraim. For I am God, and not man, the Holy One in your midst; and I will not come with terror.' Hosea 11:1, 9.

Chapter 12
The Lord Appeals to Jacob's Wrestling with the Angel of the Lord to Press Israel to Seek God Like he Did

> 'Yes, he struggled with the Angel and prevailed; he wept, and sought favor from Him. He found Him in Bethel, and there He spoke to us – that is, the LORD God of hosts. The LORD is His memorable name. So you, by the help of your God, return; observe mercy and justice, and wait on your God continually.' Hosea 12:4-6.

Chapter 13
Israel Shall be Like the Morning Cloud that Passes since this is What their Covenant Faithfulness is Like, and the Lord Reminds them that He is their Only Savior

> 'O Israel, you are destroyed, but your help is from Me. I will be your King; where is any other; that he may save you in all your cities? And your judges to whom you said, "Give me a king and princes?" I gave you a king in My anger, and I took him away in My wrath … I will ransom them from the power of the grave; I will redeem them from death. O Death, I will be your plagues! O grave, I will be your destruction! Pity is hidden from My eyes.' Hosea 13:9-11, 14.

Chapter 14
The Lord Gives Israel a Final Call to Repentance

> 'Who is wise? Let him understand these things. Who is prudent? Let him know them. For the ways of the LORD are right; the righteous walk in them, but transgressors stumble in them.' Hosea 14:9.

Joel

God judges His covenant people through a locust plague, yet promises to fulfil His covenant in sending them the Spirit

Chapter 1

The Lord will Make the Land Desolate in the Day of the Lord because of the Sins of the People, so that They Have Nothing Left to Bring Offerings to the Lord

> 'Consecrate a fast, call a sacred assembly; gather the elders and all the inhabitants of the land into the house of the LORD your God, and cry out to the LORD. Alas for the day! For the day of the LORD is at hand; it shall come as destruction from the Almighty.' Joel 1:14-15.

Chapter 2

The Lord Shall Destroy the Land through an Army of Locusts, but He will Remember His Covenant with Israel and Pour out His Spirit on the Remnant

> 'So rend your hearts and not your garments; return to the LORD your God, for He is gracious and merciful, slow to anger, and of great kindness; and He relents from doing harm … And it shall come to pass afterward that I will pour out My Spirit on all flesh; your sons and your daughters shall prophecy, your old men shall dream dreams, your young men shall see visions. And also on My menservants and on My maidservants I will pour out My Spirit in those days. And I will show wonders in the heavens and in the earth: blood and fire and pillars of smoke. The sun shall be turned into darkness, and the moon into blood, before the coming of the great and awesome day of the LORD. And it shall come to pass that whoever calls on the name of the LORD shall be saved. For in Mount Zion and

in Jerusalem there shall be deliverance, as the LORD has said, among the remnant whom the LORD calls.' Joel 2:13, 28-32.

Chapter 3

God Will Judge the Nations Surrounding Israel for Taking the Implements of His Temple

'Beat your plowshares into swords and your pruning hooks into spears; let the weak say, "I am strong." … So you shall know that I am the LORD your God, dwelling in Zion My holy mountain. Then Jerusalem shall be holy, and no aliens shall ever pass through them again.' Joel 3:10, 17.

Amos

God judges His covenant people and their enemies, promising to continue His covenant by restoring the fallen booth of David

Chapter 1

The Lord Pronounces Judgment Against Damascus, Gaza, Tyre, Edom, and Ammon, Who Did Violence to Israel and to One Another

> 'Thus says the LORD: "For three transgressions of Tyre, and for four, I will not turn away its punishment, because they delivered up the whole captivity to Edom, and did not remember the covenant of brotherhood."' Amos 1:9.

Chapter 2

Judgment Continues Against Moab, and the Lord Narrows His Focus to Judah and Israel for Breaking His Law

> "Thus says the LORD: "For three transgressions of Judah, and for four, I will not turn away its punishment, because they have despised the law of the LORD, and have not kept His commandments. Their lies lead them astray, lies which their fathers followed. But I will send a fire upon Judah, and it shall devour the palaces of Jerusalem."' Amos 2:4-5.

Chapter 3

God's Indictment Against Israel for her Unrepentant Sins, Pressing the Curses of the Covenant

> 'You only have I known of all the families of the earth; therefore I will punish you for all your iniquities.' Amos 3:2.

Chapter 4

The Lord Rebukes Israel's Golden Calf Worship and Notes that they Refused Correction for Breaking the Second Commandment, in Spite of the Afflictions He Brought Against them

> 'Come to Bethel and transgress, at Gilgal multiply transgression; bring your sacrifices every morning, your tithes every three days. Offer a sacrifice of thanksgiving with leaven, proclaim and announce the freewill offerings; for this you love, you children of Israel! Says the LORD God.' Amos 4:4-5.

Chapter 5
Amos Laments for Israel's Coming Destruction, Calling them to Repentance Before the Day of the Lord Comes Upon them in Judgment

> 'Woe to you who desire the day of the LORD! For what good is the day of the LORD to you? It will be darkness, and not light. It will be as though a man fled from a lion, and a bear met him! Or as though he went into the house, leaned his hand on the wall, and a serpent bit him! Is not the day of the LORD darkness, and not light? Is it not very dark, with no brightness in it?' Amos 5:18-20.

Chapter 6
The Lord Rebukes Israel's Security in her Prosperity, Announcing the Certainty of her Doom if she Does not Repent

> 'The LORD God has sworn by Himself, the LORD God of hosts says: "I abhor the pride of Jacob, and hate his palaces; therefore I will deliver up the city and all that is in it."' Amos 6:8.

Chapter 7
Amos Intercedes for the People When he Sees Visions of Locusts, Fire, and a Plumb Line Measuring Israel for Destruction, and Recounts his Prophetic Call Under Persecution

> 'Then Amaziah the priest of Bethel sent to Jeroboam king of Israel, saying, "Amos has conspired against you in the midst of the house of Israel. The land is not able to bear all his words."' Amos 7:10.

Chapter 8
Amos Sees a Vision of Summer Fruit Showing that the Lord Would Take Israel's Blessings from them, and the Lord Threatens to Remove His Word from those Who Will not Hear it

'Behold, the days are coming, says the LORD God, that I will send a famine on the land, not a famine of bread, nor a thirst for water, but of hearing the words of the LORD.' Amos 8:11.

Chapter 9

The Lord Gives a Final Warning that the Sinners Among His People Will Die by the Sword, yet He Promises to Restore the Fallen Booth of David, Remembering His Covenant with the Remnant, and Calling the Gentiles

'On that day I will raise up the tabernacle of David, which has fallen down, and repair its damages; I will raise up its ruins, and rebuild it as in the days of old; that they may possess the remnant of Edom, and all the Gentiles who are called by My name, says the LORD who does this thing.' Amos 9:11-12.

Obadiah

God proclaims judgment against Edom for abusing His covenant people in their distress, promising to save His people

Chapter 1

The Lord Proclaims Judgment on Edom for their Pride and Violence Against Israel, Giving Hope to Mount Zion

> 'But on Mount Zion there shall be deliverance, and there shall be holiness; the house of Jacob shall possess their possessions … Then the saviors shall come to Mount Zion to judge the mountains of Esau, and the kingdom shall be the LORD's.' Obad. 1:17, 21.

Jonah

God shows His compassion to the nations by sparing Nineveh from judgment for their sins

Chapter **1**

Jonah Refuses to Preach to the Ninevites, the Lord Brings a Storm to Set him Back on Course, Exalting Himself Among the Gentile Sailors, and Preparing a Great Fish to Swallow Jonah

> 'So he said to them, "I am a Hebrew, and I fear the LORD, the God of heaven, who made the sea and the dry land."' Jonah 1:9.

Chapter **2**

Jonah Prays to God from the Fish's Belly, Showing God's Superiority to Idols and that He is the Only Savior

> 'Then I said, "I have been cast out of Your sight; yet I will look again towards Your holy temple." ... When my soul fainted within me, I remembered the LORD; and my prayer went up to You, into Your holy temple.' Jonah 2:4, 7.

Chapter **3**

Jonah Preaches to Nineveh, the People Hear and Repent, and the Lord Spares them

> 'Then God saw their works, that they turned from their evil way; and God relented from the disaster that He had said He would bring upon them, and He did not do it.' Jonah 3:10.

Chapter **4**

Jonah is Angry at God's Compassion, and the Lord Gives and Takes a Plant to Illustrate His Character in Relation to the Salvation of the Nations

'So he prayed to the LORD, and said, "Ah, LORD, was not this what I said when I was still in my country? Therefore I fled previously to Tarshish; for I know that You are a gracious and merciful God, slow to anger and abundant in lovingkindness, One who relents from doing harm."' Jonah 4:2.

Micah

God judges His covenant people, yet promises to restore their kingdom by sending an everlasting king and remembering their sins no more

Chapter 1

The Lord Proclaims Judgment Against Israel and Judah, and Micah Mourns for them

> 'Hear, all you peoples! Listen, O earth, and all that is in it! Let the LORD God be a witness against you, the Lord from His holy temple. For behold, the LORD is coming out of His place; He will come down and tread on the high places of the earth.' Micah 1:2-3.

Chapter 2

The Lord Proclaims Judgment Against Those Doing Evil, Laying Blame at the Feet of their Lying Prophets

> '"Do not prattle," you say to those who prophesy. So they shall not prophesy to you; they shall not return insult for insult. You who are named the house of Jacob: Is the Spirit of the LORD restricted? Are these His doings? Do not My words do good to him who walks uprightly?' Micah 2:6-7.

Chapter 3

Micah is Full of the Spirit to Rebuke the Sins of the Leaders

> 'So the seers shall be ashamed, and the diviners abashed; indeed they shall all cover their lips; for there is no answer from God. But truly I am full of power by the Spirit of the LORD, and of justice and might, to declare to Jacob his transgression and to Israel his sin.' Micah 3:7-8.

Chapter 4

The Lord Shall Exalt the Kingdom in Mount Zion to Save the Nations in the Future

'Now it shall come to pass in the latter days that the mountain of the LORD's house shall be established on the top of the mountains, and shall be exalted above the hills; and peoples shall flow to it.' Micah 4:1.

Chapter 5
The Lord Shall Fulfill His Covenant by Raising up the Davidic King

'But you, Bethlehem Ephrathah, though you are little among the thousands of Judah, yet out of you shall come forth to Me the One to be Ruler in Israel, whose goings forth are from of old, from everlasting. Therefore He shall give them up, until the time that she who is in labor has given birth; then the remnant of His brethren shall return to the children of Israel. And He shall stand and feed His flock in the strength of the LORD, in the majesty of the name of the LORD His God; and they shall abide, for now He shall be great to the ends of the earth; and this One shall be peace.' Micah 5:2-5.

Chapter 6
The Lord Calls Israel to Repent of their Sins and to Trust in His Covenant Promises

'With what shall I come before the LORD, and bow myself before the High God? Shall I come before Him with burnt offerings, with calves a year old? Will the LORD be pleased with thousands of rams, ten thousand rivers of oil? Shall I give my firstborn for my transgression, the fruit of my body for the sin of my soul? He has shown you, O man, what is good; and what does the LORD require of you but to do justly, to love mercy, and to walk humbly with your God?' Micah 6:6-8.

Chapter 7
The Lord Offers One Final Rebuke, and Encourages Israel with His Forgiving Character

'For son dishonors father, daughter rises against her mother, daughter-in-law against her mother-in-law; and a man's enemies are the men of his own household. Therefore I will look to the LORD; I will wait for the God of my salvation; My God will hear me...Who is a God like You, pardoning iniquity and passing over the transgression of the remnant of His heritage? He does not retain His anger forever, because He delights in mercy. He will again have compassion on us, and will subdue our iniquities. You will cast all our sins into the depths of the sea.' Micah 7:6-7, 18-19.

Nahum

God judges Nineveh, applying His covenant name from Exodus 34

Chapter 1

Nahum Appeals to God's Divine Name in Judgment Against the Ninevites

> 'The LORD is slow to anger and great in power, and will not at all acquit the wicked. The LORD has His way in the whirlwind and in the storm, and the clouds are the dust of His feet ... Behold, on the mountains the feet of him who brings good tidings, who proclaims peace! O Judah, keep your appointed feasts, perform your vows. For the wicked one shall no more pass through you; he is utterly cut off.' Nahum 1:3, 15.

Chapter 2

The Lord will Utterly Destroy Nineveh in Spite of their Great Might

> 'Behold, I am against you, says the LORD of hosts, I will burn your chariots in smoke, and the sword shall devour your young lions; I will cut off your prey from the earth, and the voice of your messengers shall be heard no more.' Nahum 2:13.

Chapter 3

The Lord Pronounces a Final Set of Woes on Assyria

> 'Surely, your people in your midst are women! The gates of your land are wide upon for your enemies; fire shall devour the bars of your gates.' Nahum 3:13.

Habakkuk

God directs His covenant people to faith and satisfaction that He is their God, even when they do not understand His distressing providences

Chapter 1

The Prophet Asks for Understanding of the Justice of the Lord's Judgments

> 'Are You not from everlasting, O LORD my God, my Holy One? We shall not die. O LORD, You have appointed them for judgment; O Rock, You have marked them for correction. You are of purer eyes than to behold evil, and cannot look on wickedness. Why do You look on those who deal treacherously, and hold Your tongue when the wicked devours a person more righteous than he?' Hab. 1:12-13.

Chapter 2

The Lord Urges Habakkuk to Wait in Faith, Maintaining his Integrity in Patience

> 'Behold the proud, his soul is not upright in him; but the just shall live by his faith ... For the earth will be filled with the knowledge of the glory of the LORD, as the waters cover the sea' Hab. 2:4, 14.

Chapter 3

Habakkuk's Prayer and Profession of Faith in God's Good Providence

> 'Though the fig tree may not blossom, nor fruit be on the vines; though the labor of the olive may fail, and the fields yield no food; though the flock may be cut off from the fold, and there be no herd in the stalls – yet I will rejoice in the

LORD, I will joy in the God of my salvation. The LORD God is my strength; He will make my feet like deer's feet, and He will make me walk on my high hills. To the Chief Musician. With my stringed instruments.' Hab. 3:17-19.

Zephaniah

Alluding to previous covenants, God applies His covenant curses to His people, yet promises to restore them and rejoice over them

Chapter **1**
The Day of the Lord Will Resemble the Undoing of Creation

> 'Be silent in the presence of the LORD God; for the day of the LORD is at hand, for the LORD has prepared sacrifice; He has invited His guests.' Zeph. 1:7.

Chapter **2**
The Lord Calls the Meek to Repentance, Proclaiming Judgment on the Nations who Believe that they are Self-Existent and Independent

> 'See the LORD, all you meek of the earth, who have upheld His justice. Seek righteousness, seek humility. It may be that you will be hidden in the day of the LORD's anger.' Zeph. 2:3.

Chapter **3**
Jerusalem and her Wicked Rulers Have Persistently Refused to Hear the Lord, yet the Lord Will Restore His Covenant Favor

> 'The LORD your God in your midst, the Mighty One, will save; He will rejoice over you with gladness, He will quiet you with His love, He will rejoice over you with singing.' Zeph. 3:17.

Haggai

God exhorts His people to covenant faithfulness, as they look to the salvation of the nations by exalting His glory in the future in the new temple

Chapter 1

Haggai Strengthens Zerubbabel and Joshua to Finish Rebuilding the Temple, the Leaders and the People Obey the Lord, and the Lord Assures them of His Covenant

> 'Then Haggai, the LORD's messenger, spoke the LORD's message to the people, saying, "I am with you, says the LORD." So the LORD stirred up the spirit of Zerubbabel the son of Shealtiel, governor of Judah, and the spirit of Joshua the son on Jehozadak, the high priest, and the spirit of all the remnant of the people; and they came and worked on the house of the LORD of hosts, their God.' Hag. 1:13-14.

Chapter 2

Haggai Predicts that the Glory of the Latter House Shall Exceed that of the Former, even Though it is Smaller, the People Need to be Cleansed of Defilement, and God Promises to Make them Fruitful Under Zerubbabel's Leadership

> 'According to the word that I covenanted with you when you came out of Egypt, so My Spirit remains among you; do not fear! For thus says the LORD of hosts: "Once more (it is a little while) I will shake heaven and earth, the sea and dry land; and I will shake all nations, and they shall come to the Desire of All Nations, and I will fill this temple with glory," says the LORD of hosts. "The silver is Mine, and the gold is Mine," says the LORD of hosts. "The glory of this latter temple shall be greater than the former," says the LORD of hosts. "And in this place I will give peace," says the LORD of hosts.' Hag. 2:5-9.

Zechariah

God comforts the restored exiles by promising to restrain and conquer His and their enemies, and by sending a Priest who would be crowned King, exhorting them to continued repentance

Chapter 1

The Lord Requires Repentance of the Small Number of Returned Exiles, Giving the First Night Vision of Horses Surveying the Nations at Ease While Israel was in Distress, and the Second Vision of the Craftsmen Terrifying the Horns or Strength of the Nations at Ease

> 'So they answered the Angel of the LORD, who stood among the myrtle trees, and said, "We have walked to and fro throughout the earth, and behold, all the earth is resting quietly." Then the Angel of the LORD answered and said, "O LORD of hosts, how long will You not have mercy on Jerusalem and on the cities of Judah, against which You were angry these seventy years?" And the LORD answered the Angel who talked with me, with good and comforting words … Again, proclaim, saying, "Thus says the LORD of hosts: My cities shall again spread out through prosperity; the LORD will again comfort Zion, and will again choose Jerusalem."' Zech. 1:11-13, 17.

Chapter 2

The Third Night Vision of the Measuring Line and God's Promise to Protect His People as a Wall of Fire Around them, and Bringing Salvation Through them to the Nations

> 'Many nations shall be joined to the LORD in that day, and they shall become My people. And I will dwell in your midst. Then you will know that the LORD of hosts has sent Me to

you … Be silent, all flesh, before the LORD, for He is aroused from His holy habitation." Zech. 2:11, 13.

Chapter 3

The Fourth Night Vision of Cleansing Joshua the High Priest to Lead the People in Worship, While the Lord Promises that the Branch Will Take Away their Sins in a Final Day of Atonement

'Hear, O Joshua, the high priest, you and your companions who sit before you, for they are a wondrous sign; for behold, I am bringing forth My Servant the BRANCH. For behold, the stone that I have laid before Joshua: upon the stone are seven eyes. Behold, I will engrave its inscription, says the LORD of hosts, and I will remove the iniquity of that land in one day." Zech. 3:8-9.

Chapter 4

The Fifth Night Vision of the Lampstand and the Olive Trees, Showing the Endless Supply of the Spirit to Help Zerubbabel Finish his Work

'So he answered and said to me: "This is the word of the LORD to Zerubbabel: Not by might nor by power, but by My Spirit, says the LORD of hosts" … For who has despised the day of small things? For these seven rejoice to see the plumb line in the hand of Zerubbabel. These are the eyes of the LORD, which scan to and fro throughout the whole earth.' Zech. 4:6, 10.

Chapter 5

The Sixth Vision of the Flying Scroll Announcing a Curse on Covenant Breakers, and the Seventh Vision of the Woman in the Basket Going to Shinar Warns of Permanent Exile Next Time

'Then the Angel who talked with me came out and said to me, "Lift your eyes now, and see what this is that goes forth." … And he said to me, "To build a house for it in the land of Shinar; when it is ready, the basket will be set there on its base."' Zech. 5:5, 11.

Chapter 6

The Eighth and Final Vision of Four Chariots Surveying the Nations a Second Time with the Lord's Spirit Now at Rest, While the Lord Promises to Crown the Branch as a Priest-King

'Then speak to him, saying, "Thus says the LORD of hosts, saying: Behold, the Man whose name is the BRANCH! From his place He shall branch out, and He shall build the temple of the LORD; yes, He shall build the temple of the LORD. He shall bear the glory, and shall sit and rule on His throne; so He shall be a priest on His throne, and the counsel of peace shall be between them both."' Zech. 6:12-13.

Chapter 7
The People Ask Zechariah Whether they Should Continue to Fast, Remembering the Exile, but the Lord Exhorts them to Righteousness Instead

'Yes, they made their hearts like flint, refusing to hear the law and the words which the LORD of hosts had sent by His Spirit through the former prophets. Thus great wrath came from the LORD of hosts.' Zech. 7:12.

Chapter 8
The Lord Continues to Answer the Question of Fasting by Encouraging them with Restoration, Remembering His Covenant with Abraham to Make them a Blessing in His Zeal

'Thus says the LORD: "I will return to Zion, and dwell in the midst of Jerusalem. Jerusalem shall be called the City of Truth, The Mountain of the LORD of hosts the Holy Mountain … Behold, I will save My people from the land of the east and from the land of the west; I will bring them back, and they shall dwell in the midst of Jerusalem. They shall be My people and I will be their God, in truth and righteousness … And it shall come to pass that just as you were a curse among the nations, O house of Judah and house of Israel, so I will save you and you shall be a blessing. Do not fear, let your hands be strong."' Zech. 8:3, 7-8, 13.

Chapter 9
The Lord Continues to Fulfill His Covenant by Protecting Israel from their Enemies, Bringing Salvation to the Nations, and Saving His People Through their King, Who Rides on a Donkey, Quoting the Davidic Promises from Psalm 72

'Rejoice greatly, O daughter of Zion! Shout, O daughter of Jerusalem! Behold, your King is coming to you; He is just and having salvation, lowly and riding on a donkey, a colt, the foal of a donkey. I will cut off the chariot from Ephraim and the horse from Jerusalem; the battle bow shall be cut off. He shall speak peace to the nations; His dominion shall be from sea to sea, and from the River to the ends of the earth.' Zech. 9:9-10.

Chapter 10

The Lord Will Restore His Covenant People and their Children

'I will strengthen the house of Judah, and I will save the house of Joseph. I will bring them back, because I have mercy on them. They shall be as though I had not cast them aside; for I am the LORD their God, and I will hear them ... I will sow them among the peoples. And they shall remember Me in far countries; they shall live, together with their children, and they shall return.' Zech. 10:6, 9.

Chapter 11

The Lord Shall Remove the Foolish Shepherds of Israel, Symbolized by Zechariah's Two Staffs

'And the LORD said to me, "Throw it to the potter" – that princely price which they set on me. So I took the thirty pieces of silver and threw them to the house of the LORD for the potter. Then I cut in two my other staff, Bonds, that I might break the brotherhood between Judah and Israel.' Zech. 11:13-14.

Chapter 12

The Lord Will Remember His Covenant with David, Saving His People from their Enemies, and Will Pour Out His Spirit on them, Leading them to Mourn for their Sins

'The LORD will save the tents of Judah first, so that the glory of the house of David and the glory of the inhabitants of Jerusalem shall not become greater than that of Judah. In that day the LORD will defend the inhabitants of Jerusalem; the one who is feeble among them in that day shall be like David, and the house of David shall be like God, like the Angel of the LORD before them ... And I will pour on the house of David and on the inhabitants of Jerusalem the Spirit of grace and supplication; then they will look on Me whom they have pierced. Yes, they will mourn for Him as one mourns for his only son, and grieve for Him as one grieves for a firstborn.' Zech. 12:7-8, 10.

CHAPTER 13

In that Day the Lord Will Open a Fountain to Cleanse the People from Sin and Uncleanness, the People Will Reject False Prophets, the True Shepherd Will be Stricken, and the Lord Will Save the Remnant in His Covenant

> 'In that day a fountain shall be opened for the house of David and for the inhabitants of Jerusalem, for sin and for uncleanness ... Awake, O sword, against My Shepherd, against the Man who is My Companion, says the LORD of hosts. Strike the Shepherd, and the sheep will be scattered; then I will turn My hand against the little ones.' Zech. 13:1, 7.

CHAPTER 14

The Great Day of the Lord Will Come When God Judges the Nations and Will Rule Over All the Earth, His People Being Holy, Remember His Law in the Feast of Tabernacles, and His Enemies Being Cursed

> 'And the LORD shall be King over all the earth. In that day it shall be The LORD is one, and His name one ... In that day HOLINESS TO THE LORD shall be engraved on the bells of the horses. The pots in the LORD's house shall be like the bowls before the altar. Yes, every pot in Jerusalem and Judah shall be holiness to the LORD of hosts. Everyone who sacrifices shall come and take them and cook in them. In that day there shall no longer be a Canaanite in the house of the LORD of hosts.' Zech. 14:9, 20-21.

Malachi

God rebukes His restored people for falling back into covenant unfaithfulness, directing them to prepare for the coming of the Angel of the Covenant by remembering the law of Moses

Chapter 1

Malachi Assures the Restored Nation of Israel of God's Love to them, and Warns them Against Polluting the Sacrifices, Promising to Spread His Glory Among the Nations

> 'For from the rising of the sun, even to its going down, My name shall be great among the Gentiles; in every place incense shall be offered to My name, and a pure offering; for My name shall be great among the nations, says the LORD of hosts ... For I am a great King, says the LORD of hosts, and My name is to be feared among the nations.' Mal. 1:11, 14b.

Chapter 2

The Lord Exhorts the Priests to Teach the Law, Remembering His Covenant with Levi, He Rebukes them for their Divorces, and for Speaking Against His Providence

> 'The law of truth was in his mouth, and injustice was not found on his lips. He walked with Me in peace and equity, and turned many away from iniquity. For the lips of the priest should keep knowledge, and people should seek the law from his mouth; for he is the messenger of the LORD of hosts ... You have wearied the LORD with your words; yet you say, "In what way have we wearied Him?" In that you say, "Everyone who does evil is good in the sight of the LORD, and He delights in them," or, "Where is the God of justice?"' Mal. 2:6-7, 17.

Chapter 3

The Lord Proclaims that the Angel of the Covenant Will Come to His Temple to Purify the People, He Rebukes the People for Robbing God with their Tithes and Offerings, and for Complaining Against God, Remembering those who Fear Him

> 'Behold, I send My messenger, and he will prepare the way before Me. And the Lord, whom you seek, will suddenly come to His temple, even the Messenger of the covenant, in whom you delight. Behold He is coming, says the LORD of hosts … For I am the LORD, I do not change; therefore you are not consumed, O sons of Jacob.' Mal. 3:1, 6.

Chapter 4

The Great Day of the Lord Shall Come and Elijah the Prophet Will Prepare the Way by Directing the People to Remember the Law of Moses

> 'But to you who fear My name, the Sun of Righteousness shall arise with healing in His wings; and you shall go out and grow fat like stall-fed calves … Remember the Law of Moses, My servant, which I commanded him in Horeb for all Israel, with the statutes and judgments. Behold, I will send Elijah the prophet before the coming of the great and dreadful day of the LORD. And he will turn the hearts of the fathers to the children, and the hearts of the children to their fathers, lest I come and strike the earth with a curse.' Mal. 4:2, 4-6.

Matthew

God fulfills His covenant promises by sending His Son to save His people from their sins, and to spread the good news of His salvation to the ends of the earth

Chapter 1

The Lord Traces the History of His Covenant Faithfulness up to the Christ, and He is Conceived by the Spirit in Mary's Womb in Order to be Immanuel, Fulfilling the Heart of God's Covenant

> 'And she shall bring forth a Son, and you shall call His name JESUS, for He will save His people from their sins.' Matt. 1:21.

Chapter 2

Wise Men from the East Come to Worship Jesus as the Divine Christ, and Jesus Fulfills Israel's History by Being Called out of Egypt and Dwelling in Nazareth

> 'When he arose, he took the young Child and His mother by night and departed for Egypt, and was there until the death of Herod, that it might be fulfilled which was spoken by the Lord through the prophet, saying, "Out of Egypt I called My Son."' Matt. 2:14-15.

Chapter 3

John Prepares the Way for Jesus by Baptizing and Preaching Repentance, and Jesus is Baptized, Anointed with the Spirit to Fulfill His Public Office, with the Father's Approval

> 'When He had been baptized, Jesus came up immediately from the water; and behold, the heavens were opened to Him, and He saw the Spirit of God descending like a dove and alighting upon Him. And suddenly a voice came from

heaven, saying, "This is My beloved Son, in whom I am well pleased."' Matt. 3:16-17.

Chapter 4

The Spirit Leads the Anointed Christ to Overcome Temptation on Behalf of His Sinful People, Jesus Begins His Public Ministry in Accord with Scripture, Calling His First Disciples and Healing Many

> 'Then Jesus was led up by the Spirit into the wilderness to be tempted by the devil. And when He had fasted forty days and forty nights, afterward He was hungry.' Matt. 4:1-2.

Chapter 5

Jesus Begins the Sermon on the Mount, Contrasting His Interpretation of the Law with that of the Scribes and Pharisees, Illustrating that the Righteous Living Required in His Kingdom Goes Beyond What they Taught

> 'For I say to you, that unless your righteousness exceeds the righteousness of the scribes and Pharisees, you will by no means enter the kingdom of heaven ... Therefore you shall be perfect, just as your Father in heaven is perfect.' Matt. 5:20, 48.

Chapter 6

Jesus Continues to Illustrate the Superior Righteousness of His Kingdom to that of the Scribes and Pharisees by Urging His Disciples to Give, Pray, and Fast Before God Rather than Men, Encouraging them to Lay up Treasures in Heaven, Trusting that their Heavenly Father Will Provide for them as they do so

> 'Take heed that you do not do your charitable deeds before men, to be seen of them. Otherwise you have no reward from your Father in heaven ... Do not lay up for yourselves treasures on earth, where moth and rust destroy and where thieves break in and steal; but lay up for yourselves treasures in heaven, where neither moth nor rust destroys and where thieves do not break in and steal. For where your treasure is, there your heart will be also ... But seek first the kingdom of God and His righteousness, and all these things shall be added to you.' Matt. 6:1, 19-21, 33.

Chapter 7

Jesus Concludes His Sermon by Warning His Disciples to Avoid the Hypocritical Judgments of the Scribes and Pharisees, Driving them to Prayer as they Seek to Enter through the Narrow Gate, Recognizing False Teachers like the Scribes and Pharisees by their Fruits, and Concluding that only Those who Hear His Sayings and Do them Will Enter the Kingdom

> 'Enter by the narrow gate; for wide is the gate and broad is the way that leads to destruction, and there are many who go in by it. Because narrow is the gate and difficult is the way which leads to life, and there are few who find it.' Matt. 7:13-14.

Chapter 8

Jesus Shows His Glory to the Multitudes by Cleansing a Leper, Healing the Centurion's Servant and Peter's Mother-in-Law with Many Others, Teaching on the Cost of Discipleship, Showing His Power over Wind and Waves and Two Demon Possessed Men, All Illustrating the Necessity of Faith in Christ as the Promised Messiah

> 'Then Jesus said to the centurion, "Go your way; and as you have believed, so let it be done for you." And his servant was healed that same hour … that it might be fulfilled which was spoken by Isaiah the prophet, "He Himself took our infirmities and bore our sicknesses."' Matt. 8:13, 17.

Chapter 9

Jesus Shows that He is the God Who Forgives Sin and has Compassion on the Multitudes, Forgiving and Healing the Paralytic, Calling Matthew the Tax Collector, Urging Rejoicing Instead of Fasting, Raising a Dead Girl and Healing an Afflicted Woman, Healing Two Blind Men, Enabling a Mute to Speak, and Exhorting His Followers to Pray for More Laborers

> 'But that you may know that the Son of Man has power on earth to forgive sins – then He said to the paralytic, "Arise, take up your bed, and go to your house." … But when He saw the multitudes, He was moved with compassion for them, because they were weary and scattered, like sheep having no shepherd. Then He said to His disciples, "The harvest is truly plentiful, but the laborers are few. Therefore pray to the Lord of the harvest to send out laborers into His harvest."' Matt. 9:6, 36-38.

Chapter 10

Jesus Sends Out the Twelve Apostles, Teaching What to Do and Expect in Relation to the Kingdom of Heaven, Warning them of

Persecution and the Cost of Discipleship in Bearing the Cross and Doing Good to Fellow Disciples

> 'Freely you have received, freely give … Are not two sparrows sold for a copper coin? And not one of them falls to the ground apart from your Father's will. But the very hairs of your head are numbered. Do not fear therefore; you are of more value than many sparrows … He who loves father or mother more than Me is not worthy of Me. And he who loves son or daughter more than Me is not worthy of Me. And he who does not take his cross and follow after Me is not worthy of Me. He who finds his life will lose it, and he who loses his life for My sake will find it.' Matt. 10:8b, 29-31, 37-39.

Chapter **11**

Jesus Addresses John's Concerns that He is not the Kind of Messiah he Expected, Warning those Who Do not Believe in Light of His Signs, and Thanking the Father for His Sovereign Election, While Calling All Who are Weary and Heavy Laden to Come to Him

> 'And blessed is he who is not offended because of Me … At that time Jesus answered and said, "I thank You, Father, Lord of heaven and earth, that You have hidden these things from the wise and prudent and have revealed them to babes. Even so, Father, for so it seemed good in Your sight. All things have been delivered to Me by My Father, and no one knows the Son except the Father. Nor does anyone know the Father except the Son, and the one to whom the Son wills to reveal Him. Come to Me, all you who labor and are heavy laden, and I will give you rest. Take My yoke upon you, for I am gentle and lowly in heart, and you will find rest for your souls. For My yoke is easy and My burden light."' Matt. 11:6, 25-30.

Chapter **12**

Jesus Shows that He Fulfills the Servant Songs of Isaiah, After Conflict with the Pharisees Over the Purpose of the Sabbath, Illustrating that He Cast Out Demons by the Spirit of God Rather than Beelzebub, Warning Against the Sin Against the Spirit as an Illustration of the Danger of Sin and the Need to Bear Good Fruit, Concluding that Those who Hear and Keep His Word are His True Family

'Or how can one enter a strong man's house and plunder his goods, unless he first binds the strong man? And then he will plunder his house. He who is not with Me is against Me, and he who does not gather with Me scatters abroad ... For by your words you will be justified, and by your words you will be condemned ... For whoever does the will of My Father in heaven is My brother and sister and mother.' Matt. 12:29-30, 37, 50.

Chapter 13
Jesus Illustrates the Nature of the Kingdom of Heaven, Using Parables to Reveal the Truth to Some and to Hide it from Others, Showing the Need to Hear His Word, Losing All to Gain it, Concluding with His Rejection at Nazareth

'But blessed are your eyes for they see, and your ears for they hear; for assuredly, I say to you that many prophets and righteous men desired to see what you see, and did not see it, and to hear what you hear, and did not hear it ... Again, the kingdom of heaven is like a treasure hidden in a field, which a man found and hid; and for joy over it he goes and sells all that he has and buys that field.' Matt. 13:16-17, 44.

Chapter 14
After John the Baptist is Beheaded by Herod, Jesus Illustrates His Compassion by Feeding the Five-Thousand, and His Deity by Walking on the Sea, Healing Many Who Touch Him

'Then those who were in the boat came and worshiped Him, saying, "Truly You are the Son of God."' Matt. 14:33.

Chapter 15
Jesus Shows the Hypocrisy of the Scribes and Pharisees, Teaching that True Defilement Comes from Within, Contrasting them with a Gentile Woman's Faith and with Jesus' Compassion in Healing Multitudes and Feeding the Four-Thousand

'Not what goes into the mouth defiles a man; but what comes out of the mouth, this defiles a man. Then His disciples came and said to Him, "Do you know that the Pharisees were offended when they heard this saying?" But He answered and said, "Every plant which My heavenly Father has not planted will be uprooted. Let them alone. They are blind leaders of the blind. And if the blind lead the blind, both will fall into a ditch."' Matt. 15:11-14.

Chapter 16
Matthew's Gospel Reaches a Turning Point with Peter's Confession that Jesus is the Christ, the Son of the Living God, After the Pharisees and Sadducees Hypocritically Seek More Signs and Jesus Warns Against their Teaching, and Followed by Jesus Teaching on the Keys of the Kingdom, His Prediction of His Death and Resurrection, Calling His Disciples to Take up the Cross and Follow Him

'Simon Peter answered and said, "You are the Christ, the Son of the Living God." Jesus answered and said to him, "Blessed are you Simon Bar-Jonah, for flesh and blood has not revealed this to you, but My Father who is in heaven. And also I say to you that you are Peter, and on this rock I will build My church, and the gates of Hades shall not prevail against it. And I will give you the keys of the kingdom of heaven, and whatever you bind on earth will be bound in heaven, and whatever you loose on earth will be loosed in heaven."' Matt. 16:16-19.

Chapter 17
The Father Reveals Jesus' Divine Glory in His Transfiguration, While His Disciples do not Have the Faith in Him Needed to Heal a Boy, Leading Jesus to Stress the Necessity of His Death and Resurrection a Second Time, Paying Taxes for Him and Peter

'Now while they were staying in Galilee, Jesus said to them, "The Son of Man is about to be betrayed into the hands of men, and they will kill Him, and the third day He will be raised up." And they were exceedingly sorrowful.' Matt. 17:22-23.

Chapter 18
In Spite of Jesus' Revelation of His Divine Glory and Sacrificial Death, the Disciples Argue Over Who is Greatest, Warning them Against Causing Offense to Believers, Urging them to Imitate Him in Seeking Lost Sheep, Instructing them How to Use the Keys of the Kingdom to Reclaim those Going Astray, and Teaching them by Parable the Extent to which they Must be Ready to Forgive Repentant Offenders

'Moreover if your brother sins against you, go and tell him his fault between you and him alone. If he hears you, you have gained your brother. But if he will not hear you, take with you one or two more, that "by the mouth of two or three witnesses every word may be established." And if he refuses to hear them, tell it to the church. But if he refuses even to hear the church, let him be to you like a heathen and a tax collector. Assuredly, I say to you, whatever you bind on earth will be bound in heaven, and whatever you loose on earth will be loosed in heaven. Again I say to you that if two of you agree on earth concerning anything that they ask, it will be done for them by My Father in heaven. For where two or three are gathered together in My name, I am there in the midst of them.' Matt. 18:15-20.

Chapter **19**

A New Scene Opens with the Pharisees Testing Jesus with Questions Over Divorce, in Response to which Jesus Teaches about Celibacy, Blessed Little Children, and Shows the Rich Young Ruler the Impossibility of Entering the Kingdom Apart from Divine Power

'But Jesus said, "Let the little children come to Me, and do not forbid them; for of such is the kingdom of heaven." ... But Jesus looked at them and said to them, "With men this is impossible, but with God all things are possible" ... But many who are first will be last, and the last first.' Matt. 19:14, 26, 30.

Chapter **20**

Jesus Illustrates the Humility Required in His Kingdom with the Parable of the Workers in the Vineyard, Stressing His Death and Resurrection a Third Time, Exhorting His Disciples to Serve Rather than be Served, and Showing His Compassion by Healing Two Blind Men

'And whoever desires to be first among you, let him be your slave – just as the Son of Man did not come to be served, but to serve, and to give His life a ransom for many.' Matt. 20:27-28.

Chapter **21**

The People Acknowledge Jesus' Divine Glory in His Triumphal Entry into Jerusalem, Him Cleansing the Temple as His Own House, Withering the Fig Tree to Showing Coming Judgment on Unfruitful Israel, While He Answers Attacks on His Authority with the Parable of the Two Sons and Unmasking the Hypocrisy of the Priests and Pharisees with the Parable of the Wicked Vinedressers

> 'Therefore I say to you, the kingdom of God will be taken from you and given to a nation bearing the fruits of it. And whoever falls on this stone will be broken; but on whomever it falls, it will grind him to powder.' Matt. 21:43-44.

Chapter 22

Jesus Expands the Idea of the Preceding Parable Through the Parable of the Wedding Feast, and the Pharisees, Sadducees, and Scribes React by Seeking to Catch Him in His Words, Jesus Concluding by Posing a Riddle Related to His Divine-Human Identity as David's Son and David's Lord from Psalm 110

> 'While the Pharisees were gathered together, Jesus asked them, saying, "What do you think about the Christ? Whose Son is He?" They said to Him, "The Son of David." He said to them, "How then does David in the Spirit call him "Lord," saying, 'The LORD said to My Lord, sit at My right hand, till I make Your enemies Your footstool?' If David calls him 'Lord,' how is He his Son?" And no one answered Him a word, nor from that day on did anyone dare question Him anymore.' Matt. 22:41-46.

Chapter 23

Jesus Begins a New Section, Proclaiming Woes on the Scribes and Pharisees for their Hypocrisy

> 'That on you may come all the righteous blood shed on the earth, from the blood of righteous Abel to the blood of Zechariah, the son of Berechiah, whom you murdered between the temple and the altar. Assuredly, I say to you, all these things will come upon this generation. O Jerusalem, Jerusalem, the one who kills the prophets and stones those who are sent to her! How often I wanted to gather your children together, as a hen gathers her chicks under her wings, but you were not willing! See! Your house is left to you desolate; for I say to you, you shall see Me no more till you say, "Blessed is He who comes in the name of the LORD!"' Matt. 23:35-39.

Chapter 24

In Response to the Woes He Proclaimed, Jesus Predicted the Destruction of the Temple and Jerusalem as Divine Judgment on their Hypocrisy, Leading His Disciples to Look to the Final Judgment and Warning that No One Knows the Day or the Hour

> 'But he who endures to the end shall be saved ... Assuredly, I say to you, this generation will by no means pass away till all these things take place. Heaven and earth will pass away, but My words will by no means pass away.' Matt. 24:13, 34-35.

Chapter 25

Jesus Concludes this Section with Three Parables About the Final Judgment, Showing the Need to Have Divine Grace, to Use it Well, and to Serve Christ's Disciples

> 'Watch therefore, for you know neither the day nor the hour in which the Son of Man is coming ... For to everyone who has, more will be given, and he will have abundance; but from him who does not have, even what he has will be taken away ... Inasmuch as you did it to one of the least of these My brethren, you did it to Me ... Inasmuch as you did not do it to one of the least of these, you did not do it to Me.' Matt. 25:13, 29, 40, 45.

Chapter 26

The Final Scene Unfolds with the Plot to Kill Jesus, His Anointing for Burial, Judas' Betraying, the Inauguration of the New Covenant at the Lord's Supper, the Prediction of Peter's Denial, Jesus' Gethsemane Prayer, His Betrayal and the Beginning of His Trial, and Peter's Denial

> 'For this is My blood of the new covenant, which is shed for many for the remission of sins. But I say to you, I will not drink of this fruit of the vine from now on until that day when I drink it new with you in My Father's kingdom.' Matt. 26:28-29.

Chapter 27

Jesus Faces Pontius Pilate, While Judas Hangs himself in Remorse, and Jesus is Condemned While Barabbas is Set Free, and Jesus Fulfills Scripture by Dying on the Cross and Being Buried with the Rich, Opening Access to God by His Death

> 'Then, behold, the veil of the temple was torn in two from top to bottom; and the earth quaked and the rocks were split, and the graves were opened; and many bodies of the saints who had fallen asleep were raised; and coming out of the graves after

His resurrection, they went into the holy city and appeared to many.' Matt. 27:51-53.

Chapter 28

Jesus Rises from the Dead on the First Day of the Week, While the Jewish Leaders Bribe the Soldiers to Cover up the Fact, and Jesus Concludes with Commissioning the Apostles to Send the Gospel to the Nations

> 'And Jesus came and spoke to them, saying, "All authority has been given to Me in heaven and on earth. Go therefore and make disciples of all the nations, baptizing them in the name of the Father and of the Son and of the Holy Spirit, teaching them to observe all things that I have commanded you; and lo, I am with you always, even to the end of the age."' Matt. 28:18-20.

Mark

God shows that Jesus is the Christ through His many miracles, bringing people into His covenant presence, as Christ opens the way to God through His death and resurrection

Chapter **1**

The Gospel Begins with John the Baptist Preaching Repentance to Enter the Kingdom, which Message Jesus Immediately Takes up After His Baptism by the Spirit and Temptation, Calling His First Disciples, Casting out an Unclean Spirit, Healing Peter's Mother-in-Law and Many Others, Preaching and Cleansing a Leper

> 'Now after John was put in prison, Jesus came into Galilee, preaching the gospel of the kingdom of God, and saying, "The time is fulfilled, and the kingdom of God is at hand. Repent, and believe in the gospel."' Mark 1:14-15.

Chapter **2**

Jesus Shows His Divine Prerogative to Forgive Sins When He Heals the Paralytic, Showing His Compassion to Sinners by Calling Matthew the Tax Collector, Pressing for Rejoicing Instead of Fasting, and Restoring the Sabbath to its Purpose as Lord of the Sabbath

> 'Those who are well have no need of a physician, but those who are sick. I did not come to call the righteous, but sinners, to repentance … And He said, "The Sabbath was made for man, and not man for the Sabbath. Therefore the Son of Man is also Lord of the Sabbath."' Mark 2:17, 27-28.

Chapter **3**

Jesus Shows that it is Lawful to Show Mercy on the Sabbath, Many People Follow Him, He Calls the Twelve Apostles, Teaching that

He has Bound the Strong Man Satan in Order to Plunder his Goods, Warning those who Attribute His Works to Satan Against Blaspheming the Spirit, and Showing that those Doing the Will of God are His true Family

> 'For whoever does the will of God is My brother and My sister and mother.' Mark 3:35.

Chapter 4

Jesus Teaches in Parables to Reveal the Truth to Some and to Conceal it from Others, Beginning with the Parable of the Sower, Stressing the Need to Hear God's Word, Urging His Hearers to Use the Light that they Have, Warning of the Coming Judgment, Predicting the Spread of the Kingdom, and Showing His Divine Identity by Stilling the Storm

> 'Then He said to them, "Take heed what you hear. With the same measure you use, it will be measured back to you; and to you who hear, more will be given. For whoever has, to him more will be given; but whoever does not have, even what he has will be taken from him."' Mark 4:24-25.

Chapter 5

Jesus Shows His Power by Healing a Demon-Possessed Man, Restoring a Girl's Life, and Healing an Afflicted Woman, Again Telling His Disciples to Tell no one Yet

> 'Go home to your friends, and tell them what great things the Lord has done for you, and how He has had compassion on you.' Mark 5:19.

Chapter 6

After Being Rejected at Nazareth, Jesus Sends the Twelve to Preach the Repentance, While Herod Murders John the Baptist, and Jesus Shows Divine Compassion by Feeding the Five-Thousand and Divine Identity by Walking on the Sea, Concluding with More Healings as Signs of the Truth of His Teaching

> 'So they went and preached that people should repent. And they cast out many demons, and anointed with oil many who were sick, and healed them.' Mark 6:12-13.

Chapter 7

Jesus Unmasks the Hypocrisy of the Scribes and Pharisees, Showing that True Defilement Comes from Within, Contrasting them to a Gentile Woman's Persistent Faith and with His Compassion in Healing a Deaf and Mute Man

> 'And they were astonished beyond measure, saying, "He has done all things well. He makes both the deaf to hear and the mute to speak."' Mark 7:37.

Chapter **8**

Jesus Heals the Four-Thousand While the Pharisees Ironically Ask for More Signs, Leading Jesus to Warn His Disciples Against their Teaching, Illustrating that His Disciples Partly See and are Still Partly Blind by Healing a Blind Man in Stages, Stressing His Identity as the Christ through Peter's Confession, the Necessity of His Death and Resurrection, and the Need to Take Up the Cross and Follow Him

> 'Whoever desires to come after Me, let him deny himself, and take up his cross, and follow Me. For whoever desires to save his life will lose it, but whoever loses his life for My sake and the gospel's will save it. For what will it profit a man if he gains the whole world, and loses his own soul? Or what will a man give in exchange for his soul? For whoever is ashamed of Me and My words in this adulterous and sinful generation, of him the Son of Man also will be ashamed when He comes in the glory of His Father with the holy angels.' Mark 8:34b-38.

Chapter **9**

The Father Reveals Jesus' Divine Glory in His Transfiguration, While His Disciples Lack Adequate Faith in Him to Heal a Boy, Leading Jesus to Predict the Necessity of His Death and Resurrection a Second Time, Contrasting His Self-Sacrifice to the Disciples Arguing Over Who is Greatest and Forbidding those not Travelling with them from Casting Out Demons in His Name, and Jesus Warns them Against Offending Those Believing in Him

> 'For everyone will be seasoned with fire, and every sacrifice will be seasoned with salt. Salt is good, but if the salt loses its flavor, how will you season it? Have salt in yourselves, and have peace with one another.' Mark 9:49-50.

Chapter **10**

The Pharisees Question Jesus on Divorce and He Blesses the Little Children, and He Calls the Rich Young Ruler to Forsake All and

Follow Him, Illustrating the Nature of Discipleship, Predicting His Death and Resurrection a Third Time, Calling His Disciples to Follow Him in Service, and Healing Blind Bartimaeus

> 'And whoever of you desires to be first shall be slave of all. For even the Son of Man did not come to be served, but to serve, and to give His life as a ransom for many.' Mark 10:44-45.

Chapter **11**

The Crowds Acknowledge Jesus's Identity as the Christ the Son of David, Showing the Spiritual Desolation of Jerusalem in the Withered Fig Tree, Showing the Need to Cleanse the Temple and its Worship, Pressing His Disciples to the Necessity of Forgiveness, While the Jewish Leaders Question His Authority

> 'And whenever you stand praying, if you have anything against anyone, forgive him, that your Father in heaven may also forgive you your trespasses. But if you do not forgive, neither will your Father in heaven forgive your trespasses.' Mark 11:25-26.

Chapter **12**

Jesus Rebukes the Jewish Leaders with the Parable of the Wicked Vinedressers, and they Retaliate by Seeking to Catch Him in His Words with Questions about Taxes, the Resurrection, and the Law, While Jesus Poses a Riddle as to How the Christ Can Be Both David's Son and David's Lord, Concluding with the Hypocrisy of the Scribes and the Sincerity of the Poor Widow

> 'Assuredly, I say to you that this poor widow has put in more than all those who have given to the treasury; for they all put in out of their abundance, but she out of her poverty put in all that she had, her whole livelihood.' Mark 12:43-45.

Chapter **13**

Jesus Predicts the Destruction of the Jewish Temple as Divine Judgment for Rejecting Him, Pressing His Disciples to Endure Tribulation and Look to His Second Coming

> 'But of that day and hour no one knows, not even the angels in heaven, nor the Son, but only the Father. Take heed, watch and pray; for you do not know when the time is.' Mark 13:32-33.

Chapter **14**

The Jewish Leaders Plot to Murder Jesus, While a Woman Anoints Him for Burial, Judas Agreeing to Betray Jesus, and

Jesus Celebrates the Passover and Institutes the Lord's Supper in the New Covenant, and Jesus Predicts Peter's Denial, Prays in Gethsemane, is Arrested and Begins His Trial, While Peter Denies Him

> 'Assuredly, I say to you, wherever this gospel is preached in the whole world, what this woman has done will also be told as a memorial to her.' Mark 14:9.

Chapter **15**

Jesus is Condemned to Death, Taking Barabbas' Place, While the Soldiers Mock Him and He is Crucified and Dies, Granting Access to God, Being Buried with the Rich After His Death

> 'Then the veil of the temple was torn in two from top to bottom. So when the centurion, who stood opposite Him, saw that He cried out like this and breathed His last, he said, "Truly this Man was the Son of God!"' Mark 15:38-39.

Chapter **16**

Jesus is Raised from the Dead and Commissions His Disciples to Baptize and Preach the Gospel to All Nations

> 'But he said to them, "Do not be alarmed. You seek Jesus of Nazareth, who was crucified. He is risen! He is not here. See the place where they laid Him. But go, tell His disciples – and Peter – that He is going before you into Galilee; there you will see Him, as He said to You."' Mark 16:6-7.

Luke

God fulfills all of His covenant promises through sending His Son, requiring faith and repentance from all, spreading the gospel to the nations through the work of the Holy Spirit

Chapter **1**

Luke Writes to Theophilus, Beginning to Rehearse the Gospel of Christ from the Prediction of John and Jesus' Births, with Mary and John Summarizing Covenant History by Praising God for His Promises

> 'And the angel answered and said to her, "'The Holy Spirit will come upon you, and the power of the Highest will overshadow you; therefore, also, that Holy One who is to be born will be called the Son of God … As He spoke to our fathers, to Abraham and to his seed forever … And has raised up a horn of salvation for us in the house of His servant David … To perform the mercy promised to our fathers and to remember His holy covenant, the oath which He swore to our father Abraham."' Luke 1:35, 55, 69, 72-73.

Chapter **2**

Christ is Born in the City of David and the Heavenly Host Gives Glory to God in the Highest, and Simeon and Anna Praise God for Sending Salvation to the Nations, While Jesus Grows in Wisdom and Stature and in Favor with God and Men

> 'And the Child grew and became strong in spirit, filled with wisdom; and the grace of God was upon Him … And Jesus increased in wisdom and statute, and in favor with God and men.' Luke 2:40, 52.

Chapter **3**

John Preaches and Baptizes, Exhorting People to Repent of Particular Sins Particularly, and Jesus is Baptized, Receiving the

Spirit and the Father's Public Approval, Showing that His Lineage Fulfills Covenant History from Adam Onward

> 'Then he said to the multitudes that came out to be baptized by him, "Brood of vipers! Who warned you to flee from the wrath to come? Therefore bear fruits worthy of repentance, and do not begin to say to yourselves, We have Abraham as our father. For I say to you that God is able to raise up children to Abraham from these stones. And even now the ax is laid to the root of the trees. Therefore every tree which does not bear good fruit is cut down and thrown into the fire."' Luke 3:7-9.

Chapter 4

The Spirit Leads Jesus to Overcome Temptation in Place of His Sinful People, and the Same Spirit Leads Jesus to Preach the Gospel in Fulfillment of Isaiah 49, Sealing His Teaching by Casting out Unclean Spirits and Healing Many.

> 'The Spirit of the LORD is upon Me, because He has anointed Me to preach the gospel to the poor; He has sent Me to heal the brokenhearted, to proclaim liberty to the captives and recovery of sight to the blind, to set at liberty those who are oppressed; to proclaim the acceptable year of the LORD.' Luke 4:18-19.

Chapter 5

Jesus Calls His First Disciples, Cleanses a Leper, and Shows His Divine Power to Forgive Sins in Healing the Paralytic, Calling Matthew the Tax Collector and Showing that the Times Call for Rejoicing Instead of Fasting

> 'And He said to them, "Can the friends of the bridegroom fast while the bridegroom is with them? But the days will come when the bridegroom will be taken away from them; then they will fast in those days."' Luke 5:34-35.

Chapter 6

Jesus Shows that He is Lord of the Sabbath, Restoring the Sabbath to its Purposes of Worship and Mercy, Calling the Twelve Apostles, Giving a Shorter Version of the Beatitudes with Contrasting Woes, Illustrating the Necessity of Mercy in His Kingdom, and Teaching People to Keep His Commandments

> 'But why do you call me, "Lord, Lord," and do not do the things which I say?' Luke 6:46.

Chapter 7

Jesus Heals the Centurion's Servant Marveling at his Faith, He Raises the Widows Son, Leading People to Profess Hope in God's Covenant Promises, While He Reassures John in his Doubts by Pointing to the Signs, and He Forgives a Sinful Woman, Showing the Necessity of Faith in Him

> 'Then fear came upon all, and they glorified God, saying, "A great prophet has risen among us;" and, "God has visited His people."' Luke 7:16.

Chapter 8

Many Women Minister to Jesus, and He Teaches in Parables to Reveal the Truth to Some and to Conceal it from Others, Beginning with the Parable of the Sower Followed by the Parable of the Revealed Light, Showing that His True Family are Those Who Hear and Do God's Word, Revealing His Divine Identity by Calming the Wind and the Waves, Freeing the Demon-Possessed Man, and Raising a Girl from the Dead and Healing an Afflicted Woman

> 'Therefore take heed how you hear. For whoever has, to him more will be given; and whoever does not have, even what he seems to have will be taken from him.' Luke 8:18.

Chapter 9

Jesus Sends Out the Twelve While Herod Seeks to See Him, and Jesus Illustrates His Compassion by Feeding the Five-Thousand, While Peter Confesses that He is the Christ, Leading Jesus to Predict His Death and Resurrection, Calling His Disciples to Follow Him in Self-Denial, Encouraging them with His Divine Glory in the Transfiguration, Healing a Boy, Predicting His Death Again, and Contrasting His Service with the Disciple's Pride, Sectarianism, and Wrath, Pressing Home the Cost of Discipleship

> 'But Jesus said to him, "No one, having put his hand to the plow, and looking back, is fit for the Kingdom of God."' Luke 9:62.

Chapter 10

Luke Relates Material Largely Unique to him, from this Chapter Until Chapter 19, Beginning with Sending out the Seventy and Proclaiming Woes on Impenitent Cities, Showing the Vital Importance of Having their Names Written in Heaven, Rejoicing in the Father's Sovereignty Over Salvation, Teaching the Parable of the Good Samaritan to Bring Conviction of Sin, While Mary Shows the Importance of Sitting at Jesus' Feet to Learn from Him

> 'Nevertheless do not rejoice in this, that the spirits are subject to you, but rather rejoice that your names are written in heaven … And Jesus answered and said to her, "Martha, Martha, you are worried and troubled about many things. But one thing is needed, and Mary has chosen that good part, which will not be taken away from her."' Luke 10:20, 41-42.

Chapter **11**

Jesus Teaches His Disciples How to Pray, Giving a Shortened form of the Lord's Prayer and Urging Persistence in Prayer, Especially for the Holy Spirit, Showing that He has Bound Satan, and Warning those who Do not Hear Him, Urging People to Hear His Word, Rebuking those Wanting More Signs and Showing the Need to Have Light in themselves, Concluding with Woes on the Pharisees and Lawyers for their Hypocrisy

> 'If you then, being evil, know how to give good gifts to your children, how much more will your heavenly Father give the Holy Spirit to those who ask Him!' Luke 11:13.

Chapter **12**

Jesus Expands His Warnings Against the Hypocrisy of the Pharisees, Highlighting their Fear of Man, Timidity to Confess Christ and Tendency to Blaspheme the Spirit Who Leads People to Confess Him, and their Covetousness and Anxiety Over the Things of this Life, Urging People to Live in Light of His Second Coming, Showing that His Teaching Will Bring Division, that the Pharisees Cannot Discern the Times, and Exhorting All to Make Peace with God While there is Still Time

> 'I came to send fire on the earth, and how I wish it were already kindled! But I have a baptism to be baptized with, and how distressed I am till it is accomplished! Do you suppose that I came to give peace on earth? I tell you, not at all, but rather division … When you go with your adversary to the magistrate, make every effort along the way to settle with him, lest he drag you to the judge, and the judge deliver you to the officer, and the officer throw you into prison. I tell you, you shall not depart from there till you have paid the very last mite.' Luke 12:49-51, 58-59.

Chapter 13

Jesus Uses Disastrous and Wicked Events to Show the Urgency of Repentance, Gives the Parable of the Barren Fig Tree to Press the Point Home, Heals a Woman on the Sabbath to Show His Compassion to Sinners, Predicts the Spread of the Kingdom through the Parables of the Mustard Seed and the Leaven, Showing that Many Will not Enter the Narrow Gate, and Lamenting Over the Impenitence of Jerusalem

> 'Strive to enter through the narrow gate, for many, I say to you, will seek to enter and will not be able.' Luke 13:24.

Chapter 14

Jesus Shows His Compassion by Healing a Man on the Sabbath, Rebuking those Taking the Best Seats at a Supper, Showing the Rejection of the Invited Guest to God's Supper for Failing to Take His Summons Seriously, Exhorting All to Leave All Things to Follow Christ and to Have Salt in themselves

> 'If anyone comes to Me and does not hate his father and mother, wife and children, brothers and sisters, yes, and his own life also, he cannot be My disciple.' Luke 14:26.

Chapter 15

The Pharisees and Scribes Continue to Show their Hypocrisy by Grumbling About Jesus' Mercy to Sinners, and Jesus Responds with the Parables of the Lost Sheep, the Lost Coin, and the Lost Son, Showing the Value of Repentance in Contrast to their Self-Righteousness

> 'I say to you that likewise there will be more joy in heaven over one sinner who repents than over ninety-nine just persons who need no repentance.' Luke 15:7.

Chapter 16

Jesus Exhorts His Disciples to Use Unrighteous Mammon Well in Contrast to the Pharisees in their Love for Money, Leading Jesus to Show their Inability to Justify Themselves Before God Through the Example of their Approach to Divorce, and Through the Parable of the Rich Man Ending in Hell While the Beggar Lazarus Ends up in Abraham's Bosom

> 'But he said to him, "If they do not hear Moses and the prophets, neither will they be persuaded though one rise from the dead."' Luke 16:31.

Chapter 17

Jesus Warns His Disciples Against Giving Offense to Others and to Be Ready to Forgive Offenders, Telling them that the Truth of their Faith is More Important than the Strength of their Faith, Rebuking the Jewish Nations with the Gratitude of the Healed Samaritan Leper, and Urging them to Look to the Consummation of the Kingdom When Jesus Returns in Glory

> 'So Jesus answered and said, "Were there not ten cleansed? But where are the nine? Were there not any found who returned to give glory to God except this foreigner?"' Luke 17:17-18.

Chapter 18

The Parable of the Persistent Widow Illustrates Persevering Faith Through Persistent Prayer, Leading to the Tax Collector as the Model of Humble Dependence on God's Mercies in Contrast to the Pharisee, While the Rich Young Ruler Shows that Salvation is Possible to God Alone, Jesus Predicting His Death and Resurrection a Third Time and Heals a Blind Man

> 'Nevertheless, when the Son of Man comes, will He really find faith on the earth? … And the tax collector, standing afar off, would not so much as raise his eyes to heaven, but beat his breast saying, "God, be merciful to me a sinner!" I tell you, this man went down to his house justified rather than the other; for everyone who exalts himself will be humbled, and he who humbles himself will be exalted.' Luke 18:8, 13-14.

Chapter 19

Zacchaeus Illustrates that Even the Rich and their Households can Become Sons of Abraham, Leading Christ to Teach People to Use What they Have Well in the Parable of the Minas, and Showing His Glory as the Divine Messiah in the Triumphal Entry, With Jesus Weeping Over Jerusalem for its Coming Destruction and Showing the Need to Cleanse the Temple and its Worship

> 'And Jesus said to him, "Today salvation has come to this house, because he also is a son of Abraham; for the Son of Man has come to seek and to save that which was lost."' Luke 19:9-10.

Chapter 20

The Chief Priest and Scribes Question Jesus' Authority, and He Responds by Implicitly Rebuking them with the Parable of the

Wicked Vinedressers, and Puts them to Silence When they Try to Catch Him With Questions about Taxes and the Resurrection, While Jesus Poses a Riddle from Psalm 110 Regarding How the Christ can Be both David's Son and David's Lord

> 'Then some of the scribes answered and said, "Teacher, You have spoken well." But after that they dared not question Him anymore.' Luke 20:39.

Chapter 21

Jesus Contrasts the Hypocrisy of the Jewish Leaders with the Generosity of the Poor Widow, Predicting the Destruction of the Temple and His Second Coming, Urging All to Watch and Prepare for the Day

> 'But take heed to yourselves, lest your hearts be weighed down with carousing, drunkenness, and cares of this life, and that Day come on you unexpectedly. For it will come as a snare on all who dwell on the face of the whole earth. Watch therefore, and pray always that you may be counted worthy to escape all these things that will come to pass, and to stand before the Son of Man.' Luke 21:34-36.

Chapter 22

Satan Enters Judas in Order to Betray Jesus to Death, and Jesus Prepares the Passover and Institutes the Lord's Supper, Looking to the Consummation of His Kingdom Under the New Covenant, While His Disciples Argue Ironically About Greatness, Jesus Predicts Peter's Denial, Warning the Disciples to Prepare for Future Trials, Jesus Prays in Gethsemane and is Arrested and Beaten, while Peter Denies Him

> 'But you are those who have continued with Me in My trials. And I bestow upon you a kingdom, just as My Father bestowed one upon Me, that you may eat and drink at My table in My kingdom, and sit on thrones judging the twelve tribes of Israel.' Luke 22:28-30.

Chapter 23

Jesus is Tried Before Pilate and Herod, Takes Barabbas' Place on the Cross, Warning the Daughters of Jerusalem Against Coming Judgment and Prays for the Father to Forgive those Crucifying Him, Illustrating Faith Through the Penitent Thief, Jesus Then

Committing His Spirit to the Father as He Dies, as He is Buried in Joseph's Tomb

> 'But the other, answering, rebuked him, saying, "Do you not even fear God, seeing you are under the same condemnation? And we indeed justly, for we receive the due reward of our deeds; but this Man has done nothing wrong." Then he said to Jesus, "Lord, remember me when You come into Your kingdom." And Jesus said to him, "Assuredly, I say to you, today you will be with Me in Paradise."' Luke 23:40-43.

Chapter **24**

Jesus Rises from the Dead on the Third Day, The Angels Announcing the Fact to Several Women, and Then Jesus Expounds the Necessity of His Death and Resurrection from the Old Covenant Scriptures to Two Disciples on the Road to Emmaus, Appearing to His Disciples and Opening their Understanding to Read Scripture in Light of Christ's Person and Work, Exhorting them to Wait in Jerusalem for the Holy Spirit While He Ascends into Heaven

> 'Then He said to them, "These are the words which I spoke to you while I was still with you, that all things must be fulfilled which were written in the Law of Moses and the Prophets and the Psalms concerning Me." And He opened their understanding, that they might comprehend the Scriptures. Then He said to them, "Thus it is written, and thus it was necessary for the Christ to suffer and to rise from the dead the third day, and that repentance and remission of sins should be preached in His name to all nations, beginning at Jerusalem. And you are witnesses of these things. Behold, I send the Promise of My Father upon you; but tarry in the city of Jerusalem until you are endued with power from on high."' Luke 24:44-49

John

God sent His eternal Son to become flesh and tabernacle among men, fulfilling His covenant promises, and stressing the divine identity of Christ and the promise of eternal life through faith in Him

Chapter 1

John Introduces Jesus as the Eternal Word of God Who Revealed His Glory in Human Flesh, as the Lamb of God, Taking Away the Sin of the World, Making Those Who Receive Him Sons of God, and Serving as the Way Between Heaven and Earth

> 'And the Word became flesh and dwelt among us, and we beheld His glory, the glory as of the only begotten of the Father, full of grace and truth ... And of His fulness we have all received, and grace for grace. For the law was given through Moses, but grace and truth came through Jesus Christ. No one has seen God at any time. The only begotten Son, who is in the bosom of the Father, He has declared Him ... "Behold! The Lamb of God who takes away the sin of the world!"' John 1:14, 16-18, 29.

Chapter 2

Jesus' First Sign of Turning Water into Wine Illustrates the Blessings of His Coming Under the New Covenant, Jesus Showing the Need to Cleanse the People Through His Body as the True Temple, and Searching Men's Hearts Illustrating the Need for Sincere Faith

> 'Jesus answered and said to them, "Destroy this temple, and in three days I will raise it up." Then the Jews said, "It has taken forty-six years to build this temple, and will You raise it up in three days?" But He was speaking of the temple of His body. Therefore, when He had risen from the dead, His disciples remembered that He had said this to them; and they

> believed the Scripture and the word which Jesus had said.' John 2:19-22.

Chapter 3

Jesus Confronts Nicodemus with the Need to be Born of the Spirit, Echoing and Expanding Themes from Chapter 1, John Showing that Jesus Came Down From Heaven to Reveal the Father and to Save those Who Believe, Proclaiming Judgment on Those Rejecting Christ, While John Decreases in Order that Christ, Who Has the Spirit Without Measure Might Increase

> 'For God so loved the world that He gave His only begotten Son, that whoever believes in Him should not perish but have everlasting life. For God did not send His Son into the world to condemn the world, but that the world through Him might be saved ... For He whom God has sent speaks the words of God, for God does not give the Spirit by measure.' John 3:16-17, 34.

Chapter 4

Jesus Promises the Samaritan Woman at the Well a Fountain of Living Water to Come to the Father, Through His Word (Son) and Spirit, Foreshadowing His Teaching in Chapter Seven, and Expanding His Teaching on the Spirit in Chapter 3, While the Woman and the Samaritans Receive Him, and Jesus Heals a Nobleman's Son in a Way that Shows the Superiority of the Word Over Signs

> 'Woman, believe Me, the hour is coming when you will neither on this mountain, nor in Jerusalem, worship the Father. You worship what you do not know; we know what we worship, for salvation is of the Jews. But the hour is coming, and now is, when the true worshipers will worship the Father in Spirit and Truth; for the Father is seeking such to worship Him. God is Spirit, and those who worship Him must worship in Spirit and Truth.' John 4:21-24.

Chapter 5

Jesus Heals a Man on the Sabbath, Leading to a Debate Over Jesus' Eternal Relation to and Equality with the Father and Why Life Must Come Through Him, Pointing to Four Divinely Authored Witnesses Testifying to His Claims

> 'Most assuredly, I say to you, he who hears My word and believes in Him who sent Me has everlasting life, and shall not come into judgment, but has passed from death into life.

Most assuredly, I say to you, the hour is coming, and now is, when the dead will hear the voice of the Son of God; and those who hear will live. For as the Father has life in Himself, so He has granted the Son to have life in Himself, and has given Him authority to execute judgment also, because He is the Son of Man.' John 5:24-27.

CHAPTER 6

Jesus Feeds the Five Thousand and Walks on the Sea, Showing His Divine Compassion and Identity, Leading Him to Teach that He is the Bread of Life, Whom People Must Feed on by Faith if they Would Live, Resulting in Many of His Disciples Leaving Him

'And Jesus said to them, "I am the bread of life. He who comes to Me shall never hunger, and he who believes in Me shall never thirst. But I said to you that you have seen Me and yet do not believe. All that the Father gives Me will come to Me, and the one who comes to Me I will by no means cast out. For I have come down from heaven, not to do My own will, but the will of Him who sent Me. This is the will of the Father who sent Me, that of all He has given Me I should lose nothing, but should raise it up at the last day. And this is the will of Him who sent Me, that everyone who sees the Son and believes in Him may have everlasting life; and I will raise him up at the last day."' John 6:35-40.

CHAPTER 7

Jesus' Brothers, the Jewish Leaders, and the People Debate Who He Is, While Jesus Points to His Mission from the Father and the Sending of the Spirit as a Fountain of Living Water, and Nicodemus is Shut Down for Asking the Jewish Leaders to Give Jesus a Fair Hearing, Leaving the Question of His Identity Hanging

'If anyone will to do His will, he shall know concerning the doctrine, whether it is from God or whether I speak on My own authority … On the last day, that great day of the feast, Jesus stood and cried out saying, "If anyone thirsts, let him come to Me and drink. He who believes in Me, as the Scripture has said, out of his heart will flow rivers of living water." But this He spoke concerning the Spirit, whom those believing in Him would receive; for the Holy Spirit was not yet given, because Jesus was not yet glorified.' John 7:17, 37-39.

Chapter 8

Jesus Answers the Question of His Divine Identity as the Great I AM, After Forgiving the Woman Caught in Adultery, Through a Dialogue with the Pharisees, Implying the Necessity of Believing in His Divine Identity Lest they will die in their sins and Continue to Do the Will of their Father the Devil, and they Seek to Stone Him When they Finally Realize What He is Saying

> 'You are from beneath; I am from above. You are of this world; I am not of this world. Therefore I said to you that you will die in your sins; for if you do not believe that I am He, you will die in your sins ... Most assuredly, I say to you, before Abraham was, I AM. Then they took up stones to throw at Him; but Jesus hid Himself and went out of the temple, going through the midst of them, and so passed by.' John 8:23-24, 58-59.

Chapter 9

Jesus Heals a Man Born Blind to Show His Divine Glory Through Healing Him, Resulting in the Excommunication of the Man from the Synagogue After he Reasons that Jesus Must be From God, Resulting in the Man Seeing and Believing Who Jesus Really is in Contrast to the Blindness of the Pharisees

> 'For Judgment I have come into this world, that those who do not see may see, and that those who see may be made blind.' John 9:39.

Chapter 10

Jesus Expands His Teaching by Showing that Those Who See Come to God Through Christ as the Door and the Good Shepherd, Whom the Sheep Alone Hear and Who Lays Down His Life for the Sheep, Resulting in Fresh Efforts to Stone Jesus

> 'Most assuredly, I say to you, I am the door of the sheep ... I am the good shepherd. The good shepherd gives his life for the sheep ... I am the good shepherd; and I know My sheep, and am known by My own. As the Father knows Me, even so I know the Father; and I lay down My life for the sheep. And other sheep I have which are not of this fold; them also I must bring, and they will hear My voice; and there will be one flock and one shepherd.' John 10:7, 11, 14-16.

Chapter 11

Jesus Raises Lazarus from the Dead in Order to Illustrate that He is the Resurrection and the Life and that Those Who Believe in

Him Share in His Resurrection, both in this Life and the Life to Come, Leading the High Priest to Prophesy Ironically that Jesus Must Die in Order to Save their Nation

> 'Jesus said to her, "I am the resurrection and the life. He who believes in Me, though He may die, he shall live. And whoever lives and believes in Me shall never die. Do you believe this?"' John 11:25-26.

Chapter 12

Mary Anoints Jesus for His Burial, Beginning to Expose Judas' Hypocrisy, While the Jews Plot to Kill both Jesus and Lazarus, Leading to Jesus' Triumphal Entry into Jerusalem to the Consternation of the Jewish Leaders, Jesus Predicting His Death on the Cross with the Father's Verbal Approval, John Explaining Why So Few Believed in Him, and Jesus Exhorting the People to Know the Father by Walking in His Light

> 'But Jesus answered and said to them, "The hour has come that the Son of Man should be glorified. Most assuredly, I say to you, unless a grain of wheat falls into the ground and dies, it remains alone; but if it dies, it produces much grain. He who loves his life will lose it, and he who hates his life in this world will keep it for eternal life. If anyone serves Me, let him follow Me; and where I am, there My servant will be also. If anyone serves Me, him My Father will honor."' John 12:23-26.

Chapter 13

Jesus Makes the Old Commandment to Love Your Neighbor New with His Own Example, Illustrating the Principle by Washing the Disciples' Feet, Satan Enters Judas When Jesus Identifies him as His Betrayer, and Jesus Predicts Peter's Denial as Well

> 'Do you know what I have done to you? You call Me Teacher and Lord, and you say well, for so I am. If I then, your Lord and Teacher, have washed your feet, you also ought to wash one another's feet. For I have given you an example, that you should do as I have done to you. Most assuredly, I say to you, a servant is not greater than his master, nor is he who is sent greater than he who sent him. If you know these things, blessed are you if you do them.' John 13:12-17.

Chapter 14

Jesus Begins His Final Discourse to His Disciples, Assuring them that He is Leaving in Order to Prepare Rooms for them in His

Father's House, Reasserting that He is the Only Way to the Father, Telling Them to Wait for the Spirit to Enable them to Testify to Him, Exhorting them to Keep His Commandments, Assuring them that the Spirit Will Make His Teaching Clear and that He Will Give them Lasting Peace

> 'Most assuredly, I say to you, he who believes in Me, the works that I do he will do also; and greater works than these he will do, because I go to My Father. And whatever you ask in My name, that I will do, that the Father may be glorified in the Son. If you ask anything in My name, I will do it ... But the Helper, the Holy Spirit, whom the Father will send in My name, He will teach you all things and bring to your remembrance all things that I said to you.' John 14:12-14, 26.

Chapter **15**

Christ Shows that His Obedient Disciples Can Bear Fruit Only in Union with Him as the True Vine, Remaining in His Love and the Father's by Keeping His Commandments, Warning them to Trust in the Spirit as the World Will Hate and Reject them

> 'I am the vine, you are the branches. He who abides in Me, and I in him, bears much fruit; for without Me you can do nothing ... But when the Helper comes, whom I send to you from the Father, the Spirit of truth who proceeds from the Father, He will testify of Me. And you also will bear witness, because you have been with Me from the beginning.' John 15:5, 26-27.

Chapter **16**

Jesus Concludes His Discourse by Saying that He Told His Disciples These Things to Prevent them From Stumbling at His Departure and their Persecution, Telling them that the Spirit Will Glorify Him Even as He Glorifies the Father, that their Sorrow Over His Departure Will Turn to Joy, and Even Though His Disciples Misunderstand Him Again, He Assures them of His Victory Over the World for Them

> 'And when He has come, He will convict the world of sin, and of righteousness, and of judgment; of sin, because they do not believe in Me; of righteousness, because I go to My Father and you see Me no more; of judgment, because the ruler of this world is judged. I still have many things to say to you, but

you cannot bear them now. However, when He, the Spirit of truth, has come, He will guide you into all truth; for He will not speak on His own authority, but whatever He hears He will speak; and He will tell you things to come. He will glorify Me, for He will take of what is Mine and declare it to you. All things that the Father has are Mine. Therefore I said that He will take of Mine and declare it to you … These things I have spoken to you, that in Me you may have peace. In the world you will have tribulation; but be of good cheer, I have overcome the world.' John 16:8-15, 33.

Chapter 17

Jesus Closes His Discourse with a High Priestly Prayer of Application to the Holy and Righteous Father for Himself, for His Disciples, and for All Who Will Believe Through their Testimony, Pleading for the Father's Glory in the Son, that the Father Would Sanctify them in the Truth (by the Spirit of Truth), and that His Followers Would be One in Him and See His Glory

'Jesus spoke these words, lifted up His eyes to heaven, and said: "Father, the hour has come. Glorify Your Son, that Your Son also may glorify You, as You have given Him authority over all flesh, that He should give eternal life to as many as You have given Him. And this is eternal life, that they may know You, the only true God, and Jesus Christ whom You have sent. I have glorified You on the earth. I have finished the work which You have given Me to do. And now, O Father, glorify Me together with Yourself, with the glory which I had with You before the world was."' John 17:1-5.

Chapter 18

Judas Betrays Jesus and is Arrested, Giving a Glimpse of His Glory as the Great I AM Again, He Comes Before the High Priest, While Peter Denies Jesus, Jesus then Contrasting His Other-Worldly Kingdom with the Kingdoms of this World Before Pilate, Jesus Taking the Place of Barabbas to Go to the Cross

'Now when He said to them, "I am He," they drew back and fell to the ground … Jesus answered, "My kingdom is not of this world. If My kingdom were of this world, My servants would fight, so that I should not be delivered to the Jews; but now My kingdom is not from here.' John 18:6, 36.

Chapter 19

The Soldiers Mock and Scourge Jesus, Pilate Shows his Loyalty to Caesar Rather than the Christ as Pilate Begins to Realize Jesus' Divine Identity, Jesus is Crucified, Commending the Care of His Mother to John, Declaring that He has Finished the Father's Work as He Dies Voluntarily, a Soldier Pierces His Side Fulfilling Scripture, and He is Buried in Joseph's Tomb

> 'Jesus answered, "You could have no power at all against Me unless it had been given you from above. Therefore the one who delivered Me to you has the greater sin" … So when Jesus had received the sour wine, He said, "It is finished!" And bowing His head, He gave up His spirit.' John 19:11, 30.

Chapter 20

On the First Day of the Week, Peter and John Investigate the Tomb After Mary Tells them that Jesus is not There, While the Resurrected Christ Reveals Himself to Mary and Predicts His Ascension, and Jesus Reveals Himself to the Disciples, Promising the Spirit's Work in Opening the Kingdom Through Proclaiming the Forgiveness of Sins, and He Assures Thomas in his Doubts, Serving as a Pattern to All Who Believe in Him Without Seeing Him.

> 'Jesus said to him, "Thomas, because you have seen Me, you have believed. Blessed are those who have not seen and yet have believed." And truly Jesus did many other signs in the presence of His disciples, which are not written in this book; but these are written that you may believe that Jesus is the Christ, the Son of God, and that believing you may have life in His name.' John 20:29-31.

Chapter 21

Jesus Appears a Third time After His Resurrection, Recalling the Original Call of His Disciples Through a Large Catch of Fish, Specifically Restoring Peter from His Threefold Denial Through His Threefold Profession of Love to Christ, While Jesus Predicts Peter's Martyrdom and John Clears Up a Misunderstanding Concerning His Own Fate, John Assuring His Readers of the Truth of His Testimony

> 'This is the disciple who testifies to these things, and wrote these things; and we know that his testimony is true. And there are also many other things that Jesus did, which if they were written one by one, I suppose that even the world itself could not contain the books that would be written. Amen.' John 21:24-25.

Acts

God fulfills the promise giving the Spirit to Christ that He might pour Him out on all flesh, as the gospel spreads from Jerusalem, to Judea, to Samaria, and to the ends of the earth

Chapter 1

Luke Continues his Gospel Account to Theophilus by Setting the Stage for the Ascended Christ's Work in Spreading the Gospel to the Nations, Showing that the Fulfillment of the Coming of the Spirit from Luke 24 is at Hand, and Restoring the Number of the Twelve Apostles for the Work by Replacing Judas

> 'And He said to them, "It is not for you to know times or seasons which the Father has put in His own authority. But you shall receive power when the Holy Spirit has come upon you; and you shall be witnesses to Me in Jerusalem, and in all Judea and Samaria, and to the end of the earth."' Acts 1:7-8.

Chapter 2

The Promised Spirit Comes, Beginning to Spread the Gospel from Jerusalem, Gifting the Disciples to Speak in Tongues as a Sign of the Gospel Going to All Peoples Reversing the Curse of Babel, and Peter's First Sermon Sets the Tone for the Resurrected Christ Being the Core of the Gospel Message, Appealing to Joel 2, Psalm 16, and Psalm 110, and Calling Believing Families from All Nations to Repent and be Baptized for the Remission of Sins

> 'Therefore being exalted to the right hand of God, and having received from the Father the promise of the Holy Spirit, He has poured out this which you now see and hear … Then Peter said to them, "Repent, and let every one of you be baptized in the name of Jesus Christ for the remission of sins; and you shall receive the gift of the Holy Spirit. For the promise is to

you and to your children, and to all who are afar off, as many as the Lord our God will call."' Acts 2:33, 38-39.

Chapter 3

Peter and John Heal a Lame Man in the Temple, Leading them to Preach that the God of the Jews has Fulfilled His Covenant in the Death and Resurrection of Jesus, Calling Unbelieving Jews to Repent and Showing that Jesus is the Great Prophet Predicted in Deuteronomy 18

> 'The God of Abraham, Isaac, and Jacob, the God of our fathers, glorified His Servant Jesus, whom you delivered up and denied in the presence of Pilate, when he was determined to let Him go. But you denied the Holy One and the Just, and asked for a murderer to be granted to you, and killed the Prince of life, whom God raised from the dead, of which we are witnesses. And in His name, through faith in His name, has made this man strong, whom you see and know. Yes, the faith which comes through Him has given him this perfect soundness in the presence of you all.' Acts 3:13-16.

Chapter 4

Peter and John are Arrested and Stand Trial Before the Jewish Leaders, Echoing the Trial of Jesus When Peter Denied Him, Peter Preaches the Christ Boldly by the Spirit, the Leaders Warn him and John not to Preach Christ, and Peter Leads in Corporate Prayer for More Boldness Through the Spirit According to the Terms of John 14, and Barnabas Joins the Church

> 'Let it be known to you all, and to all the people of Israel, that by the name of Jesus Christ of Nazareth, whom you crucified, whom God raised from the dead, by Him this man stands here before you whole. This is the "stone which was rejected by you builders, which has become the chief cornerstone." Nor is there salvation in any other, for there is no other name under heaven given among men by which we must be saved ... And when they had prayed, the place where they were assembled together was shaken; and they were all filled with the Holy Spirit, and they spoke the word of God with boldness.' Acts 4:10-12, 31.

Chapter 5

Ananias and Saphira Lie to God the Spirit, Dying as a Result and Putting the Church in Fear of God's Holiness, While the Apostles are Imprisoned for Preaching Christ and Released by an Angel, Peter Refusing to Submit to the Command to Stop Preaching, Showing that God Fulfilled His Covenant with Israel in Jesus, Resulting in Gamaliel Exhorting the Jewish Leaders that if this Work is not from God, then it Will Fizzle Out

> 'But Peter and the other apostles answered and said: "We ought to obey God rather than men. The God of our fathers raised up Jesus whom you murdered by hanging on a tree. Him God has exalted to His right hand to be Prince and Savior, to give repentance to Israel and forgiveness of sins. And we are His witnesses to these things, and so also is the Holy Spirit whom God has given to those who obey Him."' Acts 5:29-32.

Chapter **6**

The Church Appoints the First Deacons in Order to Free the Apostles to Prayer and Preaching, While the Jews Accuse Stephen from Among this Group of Blasphemy, Using Words Similar to the Condemnation of Jesus

> 'Then the word of God spread, and the number of the disciples multiplied greatly in Jerusalem, and a great many of the priests were obedient to the faith.' Acts 6:7.

Chapter **7**

The Lord Fulfills His Promise in Luke 12 by Filling Stephen with the Spirit to Testify to Christ Under Persecution, Stephen Showing that God Fulfilled His Covenant with Israel in Jesus, in Spite of the History of Rebellion Among His People, Defending himself Against Charges of Speaking Against Moses and the Temple by Showing their Fulfillment in Jesus, Rebuking his Hearers for their Hard Hearts, and Jesus Receives Stephen into Heaven Just as the Father Received Christ on the Cross, Saul Consenting to His Death

> 'When they heard these things they were cut to the heart, and they gnashed at him with their teeth. But he, being full of the Holy Spirit, gazed into heaven and saw the glory of God, and Jesus standing at the right hand of God, and said, "Look! I see the heavens opened and the Son of Man standing at the right hand of God!" Then they cried out with a loud voice, stopped their ears, and ran at him with one accord; and they cast him out of the city and stoned him. And the witnesses laid down

> their clothes at the feet of a young man named Saul. And they stoned Stephen as he was calling on God and saying, "Lord Jesus, receive my spirit."' Acts 7:54-59.

Chapter 8

Saul Persecutes the Church, Resulting in the Spread of the Gospel to Samaria According to Jesus' Instructions in Chapter 1, the Spirit Sealing the Fact by Coming on the Samaritans through Peter and John, Peter Preaches and Confronts Simon with his Hypocrisy, and the Spirit Leads Philip to Preach the Gospel to the Ethiopian Eunuch from Isaiah 53

> 'Now when the apostles who were at Jerusalem heard that Samaria had received the word of God, they sent Peter and John to them, who, when they had come down, prayed for them that they might receive the Holy Spirit. For as yet He had fallen upon none of them. They had only been baptized in the name of the Lord Jesus. Then they laid hands on them, and they received the Holy Spirit.' Acts 8:14-17.

Chapter 9

Jesus Confronts Saul on the Damascus Road, Blinding him as a Sign of his Spiritual Blindness, and Ananias Heals and Baptizes him, Signifying his Spiritual Sight, Christ Designates him as the Apostle to the Gentiles to Promote the Progress of the Gospel to the Next Stage per Chapter 1, and Saul Suffers his First Persecution for Christ's Sake

> 'But the Lord said to him, "Go for he is a chosen vessel of Mine to bear My name before Gentiles, kings, and the children of Israel. For I will show him how many things he must suffer for My name's sake."' Acts 9:15-16.

Chapter 10

God Appears to Cornelius Who Sends a Delegation to Peter to Hear the Gospel from him, While the Lord Prepares Peter for the Inclusion of the Gentiles in the Church with a Vision from Heaven, Peter then Preaching Christ in Cornelius' House, the Holy Spirit Coming Upon the Hearers and Sealing the Fact that the Gospel is Now Spreading to the Nations

> 'And He commanded us to preach to the people, and to testify that it is He who was ordained by God to be Judge of the living

and the dead. To Him all the prophets witness that, through His name, whoever believes in Him will receive remission of sins ... Then Peter answered, "Can anyone forbid water, that these should not be baptized who have received the Holy Spirit just as we have?" And he commanded them to be baptized in the name of the Lord. Then they asked him to stay a few days.' Acts 10:42-43, 47-48.

Chapter 11

Peter Responds to Jewish Complaints About his Eating with Uncircumcised Men, Recounting his Vision and the Coming of the Spirit on Cornelius' Household, While Barnabas Encourages the Church and Takes Saul with him to Antioch, the Disciples are First Called Christians, and Agabus Prophesies a Famine

'Then I remembered the word of the Lord, how He said, "John indeed baptized with water, but you shall be baptized with the Holy Spirit." If God therefore gave them the same gift as He gave us when we believed on the Lord Jesus Christ, who was I that I could withstand God? When they heard these things they became silent; and they glorified God, saying, "Then God has also granted to the Gentiles repentance to life."' Acts 11:16-18.

Chapter 12

Herod Persecutes the Church and Kills the Apostle James, Putting Peter in Prison While the Church Gathers to Pray for him, an Angel Killing Herod and Showing God's Protection of His Church, Resulting in the Further Spread of the Word, and Barnabas and Saul Take Mark with them to Preach the Gospel

'Then immediately an angel of the Lord struck him, because he did not give glory to God. And he was eaten with worms and died. But the word of God grew and multiplied.' Acts 12:23-24.

Chapter 13

The Holy Spirit Sends Saul and Barnabas on their First Missionary Journey, Paul Ironically Blinds Elymas the Sorcerer, Recalling his Own Blindness in Chapter 9, Paul Preaches to the Jews that Jesus has Fulfilled God's Covenant with Israel, Stressing Psalm 2 and Isaiah 55, and the Jews Become Jealous When Paul Begins to Preach to the Gentiles, While John Mark Leaves them

'Then Paul and Barnabas grew bold and said, "It was necessary that the word of God should be spoken to you first; but since you reject it, and judge yourselves unworthy of everlasting life, behold, we turn to the Gentiles."' Acts 13:46.

Chapter 14

Paul and Barnabas Preach at Iconium, Lystra, and Derbe, While the Lystrans Worship Paul and Barnabas as Hermes and Zeus, and Paul is Stoned in Lystra by the Jews from Antioch, yet Survives, and Paul and Barnabas Strengthen the Churches by Appointing Elders through the Election of the People to Stabilize the Churches

> 'Men, why are you doing these things? We also are men with the same nature as you, and preach to you that you should turn from these useless things to the living God, who made the heaven, the earth, the sea, and all things that are in them, who in bygone generations allowed all nations to walk in their own ways. Nevertheless He did not leave Himself without witness, in that He did good, gave us rain from heaven and fruitful seasons, filling our hearts with food and gladness.' Acts 14:15-17.

Chapter 15

A Conflict Arises When Jewish Christians Insist on Circumcising Gentile Converts, and in Response, the Apostles and Elders Hold a General Church Council at Jerusalem to Evaluate the Matter from Scripture, the Holy Spirit Speaking Through the Elders to Welcome Gentile Believers Without Circumcision, so Long as they Remain Sensitive to the Consciences of their Jewish Brethren in Other Things, Paul and Barnabas then Preaching in Antioch Before they Separate Over Whether to Take John Mark with them to Strengthen the Churches

> 'Since we have heard that some who went out from us have troubled you with words, unsettling your souls, saying, "You must be circumcised and keep the law" – to whom we gave no such commandment – it seemed good to us, being assembled with one accord, to send chosen men to you with our beloved Barnabas and Paul, men who have risked their lives for the name of the Lord Jesus Christ. We have therefore sent Judas and Silas, who will also report the same things by word of mouth. For it seemed good to the Holy Spirit, and to us, to lay upon you no greater burden than these necessary things: that you abstain from things offered to idols, from blood, from

things strangled, and from sexual immorality. If you keep yourselves from these, you do well. Farewell.' Acts 15:24-29.

Chapter 16

Paul Circumcises Timothy Due to his Jewish Heritage, While Delivering the Decrees of the Council to be Kept by All the Churches, Receiving the Spirit's Call to Preach in Macedonia, Baptizing the Households of Lydia and the Jailer at Philippi, Paul and Silas Stressing their Roman Citizenship Before the Magistrates Who Mistreated them

'And he brought them out and said, "Sirs, what must I do to be saved?" So they said, "Believe on the Lord Jesus Christ, and you will be saved, you and your household." Then they spoke the word of the Lord to him and to all who were in his house. And he took them the same hour of the night and washed their stripes. And immediately he and all his family were baptized. Now when he had brought them into his house, he set food before them; and he rejoiced, having believed in God with all his household.' Acts 16:30-34

Chapter 17

Paul Preaches at Thessalonica Where Many Come to Faith, While the Jews Retaliate by Inciting a Mob, then Many in Berea Come to Faith by Searching the Scriptures in Response to Paul's Preaching, and Paul Preaches at the Areopagus in Athens, Who Have a Mixed Reception of the Gospel Message

'Truly, these times of ignorance God overlooked, but now commands all men everywhere to repent, because He has appointed a day on which He will judge the world in righteousness by the Man whom He has ordained. He has given assurance of this to all by raising Him from the dead.' Acts 17:30-31.

Chapter 18

The Lord Sends Paul to Minister at Corinth, While the Jews Accuse him Before Gallio, After which Paul Travels Through Syria, Ephesus, Galatia, and Phrygia on his Way to Jerusalem, and Apollos, a Disciple of John the Baptist, Refutes the Jews from the Scriptures

'Now the Lord spoke to Paul in the night by a vision, "Do not be afraid, but speak, and do not keep silent; for I am with you, and no one will attack you or hurt you, for I have many people in this city."' Acts 18:9-10.

Chapter 19

Paul Baptizes Twelve Men in Ephesus Who Falsely Claimed to be Disciples of John the Baptist (like Apollos), some Jewish Exorcists are Overcome by Demons when they Seek to Imitate the Apostles, and the Craftsmen at Ephesus Start a Riot When Many Turn from Idols, Calling their Trade into Question, the Clerk Dispersing them

> 'And many who had believed came confessing and telling their deeds. Also, many of those who had practiced magic brought their books together and burned them in the sight of all. And they counted up the value of them, and it totaled fifty thousand pieces of silver. So the word of the Lord grew mightily and prevailed.' Acts 19:18-20.

Chapter 20

Paul Travels Through Greece, Macedonia, and Troas, Gathering on the First Day of the Week and Healing a Young Man Who Fell from a Window and Died During his Preaching, then Paul Calls and Exhorts the Ephesian Elders from Miletus to Take Heed to themselves and to the Church as he Prepares to be Imprisoned in Jerusalem

> 'Therefore take heed to yourselves and to all the flock, among which the Holy Spirit has made you overseers, to shepherd the church of God which He purchased with His own blood.' Acts 20:28.

Chapter 21

Paul Continues to Travel to Jerusalem, Agabus Warning About his Impending Imprisonment, the Leaders in Jerusalem Urging Paul to Make Peace with the Jews when he Arrives, yet Paul is Beaten by an Angry Mob and Imprisoned by a Roman Commander, and Paul Asks if he can Address the Crowd

> 'Then Paul answered, "What do you mean by weeping and breaking my heart? For I am ready not only to be bound, but also to die at Jerusalem for the name of the Lord Jesus."' Acts 21:13.

Chapter 22

Paul Preaches to the Jews in Hebrew, Recounting his Former Life and Conversion to Christ, and the Mob Begins to Riot Again

When he Mentions his Commission to the Gentiles, and Paul Appeals to his Roman Citizenship as the Centurion Prepares to Question him

> 'And when the blood of Your martyr Stephen was shed, I also was standing by consenting to his death, and guarding the clothes of those who were killing him. Then He said to me, "Depart, for I will send you far from here to the Gentiles."' Acts 22:20-21.

Chapter 23

Paul Appears Before the Chief Priests and the Jewish Council, Playing the Pharisees and Sadducees Against Each Other Over the Resurrection of the Dead, and Christ Strengthens Paul in a Vision While the Jews Plot to Kill him, Paul's Nephew Intervening with the Centurion, who Sends Paul Caesarea to Stand Before Felix

> 'But the following night the Lord stood by him and said, "Be of good cheer, Paul; for as you have testified for Me in Jerusalem, you must also bear witness at Rome."' Acts 23:11.

Chapter 24

Tertullus the Orator Flatters Felix, Accusing Paul of Disturbing the Peace that he Created, Paul Defends his Hope in the Resurrection of the Dead in Christ, and Paul Preaches the Gospel to Felix

> 'And after some days when Felix came with his wife Drusilla, who was Jewish, he sent for Paul and heard him concerning the faith in Christ. Now as he reasoned about righteousness, self-control, and the judgment to come, Felix was afraid and answered, "Go away for now; when I have a convenient time I will call for you." Meanwhile he also hoped that money would be given him by Paul, that he might release him. Therefore he sent for him more often and conversed with him.' Acts 24:24-26.

Chapter 25

Paul Appeals to Caesar in Order to Preach the Gospel in Rome, According to Christ's Promise in Chapter 23, While King Agrippa and Bernice Prepare to Hear Paul

> 'So Paul said, "I stand at Caesar's judgment seat, where I ought to be judged. To the Jews I have done no wrong, as you very well know. For if I am an offender, or have committed anything

deserving of death, I do not object to dying; but if there is nothing in these things of which these men accuse me, no one can deliver me to them. I appeal to Caesar."' Acts 25:10-11.

CHAPTER **26**

Paul Preaches Before Agrippa, Affirming that Jesus Fulfilled God's Covenant with Israel, Stressing the Resurrection, While Paul Recounts his Conversion to Christ Again, Including his Mission to Jews and Gentiles, and Paul Calls Agrippa to Faith in Christ

'I will deliver you from the Jewish people, as well as from the Gentiles, to whom I now send you, to open their eyes, in order to turn them from darkness to light, and from the power of Satan to God, that they may receive forgiveness of sins and an inheritance among those who are sanctified by faith in Me.' Acts 26:17-18.

CHAPTER **27**

Paul is Sent to Italy, While Paul Warns the Sailors of Impending Shipwreck, yet the Sailors Press on While the Lord Answers Paul's Prayers to Save the Men on the Ship, so Long as they Stay on the Ship, and the Soldiers Spare Paul and the Other Prisoners When they are Shipwrecked on Malta, Jesus Preserving Paul to Preach the Gospel in Rome

'And the soldiers' plan was to kill the prisoners, lest any of them should swim away and escape. But the centurion, wanting to save Paul, kept them from their purpose, and commanded that those who could swim should jump overboard first and get to land, and the rest, some on boards and some on parts of the ship. And so it was that they all escaped safely to land.' Acts 27:42-44.

CHAPTER **28**

Paul is bit by a Serpent and the Natives Conclude that he is a god When he Does not Die, and Paul Heals Many, Confirming his Apostolic Call, Paul then Moving to Rome and Gathering the Jews to Preach the Gospel to them, Summarizing the Theme of Acts and Setting the Stage for the Church's Ongoing Mission When the Jews are Divided in their Response to Paul

'So when they did not agree among themselves, they departed after Paul and said one word: "The Holy Spirit spoke rightly through Isaiah the prophet to our fathers ... Therefore let it be known to you that the salvation of God has been sent to the Gentiles, and they will hear it!" And when he had said these words, the Jews departed and had a great dispute among themselves. Then Paul dwelt two whole years in his own rented house, and received all who came to him, preaching the kingdom of God and teaching the things which concern the Lord Jesus Christ with all confidence, no one forbidding him.' Acts 28:25, 28-31.

Romans

God summarizes the core of the gospel of His Son through Paul, moving from God's judgment against sin, through Christ's atoning work and justification by faith alone, pressing sanctification in union with Christ, exalting God for His promises of glorification, explaining why so few Jews believed, and exhorting the church to pursue godliness

Chapter **1**

Paul Proclaims his Readiness to Preach the Gospel to the Roman Christians without Shame, Identifying Jesus as the Son of David, Whom the Spirit Declared to be the Son of God by His Resurrection, Setting forth the Gospel as Displaying God's Righteousness, Remedying God's Wrath, which is Presently Revealed in What People Think and How they Live

> 'For I am not ashamed of the gospel of Christ, for it is the power of God to salvation for everyone who believes, for the Jew first and also for the Greek. For in it the righteousness of God is revealed from faith to faith, as it is written, "The just shall live by faith." For the wrath of God is revealed from heaven against all ungodliness and unrighteousness of men, who suppress the truth in unrighteousness ... And even as they did not like to retain God in their knowledge, God gave them over to a debased mind, to do those things which are not fitting.' Rom. 1:16-18, 28.

Chapter **2**

Paul Continues to set the Stage for the Gospel by Convincing Jews as Well as Greeks that they are Under Sin, Showing that True Circumcision Lies in the Heart, Alluding to OT Teaching from Texts like Deuteronomy 10 and 30 and Jeremiah 4

> 'For circumcision is indeed profitable if you keep the law; but if you are a breaker of the law, your circumcision has become uncircumcision. Therefore if an uncircumcised man keeps the righteous requirements of the law, will not his uncircumcision be counted circumcision? And will not the physically uncircumcised, if he fulfills the law, judge you how, even with your written code and circumcision, are a transgressor of the law? For he is not a Jew who is one outwardly, nor is circumcision that which is outward in the flesh; but he is a Jew who is one inwardly; and circumcision is that of the heart, in the Spirit, not in the letter; whose praise is not from men but from God.' Rom. 2:25-29.

Chapter 3

Paul Concludes his Argument for the Conviction of Sin, Noting the Profit of Being a Circumcised Jew in Having the Oracles of God, yet Concluding that All Have Sinned, Requiring Justification by Faith in Christ, Who Atoned for Sin and Satisfied God's Righteousness, and Receiving Him by Faith, Without the Deeds of the Law

> 'For all have sinned and fall short of the glory of God, being justified freely by His grace through Redemption that is in Christ Jesus, whom God set forth as a propitiation by His blood, through faith, to demonstrate His righteousness, because in His forbearance God had passed over the sins that were previously committed, to demonstrate at the present time His righteousness, that He might be just and the justifier of the one who has faith in Christ ... Therefore we conclude that a man is justified by faith apart from the deeds of the law.' Rom. 3:23-26, 28.

Chapter 4

Paul Expands Justification by Faith in Christ Alone by Citing Examples from Abraham (Genesis 15) and David (Psalm 32), Showing that All who Believe are Abraham's True Seed

> 'And he received the sign of circumcision, a seal of the righteousness of the faith which he had while still uncircumcised, that he might be the father of all those who believe, though they are uncircumcised, that righteousness might be imputed to them also ... who was delivered up because of our offenses, and was raised because of our justification.' Rom. 4:11, 25.

Chapter 5

After Extolling the Peace that Comes Through Communion with God through His Son and by His Spirit, Paul Explains How God Could Impute Christ's Righteousness to us by Explaining His Covenantal Role as the Second Adam

> 'Therefore, having been justified by faith, we have peace with God through our Lord Jesus Christ, through whom also we have access by faith into this grace in which we stand, and rejoice in hope of the glory of God. And not only that, but we also glory in tribulations, knowing that tribulation produces perseverance; and perseverance, character; and character, hope. Now hope does not disappoint, because the love of God has been poured out in our hearts by the Holy Spirit who was given us ... For as by one man's disobedience many were made sinners, so also by one Man's obedience many will be made righteous.' Rom. 5:1-5, 19.

Chapter 6

Paul Shows that Union with Christ by Faith Does not Mean that Those Justified Should Live in Sin, but he Shows the Implications of Union with Christ in our Sanctification, our Baptism Signifying Union with Him in His Death and Resurrection

> 'Therefore we were buried with Him through baptism into death, that just as Christ was raised from the dead by the glory of the Father, even so we also should walk in newness of life ... For the wages of sin is death, but the gift of God is eternal life in Christ Jesus our Lord.' Rom. 6:4, 23.

Chapter 7

Paul Concludes his Teaching on Sanctification Through Union with Christ with an Analogy to Marriage, Shifting to a Pastoral Question About the Goodness of the Law in Spite of our Sin, and how Believers Retain Confidence Before God in Spite of their Indwelling Sin

> 'I find then a law, that evil is present with me, the one who wills to do good. For I delight in the law of God according to the inward man. But I see another law in my members, warring against the law of my mind, and bringing me into captivity to the law of sin which is in my members. O wretched man that I am! Who will deliver me from this body of death? I thank

> God – through Jesus Christ our Lord! So then, with the mind I myself serve the law of God, but with my flesh the law of sin.' Rom. 7:21-25.

Chapter 8

Paul Concludes that there is no Condemnation for Those United to Christ, Who Walk by the Spirit, and who Hope in God as their Adopting Father, Showing that the Spirit Helps us Pray to Endure Suffering, as we Look to the Final Fruits of Adoption in the Resurrection of our Bodies and of the World, Being Confident that Nothing Can Separate us from God's Love in Christ Along the Way to Glory

> 'There is therefore now no condemnation to those who are in Christ Jesus, who do not walk according to the flesh, but according to the Spirit. For the law of the Spirit of life in Christ Jesus has made me free from the law of sin and death. For what the law could not do in that it was weak through our flesh, God did by sending His own Son in the likeness of sinful flesh, on account of sin: He condemned sin in the flesh, that the righteous requirement of the law might be fulfilled in us who do not walk according to the flesh but according to the Spirit ... And we know that all things work together for good to those who love God, to those who are called according to His purpose.' Rom. 8:1-4, 28.

Chapter 9

Paul Abruptly Transitions from Great Joy Over the Gospel to Great Sorrow Over so Many Unbelieving Jews, Explaining Why so Few of them Believed in Christ in Three Parts, the First Argument Being God's Purpose in Election

> 'But it is not that the word of God has taken no effect. For they are not all Israel who are of Israel, nor are they all children because they are the seed of Abraham; but "In Isaac shall your seed be called." That is, those who are the children of the flesh, these are not the children of God; but the children of the promise are counted as the seed ... Therefore He has mercy on whom He wills, and whom He wills He hardens.' Rom. 9:6-8, 18.

Chapter 10

Paul's Second Argument Why so Many Jews did not Believe is that they Were Responsible to Receive Christ's Voice in the Gospel, but they Refused Him

'How then shall they call on Him in whom they have not believed? And how shall they believe in Him of whom they have not heard? And how shall they hear without a preacher? And how shall they preach unless they are sent? As it is written, ""How beautiful are the feet of those who preach the gospel of peace, who bring glad tidings of good things!"" But they have not all obeyed the gospel. For Isaiah says, ""LORD, who has believed our report?"" So then faith comes by hearing, and hearing by the word of God.' Rom. 10:14-17.

Chapter 11
Paul's Third and Final Argument Why so Many Jews Rejected Christ is that God used their Fall to Bring in the Gentiles, Which in Turn Will Result in a Future Calling of the Jews, Leading Paul to Praise God for His Unsearchable Wisdom

'I say then, have they stumbled that they should fall? Certainly not! But through their fall, to provoke them to jealousy, salvation has come to the Gentiles. Now if their fall is riches for the world, and their failure riches for the Gentiles, how much more their fullness! ... Oh, the depth of the riches both of the wisdom and knowledge of God! How unsearchable are His judgments and His ways past finding out! "For who has known the mind of the LORD? Or who has become His counsellor? Or who has first given to Him and it shall be repaid to him?" For of Him and through Him and to Him are all things, to whom be glory forever. Amen.' Rom. 11:11-12, 33-36.

Chapter 12
Paul Stresses Our Response to this Glorious Gospel for the Remainder of the Book, Beginning with the Need to Serve One Another in the Church, which is Christ's Body, with Gifts and Graces

'I beseech you therefore, brethren, by the mercies of God, that you present your bodies a living sacrifice, holy, acceptable to God, which is your reasonable service. And do not be conformed to this world, but be transformed by the renewing of your mind, that you may prove what is that good and acceptable and perfect will of God. For I say, through the grace given to me, to everyone who is among you, not to think of himself more highly than he ought to think, but to think soberly, as God has dealt to each one a measure of faith.' Rom. 12:1-3.

Chapter 13

Paul Extends Christian Holiness into Submission to Civil Authority, Fulfilling the Law Through Love, and Putting on Christ as we Anticipate His Return, Building on his Teaching from Chapters 6-7

> 'And do this, knowing the time, that now it is high time to awake out of sleep; for now our salvation is nearer than when we first believed. The night is far spent, the day is at hand. Therefore let us cast off the works of darkness, and let us put on the armor of light. Let us walk properly, as in the day, not in revelry and drunkenness, not in lewdness and lust, not in strife and envy. But put on the Lord Jesus Christ, and make no provision for the flesh, to fulfill its lusts.' Rom. 13:11-14.

Chapter 14

Paul Continues to Press for Holiness in How Jews and Gentiles Address Difference of Conscience in the Church, Expanding the Teaching of Acts 15 into Holy Days and Food Restrictions

> 'Therefore let us pursue the things which make for peace and the things by which one may edify another ... But he who doubts is condemned if he eats, because he does not eat from faith; for whatever is not of faith is sin.' Rom. 14:19, 23.

Chapter 15

Paul Solidifies his Instructions from the Preceding Chapter by Pointing to Christ's Example in Fulfilling God's Covenant as God's Servant, Shifting to his Concluding Remarks About Christ Sending him to the Gentiles to Bring them to God by the Spirit, Noting his Plans to Visit Rome and Asking for their Prayers

> 'Therefore receive one another, just as Christ also received us, to the glory of God. Now I say that Jesus Christ has become a servant to the circumcision for the truth of God, to confirm the promises made to the fathers ... that I might be a minister of Jesus Christ to the Gentiles, ministering the gospel of God, that the offering of the Gentiles might be acceptable, sanctified by the Holy Spirit.' Rom. 15:7-8, 16.

Chapter 16

Paul Closes the Book by Greeting Many Saints by Name, Exhorting them to Avoid Divisive Persons and Encouraging them that

God will Crush Satan Under their Feet Shortly, Ending with a Doxology to God for His Glorious Gospel

> 'For those who are such do not serve our Lord Jesus Christ, but their own belly, and by smooth words and flattering speech deceive the hearts of the simple ... Now to Him who is able to establish you according to my gospel and the preaching of Jesus Christ, according to the revelation of the mystery kept secret since the world began but now made manifest, and by the prophetic Scriptures made known to all nations, according to the commandment of the everlasting God, for obedience to the faith – to God, alone wise, be glory through Jesus Christ forever. Amen.' Rom. 16:18, 25-27.

1 Corinthians

God exhorts the church to walk according to His wisdom in Christ, taught by the Spirit, to remedy the devastating effects of their worldly wisdom

Chapter 1

Paul Recounts his Apostolic Call and Thanks God for the Corinthian Church, Immediately Addressing their Divisions, and Setting forth Christ as the Wisdom of God to Combat their Worldly Thinking, which Becomes the Key to Remedying Every Problem Facing their Church

> 'But of Him you are in Christ Jesus, who became for us wisdom from God – and righteousness and sanctification and redemption – that, as it is written, "He who glories, let him glory in the LORD."' 1 Cor. 1:30 31.

Chapter 2

Paul Explains that he Preached Christ Alone as the Wisdom and Power of God by the Holy Spirit, so that their Faith Would not Rest in the Wisdom of Men but in the Power of God, Reminding them that they Could not Know the Things that the Spirit Alone Could Reveal About Christ Unless the Spirit had Taught them and Enabled them to Receive it

> 'But we speak the wisdom of God in a mystery, the hidden wisdom which God ordained before the ages for our glory, which none of the rulers of this age knew; for had they known, they would not have crucified the Lord of glory. But as it is written, "Eye has not seen, nor ear heard, nor have entered into the heart of man the things which God has prepared for those who love Him." But God has revealed them to us through His

> Spirit. For the Spirit searches all things, yes, the deep things of God.' 1 Cor. 2:7-10.

Chapter 3

Paul Illustrates Why their Divisions Display Worldly Wisdom Rather than the Wisdom of God in Christ, Pointing out that Ministers are Only Servants of Christ to the Church, Warning them Against Dividing the Church, which is the Temple of the Holy Spirit

> 'Do you not know that you are the temple of God and that the Spirit of God dwells in you? If anyone defiles the temple of God, God will destroy him. For the temple of God is holy, which temple you are.' 1 Cor. 3:16.

Chapter 4

Paul Finalizes his Teaching on their Divisions, Rebuking them with Sarcasm to Shock them out of their Worldly Thinking, Reminding them of his Pastoral Care for them and Urging them to Repent Before he Visits them

> 'For I know nothing against myself, yet I am not justified by this; but He who judges me is the Lord. Therefore judge nothing before the time, until the Lord comes, who will both bring to light the hidden things of darkness and reveal the counsels of the hearts. Then each one's praise will come from God.' 1 Cor. 4:4-5.

Chapter 5

Paul Next Shows the Effects of the Worldly Wisdom of the Corinthians on Church Discipline, in their Failure to Recognize that Failing to Excommunicate an Incestuous man Affects the Whole Church

> 'Your glorying is not good. Do you not know that a little leaven leavens the whole lump? Therefore purge out the old leaven, that you may be a new lump, since you truly are unleavened. For indeed Christ, our Passover, was sacrificed for us. Therefore let us keep the feast, not with old leaven, not with the leaven of malice and wickedness, but with the unleavened bread of sincerity and truth.' 1 Cor. 5:6-8.

Chapter 6

Paul Builds on the Theme of their Failure, through Worldly Wisdom, to Judge those Among them, by Rebuking their Lawsuits

Against One Another Outside of the Church, Reminding them that they Were Washed and Sanctified by Christ and the Spirit of God, and that they Should Flee Sexual Immorality Because their Bodies are Temples of the Holy Spirit

> 'And such were some of you, but you were washed, but you were sanctified, but you were justified, in the name of the Lord Jesus and by the Spirit of our God ... Or do you not know that your body is the temple of the Holy Spirit who is in you, whom you have from God, and you are not your own? For you were bought at a price; therefore glorify God in your body and in your spirit, which are God's.' 1 Cor. 6:11, 19-20.

Chapter 7

Paul Shifts Attention to Questions that they Sent him About Marriage, Showing that Marriage is the Proper Outlet for Sexual Desire, Repeating Christ's Teaching About Marriage and Divorce, and Adding his Own Counsel Regarding the Advantages of Singleness Under Persecution

> 'You were bought at a price; do not become slaves of men. Brethren, let each one of you remain with God in that state in which he was called.' 1 Cor. 7:23-24.

Chapter 8

Paul Shifts Again to a Three Chapter Discussion about Asserting One's Rights in Relation to Eating Food Offered to Idols, Showing that Idols are Nothing and that Food is Food, but that they Should Avoid Leading the Weak into Idolatry, Pushing Towards the Wisdom of God in Christ as the Path Forward

> 'Yet for us there is one God, the Father, of whom are all things, and we for Him; and one Lord Jesus Christ, through whom are all things, and through whom we live ... And because of your knowledge shall the weak brother perish, for whom Christ died? But when you thus sin against the brethren, and wound their weak conscience, you sin against Christ.' 1 Cor. 8:6, 11-12.

Chapter 9

Paul Exemplifies his Principles by Showing that he and the Other Apostles did not Insist on their Rights, Setting Forth a Principle that Christians Should Become All Things to All Men to Save Some

> 'For though I am free from all men, I have made myself a servant to all, that I might win the more; and to the Jews I became as a Jew, that I might win Jews; to those who are under the law, as under the law, that I might win those who are under the law; to those who are without law, as without law (not being without law toward God, but under law toward Christ), that I might win those who are without law; to the weak I became as weak, that I might win the weak. I have become all things to all men, that I might by all means save some.' 1 Cor. 9:19-22.

Chapter **10**

Paul Concludes his Argument About Food Offered to Idols by Warning Against Idolatry from Old Testament Examples and from the Fellowship they Have with Christ and One Another in the Lord's Supper, Urging them to Eat and Drink to God's Glory

> 'No temptation has overtaken you except such as is common to man; but God is faithful, who will not allow you to be tempted beyond what you are able, but with the temptation will also make a way of escape, that you may be able to bear it … The cup of blessing which we bless, is it not the communion of the blood of Christ? The bread which we break, is it not the communion of the body of Christ? For we, though many, are one bread and one body; for we all partake of that one bread … Therefore whether you eat or drink, or whatever you do, do all to the glory of God.' 1 Cor. 10:13, 16-17, 31.

Chapter **11**

Paul Shifts Attention for the Next Four Chapters to Evidences of their Worldly Wisdom in Public Worship, Beginning with their Confusion Over the Roles of Men and Women in the Church and their Abuses of One Another at the Lord's Supper, Showing the Implications of their Communion with one Another in Christ

> 'Imitate me, just as I also imitate Christ … Therefore whoever eats this bread or drinks this cup of the Lord in an unworthy manner will be guilty of the body and blood of the Lord. But let a man examine himself, and so let him eat of the bread and drink of the cup. For he who eats and drinks in an unworthy manner eats and drinks judgment to himself, not discerning the Lord's body. For this reason many are weak and sick among you, and many sleep. For if we would judge

ourselves, we would not be judged. But when we are judged, we are chastened by the Lord, that we may not be condemned with the world.' 1 Cor. 11:1, 27-32.

Chapter 12

Paul Stresses the Proper Use of the Extraordinary Gifts of the Spirit in Public Worship, Showing that the Wisdom of God in Christ Unites them in Gifts, While their Worldly Wisdom Divided them

> 'For as the body is one and has many members, but all the members of that one body, being many, are one body, so also is Christ. For by one Spirit we were all baptized into one body – whether Jews or Greeks, whether slaves or free – and have all been made to drink into one Spirit.' 1 Cor. 12:12-13.

Chapter 13

Paul Next Prioritizes Love, in Order to Show that the Wisdom of God in Christ Leads them to Prioritize Graces Over Gifts, Showing that their Worldly Wisdom has Made them Childish

> 'When I was a child, I spoke as a child, I understood as a child, I thought as a child; but when I became a man, I put away childish things. For now we see in a mirror dimly, but then face to face. Now I know in part, but then I shall know just as I also am known. And now abide faith, hope, and love, these three; but the greatest of these is love.' 1 Cor. 13:11-13.

Chapter 14

Paul Concludes his Critique of their Practices in Public Worship, Laying Down Principles of how the Wisdom of God in Christ Should Lead them to do All Things Decently and in Order, Preferring Others Above themselves

> 'Even so you, since you are zealous for spiritual gifts, let it be for the edification of the church that you seek to excel … Brethren, do not be children in understanding; however, in malice be babes, but in understanding be mature … Let all things be done decently and in order.' 1 Cor. 14:12, 20, 40.

Chapter 15

Paul Reiterates the Central Importance of Christ's Resurrection for our Salvation, in the Face of Some Who Questioned the

Resurrection from the Dead, Cautioning the Church Against Speculation, and Urging them to Perseverance in Hope

> 'For if the dead do not rise, then Christ is not risen. And if Christ is not risen, your faith is futile; you are still in your sins! ... For since by man came death, by Man also came the resurrection of the dead. For as in Adam all die, even so in Christ all shall be made alive ... Therefore, my beloved brethren, be steadfast, immovable, always abounding in the work of the Lord, knowing that your labor is not in vain in the Lord.' 1 Cor. 15:16-17, 21-22, 58.

Chapter **16**

Paul Gives Final Instructions for the Collection Every First Day of the Week, Detailing his Travel Plans, Giving a Final Exhortation Towards Faith and Love, Closing with God's Benediction to Those who Love Christ

> 'If anyone does not love the Lord Jesus Christ, let him be accursed. O Lord, come! The grace of the Lord Jesus Christ be with you. My love be with you all in Christ Jesus. Amen.' 1 Cor. 16:22-23.

2 Corinthians

God establishes Paul's apostleship against false apostles, in order to uphold the integrity of the gospel and the ministry of the Spirit under the new covenant

Chapter 1

Paul Begins Implicitly to Defend his Integrity and Apostolic Call Against Detractors, Recounting the Purposes of his Affliction and his Trustworthiness, Even Though his Plans to go to Corinth Were Hindered, Stressing God's Comforting Work in the Church, Through His Son, and by His Spirit

> 'Blessed be the God and Father of our Lord Jesus Christ, the Father of mercies and God of all comfort, who comforts us in all our tribulation, that we may be able to comfort those who are in any trouble, with the comfort with which we ourselves are comforted by God. For as the sufferings of Christ abound in us, so our consolation also abounds through Christ ... For all the promises of God in Him are Yes, and in Him Amen, to the glory of God through us. Now He who establishes us with you in Christ and has anointed us is God, who has also sealed us and given us the Spirit in our hearts as a guarantee.' 2 Cor. 1:3-5, 20-21.

Chapter 2

Paul Further Explains that he did not Visit them Because he Gave them Time to Restore a Repentant Excommunicated Brother, Contrasting his Sincere Preaching with his Opponents, who Preach for Financial Gain, Noting his own Insufficiency for the Task

> 'Lest Satan should take advantage of us; for we are not ignorant of his devices ... Now thanks be to God who always leads us

> in triumph in Christ, and through us diffuses the fragrance of His knowledge in every place. For we are to God the fragrance of Christ among those who are being saved and among those who are perishing. To the one we are the aroma of death leading to death, and to the other the aroma of life leading to life. And who is sufficient for these things?' 2 Cor. 2:11, 14-16.

Chapter 3
Contrasting his Ministry with False Teachers, who Commend themselves, Paul Notes that God Made him Sufficient to be a Minister of the New Covenant, Which is a Ministry of the Spirit's Power

> 'And we have such trust through Christ toward God. Not that we are sufficient of ourselves to think of anything as being from ourselves, but our sufficiency is from God, who also made us sufficient as ministers of the new covenant, not of the letter but of the Spirit; for the letter kills, but the Spirit gives life ... But we all, with unveiled face, beholding as in a mirror the glory of the Lord, are being transformed into the same image from glory to glory, just as by the Spirit of the Lord.' 2 Cor. 3:4-6, 18.

Chapter 4
Paul's True Commendation to the Church is not by Letter, Like the False Teachers, but in the Conscience of Believers who Witness the Treasure of the Gospel in him Under his Affliction, Urging them to Follow his Example in Looking Towards an Eternal Weight of Glory

> 'For we do not preach ourselves, but Christ Jesus the Lord, and ourselves your bondservants for Jesus' sake. For it is the God who commanded light to shine out of darkness, who has shone in our hearts to give the light of the glory of God in the face of Jesus Christ. But we have this treasure in earthen vessels, that the excellence of the power may be of God and not of us.' 2 Cor. 4:5-7.

Chapter 5
Paul Stresses the Fact that he Conducted his Ministry Looking to the Resurrection, and Being Willing to Lose his Life to be with Christ, Refusing to Commend himself as the False Teachers do, but Ministering in the Fear of the Lord as an Ambassador of

God, through Whom God Pleads with Men to be Reconciled to Himself in Christ

> 'Knowing, therefore, the terror[1] of the Lord, we persuade men; but we are well known to God, and I also trust are well known in your consciences ... Now then, we are ambassadors for Christ, as though God were pleading through us: we implore you on Christ's behalf, be reconciled to God. For He made Him who knew no sin to be sin for us, that we might become the righteousness of God in Him.' 2 Cor. 5:11, 20-21.

Chapter 6

After Driving Home the Urgency of Hearing God's Call, Paul Commends his Ministry Through Sincerity and Suffering for Christ, Urging the Corinthians not to Have Fellowship with Ungodly False Teachers

> 'We give no offense in anything, that our ministry may not be blamed. But in all things we commend ourselves as ministers of God: in much patience, in tribulations, in needs, in distresses ... Do not be unequally yoked together with unbelievers. For what fellowship has light with darkness? And what accord has Christ with Belial? And what agreement has the temple of God with idols? For you are the temple of the living God.' 2 Cor. 6:3, 14-16a.

Chapter 7

Paul Urges Holiness and Open-Heartedness Between himself and the Church, Expressing his Concerns Over their Genuine Repentance, yet Being Encouraged by Titus' Testimony to the Marks of their Sincerity

> 'Therefore having these promises, beloved, let us cleanse ourselves from all filthiness of the flesh and spirit, perfecting holiness in the fear of God.' 2 Cor. 7:1.

Chapter 8

Interjecting Instructions About Contributing to a Gift to Supply the Needs of Believers in Need, Pressing the Examples of the Macedonians and of Christ Giving Himself for their Salvation, in Order to Receive the Delegates and to be Ready to Contribute Freely

---

1. 'Fear' is a better translation in this case.

'I speak not by commandment, but I am testing the sincerity of your love by the diligence of others. For you know the grace of our Lord Jesus Christ, that though He was rich, yet for your sakes He became poor, that you through His poverty might become rich.' 2 Cor. 8:8-9.

Chapter 9

Paul Reminds them of their Former Promises to Give, Encouraging then to Give Cheerfully, Being Confident that God will Supply both their Physical and Spiritual Needs, and that their Participation will Strengthen the Fellowship of the Church, and Reflect God's Character in Giving Christ

'Now may He who supplies seed to the sower, and bread for food, supply and multiply the seed you have sown and increase the fruits of your righteousness, while you are enriched in everything for all liberality, which causes thanksgiving through us to God … Thanks be to God for His indescribable gift!.' 2 Cor. 9:10-11, 15.

Chapter 10

Paul Shifts Towards Attacking the Problem of False Teacher/ Apostles More Directly, Urging the Use of Spiritual Weapons for Spiritual Warfare in Doing so, Appealing to God's Commendation of his own Apostolic Authority, Against Accusations that his Bodily Presence and Speech are Contemptible

'For we dare not class ourselves or compare ourselves with those who commend themselves. But they, measuring themselves by themselves, and comparing themselves among themselves, are not wise … For not he who commends himself is approved, but whom the Lord commends.' 2 Cor. 10:12, 18.

Chapter 11

Paul is Worried that the Corinthians are too Ready to Accept a Different Gospel and Another Jesus than What he Preached to them, Reluctantly Contrasting his Apostolic Credentials to that of the False Teachers, who, Like Satan, Appear as Ministers of Light

'But what I do, I will also continue to do, that I may cut off the opportunity from those who desire an opportunity to be regarded just as we are in the things of which they boast. For such are false apostles, deceitful workers, transforming themselves into apostles of Christ. And no wonder! For Satan himself transforms himself into an angel of light. Therefore it is no great thing if his ministers also transform themselves into ministers of righteousness, whose end will be according to their works.' 2 Cor. 11:12-15.

CHAPTER **12**

Paul Establishes his Apostolic Credentials with his Visions of the Third Heaven, Accompanied by a Thorn in the Flesh to Humble him, Pointing to the Signs of an Apostle Displayed in his Ministry, and Contrasting his Love for the Church with the Abuses of the False Apostles

'And He said to me, 'My grace is sufficient for you, for My strength is made perfect in weakness.' Therefore most gladly I will rather boast in my infirmities, that the power of Christ may rest upon me ... Truly the signs of an apostle were accomplished among you with all perseverance, in signs and wonders and mighty deeds ... And I will very gladly spend and be spent for your souls; though the more abundantly I love you, the less I am loved.' 2 Cor. 12:9, 12, 15.

CHAPTER **13**

Paul Warns the Corinthians to be Ready for his Third Visit, Re-affirming his Care for the Church as he Exhorts them to Examine their Ways, Closing with Greetings and a Trinitarian Benediction

'For we are glad when we are weak and you are strong. And this also we pray, that you may be made complete. Therefore I write these things being absent, lest being present I should use sharpness, according to the authority which the Lord has given me for edification and not for destruction ... The grace of the Lord Jesus Christ, and the love of God, and the communion of the Holy Spirit be with you all. Amen.' 2 Cor. 13:9-10, 14.

Galatians

God stresses the necessity of justification by faith alone in Christ alone against false Jewish teaching, directing the believers to walk in the Spirit rather than the works of the flesh

Chapter 1

Paul Stresses his Apostolic Call, to Prevent the Galatians from Turning Aside to Another Gospel, Stressing the Divine Origin of his Gospel

> 'But even if we, or an angel from heaven, preach any other gospel to you than what we have preached to you, let him be accursed. As we have said before, so now I say again, if anyone preaches any other gospel to you than what you have received, let him be accursed. For do I now persuade men, or God? Or do I seek to please men? For if I still pleased men, I would not be a bondservant of Christ.' Gal. 1:8-10.

Chapter 2

Continuing to Recount his Apostolic Call, Paul Emphasizes the Fact that Christ Called him Independently of the Other Apostles, Hinting at the Problem at Hand When he Rebuked Peter's Hypocritical Interaction with Gentiles in Light of Jewish Pressure, Pressing the Galatians to Look to the Righteousness that Comes Through Faith in Christ Rather than Through the Law

> 'I have been crucified with Christ; it is no longer I who live, but Christ lives in me; and the life which I now live in the flesh I live by faith in the Son of God, who loved me and gave Himself for me. I do not set aside the grace of God; for if righteousness comes through the law, then Christ died in vain.' Gal. 2:20-21.

Chapter 3

Pushing to the Heart of the Problem, Paul Defends Justification Through Faith in Christ in Fulfilment of God's Covenant with

Abraham, Explaining that God Gave the Law to Reveal Sin and to Drive People to Sonship Through Faith in Christ

> 'Christ redeemed us from the curse of the law, having become a curse for us (for it is written, "Cursed is everyone who hangs on a tree"), that the blessing of Abraham might come upon the Gentiles in Christ Jesus, that we might receive the promise of the Spirit through faith … For you are all sons of God through faith in Christ Jesus. For as many of you as were baptized into Christ have put on Christ. There is neither Jew nor Greek, there is neither slave nor free, there is neither male nor female; for you are all one in Christ Jesus. And if you are Christ's, then you are Abraham's seed, and heirs according to the promise.' Gal. 3:13-14, 26-29.

Chapter **4**

Paul Shows that God Sent His Son so that we Might Receive the Spirit of Adoption, as he Expresses his Fears of their Caving into Jewish Pressures to Compromise the Gospel, Illustrating Two Opposing Ways of Pleasing God Through an Allegory of Hagar and Sarah

> 'But when the fullness of time had come, God sent forth His Son, born of a woman, born under the law, to redeem those who were under the law that we might receive the adoption as sons. And because you are sons, God has sent forth the Spirit of His Son into your hearts, crying out, "Abba, Father!" Therefore you are no longer a slave, but a son, and if a son, then an heir of God through Christ.' Gal. 4:4-7.

Chapter **5**

Paul Presses the Galatians to Stand Fast in their Liberty in Christ, Refusing Circumcision and Shunning False Teachers, Exhorting them to Put Off the Works of the Flesh and to Bear the Fruit of the Spirit in Christ

> 'Indeed I, Paul, say to you that if you become circumcised, Christ will profit you nothing … But the fruit of the Spirit is love, joy, peace, longsuffering, kindness, goodness, faithfulness, gentleness, self-control. Against such there is no law. And those who are Christ's have crucified the flesh with its passions and desires. Let us not become conceited, provoking one another, envying one another.' Gal. 5:2, 22-26.

CHAPTER 6

Paul Encourages them to Bear One Another's Burdens, to Promote the Work of Sound Teachers, and to Persevere in Doing Good, Boasting in Christ's Cross Alone, and Wishing Peace on the Church, as the Israel of God, as a Final Blow Against False Jewish Teachers

> 'But God forbid that I should boast except in the cross of our Lord Jesus Christ, by whom the world has been crucified to me, and I to the world. For in Christ Jesus neither circumcision nor uncircumcision avails anything, but a new creation.' Gal. 6:14-15.

Ephesians

God sets forth His Triune glory in the gospel message and in the church and its life, directing believers how to walk worthy of their calling

Chapter **1**

Paul Greets the Ephesian Church as Saints and Faithful, Blessing the Father in His Glorious Grace for Election to the Adoption as Sons, for Sending Christ to Bring Redemption Through His Blood, and for Sealing Believers with the Spirit as a Downpayment of their Inheritance, Praying that They Would Grow in Spiritual Wisdom in Christ, Who is Head Over All Things for the Sake of the Church

> 'In Him also we have obtained an inheritance, being predestined according to the purpose of Him who works all things according to the counsel of His will, that we who first trusted in Christ should be to the praise of His glory ... And He put all things under His feet, and gave Him to be head over all things to the church, which is His body, the fullness of Him who fills all in all.' Eph. 1:11-12, 22-23.

Chapter **2**

Continuing to Extol the Grace of God, Paul Reminds them that God Made them Alive When they Were Dead in Sin, Without Christ, and, as Gentiles, Strangers to God's Covenant Promises, Showing How Christ Made Peace Between them and God Through His Blood, so that they Might Come to God through Christ by One Spirit, God Bringing them into the Church as His Household and the Temple of the Holy Spirit, Christ Being its Foundation

> 'For through Him we both have access by one Spirit to the Father. Now, therefore, you are no longer strangers and foreigners, but

> fellow citizens with the saints and members of the household of God, having been built on the foundation of the apostles and prophets, Jesus Christ Himself being the chief cornerstone, in whom the whole building, being fitted together, grows into a holy temple to the Lord, in whom you are also being built together for a dwelling place of God in the Spirit.' Eph. 2:18-22.

Chapter 3

Paul Recounts the Purpose of his Ministry in Declaring the Unsearchable Riches of God in Christ by the Holy Spirit, Praying that the Spirit Would Enable them to Know the Love of Christ, which Passes Knowledge, in Order to be Filled with the Fullness of God, Giving Glory to the God Who Answers Better than we Could Ask or Think

> 'Now to Him who is able to do exceedingly abundantly above all that we ask or think, according to the power that works in us, to Him be glory in the church by Jesus Christ to all generations, forever and ever. Amen.' Eph. 3:20-21.

Chapter 4

Grounding the Church in the Work of the Triune God, Paul Shows that Christ Distributed Gifts to the Church, Especially Teaching Gifts to Prevent them from Being Tossed About by Every Wind of Doctrine and to Build them Up into Unity and Maturity in Christ, Exhorting them to Put Off Ungodly Practices, Replacing them with Godly Ones, Walking Worthy of their Calling in Christ and not Grieving the Spirit Who Sealed us for the Day of Redemption

> 'I, therefore, the prisoner of the Lord, beseech you to walk worthy of the calling with which you were called, with all lowliness and gentleness, with longsuffering, bearing with one another in love, endeavoring to keep the unity of the Spirit in the bond of peace. There is one body and one Spirit, just as you were called in one hope of your calling; one Lord, one faith, one baptism; one God and Father of all, who is above all, and through all, and in you all.' Eph. 4:1-6.

Chapter 5

We Must Imitate God as His Beloved Children in Christ, Walking in Love as those who Were Once Darkness but Now are Light in the Lord, Redeeming the Time and Being Thankful, as We Honor Christ in our Relationships with Others, Beginning with Marriage

> 'Therefore be imitators of God as dear children … For you were once darkness, but now you are light in the Lord. Walk as children of light … And do not be drunk with wine, in which is dissipation; but be filled with the Spirit, speaking to one another in psalms and hymns and spiritual songs, making melody in your heart to the Lord, giving thanks always for all things to God the Father in the name of our Lord Jesus Christ, submitting to one another in the fear of God.' Eph. 5:1, 8, 18-21.

Chapter 6

Continuing our Relationships with Others, Children Must Obey their Parents in the Lord, Fathers Must Train Children in the Nurture and Admonition of the Lord, Bondservants Must Obey Christ in Obeying their Masters, Masters Must Imitate their Master in Heaven, and the Saints in General Must Stand in the Faith by Putting on the Whole Armor of God, Concluding with Paul's Greetings and Benediction

> 'Stand therefore, having girded your waist with truth, having put on the breastplate of righteousness, and having shod your feet with the preparation of the gospel of peace; above all, taking the shield of faith with which you will be able to quench all the fiery darts of the wicked one. And take the helmet of salvation, and the sword of the Spirit, which is the word of God; praying always with all prayer and supplication in the Spirit, being watchful to this end with all perseverance and supplication for all the saints.' Eph. 6:14-18.

Philippians

God sets forth Christ, as the ground of heavenly citizenship, and as the pattern of Christian living, exhorting a faithful church to remain faithful

Chapter 1

Paul Addresses the Elders and Deacons in Philippi, Thanking God for their Partnership with him in the Gospel and Praying for their Love to Abound In Knowledge, Recounting his Persecution in Prison and the Sincerity of Some and the Hypocrisy of Others, Testifying his Desire to be with Christ and his Confidence that God will Answer their Prayers for his Release, and Urging them to Walk Worthy of the Gospel Under Suffering

> 'Being confident of this very thing, that He who began a good work in you will complete it until the day of Christ Jesus … For to me, to live is Christ, and to die is gain … For to you it has been granted on behalf of Christ, not only to believe in Him, but also to suffer for His sake, having the same conflict which you saw in me and now hear is in me.' Phil. 1:6, 21, 29-30.

Chapter 2

In Light of Our Comfort in Christ and Fellowship in the Spirit, Believers Must Pursue Like-Minded Humility, Looking to Christ's Incarnation as the Highest Example and Pattern to Follow, Doing All Things Without Complaining or Arguing, and Looking to the Further Examples of Paul, Timothy, and Epaphroditus, as they Imitate Christ

> 'Let this mind be in you which was also in Christ Jesus, who, being in the form of God, did not consider it robbery to be equal with God, but made Himself of no reputation, taking the form of a bondservant, and coming in the likeness of men.

> And being found in appearance as a man, He humbled Himself and became obedient to the point of death, even the death of the cross. Therefore God also has highly exalted Him and given Him the name which is above every name, that at the name of Jesus every knee should bow, of those in heaven, and of those on earth, and of those under the earth, and that every tongue should confess that Jesus Christ is Lord, to the glory of God the Father.' Phil. 2:5-11.

Chapter 3

The Philippian Christians Must Rejoice in the Lord, Taking Precautions Against False Jewish Teachers, Remembering that they are the True Circumcision, which Paul Illustrates Through his Own Conversion to Christ, Urging them to Press Towards Perfection at the Resurrection of the Dead, Knowing that their Citizenship is in Heaven and that Some Enemies of Christ are Among them

> 'For we are the circumcision, who worship God in the Spirit, rejoice in Christ Jesus, and have no confidence in the flesh … Yet indeed I count all things loss for the excellence of the knowledge of Christ Jesus my Lord, for whom I have suffered the loss of all things, and count them as rubbish, that I may gain Christ … For our citizenship is in heaven, from which we also eagerly wait for the Savior, the Lord Jesus Christ, who will transform our lowly body that it might be conformed to His glorious body, according to the working by which He is able to subdue all things to Himself.' Phil. 3:3, 8, 20-21.

Chapter 4

Paul Urges them to Stand Fast in the Lord, Pressing Euodia and Syntyche to Reconcile, Exhorting the Church to Rejoice in the Lord Always, Praying Through Anxiety with Thanksgiving and Faith, Meditating on Good Things with Assurance of God's Presence, Thanking the Church for their Generosity, and Closing with a Greeting and Benediction

> 'Rejoice in the Lord always. Again I will say, rejoice! Let your gentleness be known to all men. The Lord is at hand. Be anxious for nothing, but in everything by prayer and supplication, with thanksgiving, let your requests be made known to God; and the peace of God, which surpasses all understanding, will guard your hearts and minds through Christ Jesus.' Phil. 4:4-7.

Colossians

God exalts the preeminence of Christ in the church, protecting His covenant people from dangerous philosophies and practices, teaching them how to live in union with Christ in every area of life

Chapter **1**

Paul Thanks the Father for the Colossians' Faith in Christ and Love in the Spirit, Extolling Christ as Redeemer and as the God of Creation and Providence, Reminding them of what they Were Without Christ and Who they are Now in Christ, Paul Rejoicing in his Suffering for Christ and Outlining his Goals in Preaching

> 'I now rejoice in my sufferings for you, and fill up in my flesh what is lacking in the afflictions of Christ, for the sake of His body, which is the church, of which I became a minister according to the stewardship from God which was given to me for you, to fulfill the word of God, the mystery which has been hidden from ages and from generations, but now has been revealed to His saints. To them God willed to make known what are the riches of the glory of this mystery among the Gentiles: which is Christ in you, the hope of glory. Him we preach, warning every man and teaching every man in all wisdom, that we may present every man perfect in Christ Jesus. To this end I also labor, striving according to His working which works in me mightily.' Col. 1:24-29.

Chapter **2**

Rejoicing in their Steadfastness in the Lord, Paul Warns them Against Empty Philosophy and Jewish Traditions, Reminding them that they are the True Circumcision, and that they Should Pursue True Godliness

'Beware lest anyone cheat you through philosophy and empty deceit, according to the tradition of men, according to the basic principles of this world, and not according to Christ. For in Him dwells all the fullness of the Godhead bodily; and you are complete in Him, who is the head of all principality and power. In Him you were also circumcised with the circumcision made without hands, by putting off the body of the sins of the flesh, by the circumcision of Christ, buried with Him in baptism, in which you were also raised with Him through faith in the working of God, who raised Him from the dead.' Col. 2:8-12.

Chapter 3

Believers Must Live as Those Raised with Christ and Whose Lives are Hidden with Christ in God, Putting to Death Ungodly Practices, and Replacing them with Godly Ones, Stressing Love as the Bond of Perfection, and Carrying these Principles into their Relationships

'If then you were raised with Christ, seek those things which are above, where Christ is, sitting at the right hand of God. Set your mind on things above, not on things on the earth. For you died, and your life is hidden with Christ in God. When Christ who is our life appears, then you also will appear with Him in glory.' Col. 3:1-4.

Chapter 4

Paul Exhorts the Church to Prayer and Watchfulness, Commending Tychicus, Aristarchus, and Epaphras to them, Exhorting them to Exchange his Letters with the Church in Laodicea, Closing with a Benediction

'Walk in wisdom toward those who are outside, redeeming the time. Let your speech always be with grace, seasoned with salt, that you may know how you ought to answer each one.' Col. 4:5-6.

1 Thessalonians

God encourages a faithful church to increase in the love of the Spirit as they hope in Christ through death and look to His return

CHAPTER **1**

Paul Thanks God for the Faith, Hope, and Love in Christ Among the Thessalonian Church, their Receiving the Word in the Power of the Spirit as Evidence of their Election by God, Serving as Examples to Other Churches

> 'We give thanks to God always for you, making mention of you in our prayers, remembering without ceasing your work of faith, labor of love, and patience of hope in our Lord Jesus Christ in the sight of our God and Father, knowing, beloved brethren, your election by God. For our gospel did not come to you in word only, but also in power, and in the Holy Spirit and in much assurance, as you know what kind of men we were among you for your sake.' 1 Thess. 1:2-5.

CHAPTER **2**

Paul Reminds them of the Character of his Ministry Among them, Like a Gentle Mother and Exhorting Father, Praising God for their Reception of the Word Under Jewish Persecution, Expressing his Longing to See them Again

> 'For this reason we also thank God without ceasing, because when you received the word of God which you heard from us, you welcomed it not as the word of men, but as it is in truth, the word of God, which also effectively works in you who believe.' 1 Thess. 2:13.

Chapter 3

Paul Recounts that Timothy Brought him Good News of their Perseverance Under Persecution, Praying that God Would Continue to Establish them in Holiness Until Christ's Return

> 'Now may our God and Father Himself, and our Lord Jesus Christ, direct our way to you. And may the Lord make you increase and abound in love to one another and to all, just as we do to you, so that He may establish your hearts blameless in holiness before our God and Father at the coming of our Lord Jesus Christ with all His saints.' 1 Thess. 3:11-13.

Chapter 4

Sanctification is God's Will Revealed by the Spirit, which they Must Continue to Express in Brotherly Love, Taking Comfort that Those who Have Died in Christ Will Rise with them at the Last Day and that they Shall Always be with the Lord

> 'For this we say to you by the word of the Lord, that we who are alive and remain until the coming of the Lord will by no means precede those who are asleep. For the Lord Himself will descend from heaven with a shout, with the voice of an archangel, and with the trumpet of God. And the dead in Christ will rise first. Then we who are alive and remain shall be caught up together with them in the clouds to meet the Lord in the air. And thus we shall always be with the Lord. Therefore comfort one another with these words.' 1 Thess. 4:15-18.

Chapter 5

Yet Paul Warns that No One Knows When Christ Will Return, and that Instead Believers Should Watch for the Day by Walking in the Light, Being Confident that Christ who Died for them will Also Raise them from the Dead, Leading Paul to Conclude with Final Specific Exhortations, Closing with a Benediction

> 'But let us who are of the day be sober, putting on the breastplate of faith and love, and as a helmet the hope of salvation. For God did not appoint us to wrath, but to obtain salvation through our Lord Jesus Christ, who died for us, that whether we wake or sleep, we should live together with Him.' 1 Thess. 5:8-10.

2 Thessalonians

God encourages believers persevering through persecution to remember that the resurrection is still future, pressing them to live Spirit-filled lives just as God called them to Christ by the Spirit

Chapter **1**

Paul Thanks God for the Perseverance of the Thessalonians Under Jewish Persecution, Reminding them that God will Judge their Persecutors, and Praying for their Continued Perseverance

> 'These shall be punished with everlasting destruction from the presence of the Lord and from the glory of His power, when He comes, in that Day, to be glorified in His saints and to be admired among all those who believe, because our testimony among you was believed.' 2 Thess. 1:9-10.

Chapter **2**

Countering those who Say that the Day of the Lord has Come Already, Paul Shows the Church Some Things that Must Take Place Before that Day, Warning them Against Deception, Thanking God for Electing them, Sanctifying them in the Spirit, and Calling them to Christ Through Gospel Preaching, Commending them to Christ and the Father to Establish them in Every Good Word and Work

> 'But we are bound to give thanks to God always for you, brethren beloved by the Lord, because God from the beginning chose you for salvation through sanctification by the Spirit and belief in the truth, to which He called you by our gospel, for the obtaining of the glory of our Lord Jesus Christ. Therefore, brethren, stand fast and hold the traditions which you were taught, whether by word or our epistle.' 2 Thess. 2:13-15.

Chapter 3

Paul Asks for Prayer for the Spread of the Word Through his Preaching, Encouraging them to Press on with Confidence in God's faithfulness to them, Urging them to Avoid Idleness and to Persevere in Doing Good, Closing with a Benediction

> 'But the Lord is faithful, who will establish you and guard you from the evil one. And we have confidence in the Lord concerning you, both that you do and will do the things we command you.' 2 Thess. 3:3-4.

1 Timothy

God, through Paul, instructs Timothy how to establish order in the church, all the while keeping His covenant people grounded in the central promises of the gospel

Chapter **1**

Paul Reminds Timothy of his Charge to Care for the Church in Ephesus, Charging Some not to Teach False Doctrine Related to Jewish Abuses of the Law, Showing the Use of the Law in Convicting People of Sin, Reminding Timothy that God had Mercy on Paul in his Sin as a Pattern of Mercy to Others, Pressing Timothy to Fight the Good Fight of Faith, Taking Warning from those Who Made Shipwreck of the Faith

> 'This is a faithful saying and worthy of all acceptance, that Christ Jesus came into the world to save sinners, of whom I am chief. However, for this reason I obtained mercy, that in me Jesus Christ might show all longsuffering, as a pattern to those who are going to believe on Him for everlasting life. Now to the King eternal, immortal, invisible, to God who alone is wise, be honor and glory forever and ever. Amen.' 1 Tim. 1:15-17.

Chapter **2**

Christians Must Pray and Give Thanks for All, God Desiring All Kinds of Men to be Saved Through Christ, the Only Mediator Between God and Men, Instructing Timothy on the Conduct of Men and Women in the Church, Forbidding Women to Teach or Hold Authority Over Men

> 'For there is one God and one Mediator between God and men, the Man Christ Jesus, who gave Himself a ransom for all, to be testified in due time, for which I was appointed a preacher and

> an apostle – I am speaking the truth in Christ and not lying – a teacher of the Gentiles in faith and truth.' 1 Tim. 2:5-7.

Chapter 3
Paul Gives Timothy Criteria for the Godliness Required of Elders and Deacons in the Church, Showing him How to Order the Church of the Living God, and Reminding him of the Substance of the Gospel, on which the Church Rests

> 'These things I write to you, though I hope to come to you shortly; but if I am delayed, I write so that you may know how you ought to conduct yourself in the house of God, which is the church of the living God, the pillar and ground of the truth. And without controversy, great is the mystery of godliness: God was manifested in the flesh, justified in the Spirit, seen by angels, preached among the Gentiles, believed on in the world, received up in glory.' 1 Tim. 3:14-16.

Chapter 4
Timothy Must be a Good Minister of Christ in Light of the Spirit's Warnings of Coming Apostasy Through False Teachers, Urging him to Remember his Ordination to Ministry, Letting no one Despise his Youth

> 'Now the Spirit expressly says that in latter times some will depart from the faith, giving heed to deceiving spirits and doctrines of demons, speaking lies in hypocrisy, having their own conscience seared with a hot iron, forbidding to marry, and commanding to abstain from foods which God created to be received with thanksgiving by those who believe and know the truth. For every creature of God is good, and nothing is to be refused if it is received with thanksgiving; for it is sanctified by the word of God and prayer. If you instruct the brethren in these things, you will be a good minister of Jesus Christ, nourished in the words of faith and of the good doctrine which you have carefully followed.' 1 Tim. 4:1-6.

Chapter 5
Timothy Must Treat Older Men with Respect, and Paul Instructs him How to Evaluate the Church's Care for Widows, Urging him to Teach the Church to Support Good Elders Financially, Cautioning him Against Ordaining Men Hastily to Office

'I charge you before God and the Lord Jesus Christ and the elect angels that you observe these things without prejudice, doing nothing with partiality. Do not lay hands on anyone hastily, nor share in other people's sins; keep yourself pure.' 1 Tim. 5:22-23.

Chapter 6

Bondservants Must Honor God by Honoring their Masters, False Teaching is Marked by Ungodliness, While the Truth Timothy Must Preach Accords with it, Being Aware that Some will Preach the Gospel Hoping for Financial Gain, Paul Exhorting Timothy to Confess the Good Confession Before Men Just as Christ Did Before Pilate, Giving Instructions to the Rich to be Generous, and Closing With a Final Warning and Benediction

'I urge you in the sight of God who gives life to all things, and before Jesus Christ who witnessed the good confession before Pontius Pilate, that you keep this commandment without spot, blameless until our Lord Jesus Christ's appearing, which He will manifest in His own time, He who is the blessed and only Potentate, the King of kings and Lord of lords, who alone has immortality, dwelling in unapproachable light, whom no man has seen nor can see, to whom be honor and everlasting power. Amen.' 1 Tim. 6:13-16.

2 Timothy

God, through Paul, presses Timothy to persevere in preaching the Word in the face of persecution and Paul's imminent death

Chapter **1**

Paul Thanks God for Timothy's Genuine Faith, Following his Mother and Grandmother, Pressing him not to be Ashamed of the Testimony of Christ, to Which God Calls Believers According to His Purpose and Grace, and to Fulfill his Call to the Ministry by the Spirit's Power

> 'Hold fast the pattern of sound words which you have heard from me, in faith and love which are in Christ Jesus. That good thing which was committed to you, keep by the Holy Spirit who dwells in us.' 2 Tim. 1:13-14.

Chapter **2**

Timothy Must Endure Hardship as a Good Soldier of Christ, Committing Paul's Teaching to Faithful Men Who Can Teach Others, Shunning the Idle Babblings of False Teachers, and Being Confident that the Lord Knows Who are His in Spite of the Apostasy of Others in the Church

> 'Therefore I endure all things for the sake of the elect, that they also may obtain the salvation which is in Christ Jesus with eternal glory. This is a faithful saying: For if we died with Him, we shall also live with Him. If we endure, we shall also reign with Him. If we deny Him, He will also deny us. If we are faithless, He remains faithful; He cannot deny Himself.' 2 Tim. 2:10-13.

Chapter **3**

Ungodly Men Will Increase, who Profess Godliness but Deny its Power, While Timothy Must Remember Paul's Example of

Enduring Persecution, Resisting Evil Men and Imposters by Holding to Scripture

> 'But evil men and imposters will grow worse and worse, deceiving and being deceived. But you must continue in the things which you have learned and been assured of, knowing from whom you have learned them, and that from childhood you have known the Holy Scriptures, which are able to make you wise for salvation through faith which is in Christ Jesus. All Scripture is given by inspiration of God, and is profitable for doctrine, for reproof, for correction, for instruction in righteousness, that the man of God may be complete, thoroughly equipped for every good work.' 2 Tim. 3:13-17.

Chapter 4

Therefore Paul Puts Timothy Under Oath to Preach the Word Continually, Noting his Imminent Death and Present Abandonment by his Friends, Taking Courage that Christ Stood With him and Always Will, Concluding with Greetings and a Benediction

> 'But the Lord stood with me and strengthened me, so that the message might be preached fully through me, and that all the Gentiles might hear. Also I was delivered out of the mouth of the lion. And the Lord will deliver me from every evil work and preserve me for His heavenly kingdom. To Him be glory forever and ever. Amen!' 2 Tim. 4:17-18.

Titus

Through Paul, God instructs Titus to appoint elders in the churches and to remind believers that the grace by which God saves them also teaches them to be zealous for good works

Chapter 1

After Noting his Apostolic Call to Preach as it Relates to the Faith of God's Elect, the Truth that Accords with Godliness, and God's Eternal Promise of Eternal Life, Paul Gives Titus Instructions to Help Order the Churches, Outlining the Qualifications of Elders, who are Bishops or Overseers of the Churches, to Counter False Jewish Teachers, who are Marked by Ungodly Conduct

> 'Paul, a bondservant of God and an apostle of Jesus Christ, according to the faith of God's elect and the acknowledgement of the truth which accords with godliness, in hope of eternal life which God, who cannot lie, promised before time began, but has in due time manifested His word through preaching, which was committed to me according to the commandment of God our Savior.' Titus 1:1-3.

Chapter 2

Titus Must Teach Sound Doctrine, Instructing People of Both Sexes and All Ages How to Behave in the Church, Reminding the Church that Christ Redeemed the Church to Make His People Zealous for Good Works, Being Motivated by Christ's Second Coming

> 'For the grace of God that brings salvation has appeared to all men, teaching us that, denying ungodliness and worldly lusts, we should live soberly, righteously, and godly in the present age, looking for the blessed hope and glorious appearing of our great God and Savior Jesus Christ, who gave Himself for

> us, that He might redeem us from every lawless deed and purify for Himself His own special people, zealous for good works.' Titus 2:11-14.

Chapter 3

Titus Must Remind Believers of the Kindness and Love of God to them, who Saved them by Grace Rather than by Works, by the Regeneration of the Spirit, Being Justified Through Faith in Christ, so that they Might Maintain Good Works, Rejecting Divisive People, Paul Concluding with Greetings and a Benediction

> 'But when the kindness and love of God our Savior toward man appeared, not by works of righteousness which we have done, but according to His mercy He saved us, through the washing of regeneration and renewing of the Holy Spirit, whom He poured out on us abundantly through Jesus Christ our Savior, that having been justified by His grace we should become heirs according to the hope of eternal life.' Titus 3:4-7.

Philemon

Paul reflects God's care for a new convert and for the social relationships of believers

Chapter 1

Paul Addresses Philemon from Prison, Thanking God for his Evident Love and Faith, Appealing to him to Receive and Free Onesimus, Philemon's Escaped Slave Who Came to Christ Through Paul While in Prison, Expressing Confidence that Philemon Will Do So, Closing with Greetings and a Benediction

> 'For perhaps he departed for a while for this purpose, that you might receive him forever, no longer as a slave, but more than a slave – a beloved brother, especially to me but how much more to you, both in the flesh and in the Lord.' Philem. 15-16.

Hebrews

God perfects all of the promises of the old covenant by fulfilling them through Christ in the new covenant, in order to prevent Jewish believers from the temptation to return to Judaism

Chapter 1

The Author Establishes the Superiority of God's Revelation Through Christ Over His Former Revelation to the Prophets Through the Ministry of Angels, Contrasting the Son's Divine Identity with the Role of the Angels as Ministering Servants

> 'God, who at various times and in various ways spoke in time past to the fathers by the prophets, has in these last days spoken to us by His Son, whom He has appointed heir of all things, through whom also He made the worlds; who being the brightness of His glory and the express image of His person, and upholding all things by the word of His power, when He had by Himself purged our sins, sat down at the right hand of the Majesty on high, having become so much better than the angels, as He has by inheritance obtained a more excellent name than they.' Heb. 1:1-4.

Chapter 2

The Reason for Establishing the Superiority of God's Revelation in Christ Over that which Came Through the Ministry of Angels, is to Press Jewish Christians not to Apostatize Back into Judaism, but to Look to the Incarnate Christ, Who Became Lower than the Angels as Man, Though He is Higher than them as God, in Order to Save the Children of Abraham Through His Sufferings

> 'Inasmuch then as the children have been partakers of flesh and blood, He Himself likewise shared in the same, that through death He might destroy him who had the power of death, that

> is, the devil, and release those who through fear of death were all their lifetime subject to bondage. For indeed He does not give aid to angels, but He does give aid to the seed of Abraham. Therefore, in all things He had to be made like His brethren, that He might be a merciful and faithful High Priest in things pertaining to God, to make propitiation for the sins of the people. For in that He Himself has suffered, being tempted, He is able to aid those who are tempted.' Heb. 2:14-18.

Chapter 3

Christ's Divine Identity and Superiority to Moses is Another Reason Why Jewish Believers Should not Apostatize from Christ by Returning to Temple Worship, Warning them From Psalm 95 not to Fail to Enter God's Promised Rest by Departing from God

> 'Beware, brethren, lest there be in any of you an evil heart of unbelief in departing from the living God; but exhort one another daily, while it is called "Today," lest any of you be hardened through the deceitfulness of sin. For we have become partakers of Christ if we hold the beginning of our confidence steadfast to the end.' Heb. 3:12-14.

Chapter 4

Though God Promised Eternal Rest in the First Sabbath in Creation, Joshua Bringing Israel into the Promised Land was not that Rest, but God Secured Eternal Sabbath Rest Through Christ's Finished Work, and Believers Must Look to Christ Through the Word as they Seek Diligently to Enter God's Rest

> 'For he who has entered His rest has himself also ceased from his works as God did from His. Let us therefore be diligent to enter that rest, lest anyone fall according to the same example of disobedience ... Seeing then that we have a great High Priest who has passed through the heavens, Jesus the Son of God, let us hold fast our confession. For we do not have a High Priest who cannot sympathize with our weaknesses, but was in all points tempted as we are, yet without sin. Let us therefore come boldly to the throne of grace, that we may obtain mercy and find grace to help in time of need.' Heb. 4:10-11, 14-16.

Chapter 5

The Author Encourages his Readers to Persevere by Considering Christ's Call by God to be a Unique High Priest After the Order of Melchizedek, Citing Psalms 2 and 110, Christ Securing Eternal Salvation Through Obedient Suffering, Rebuking them for their Spiritual Immaturity by their Temptation to Return to Judaism

> 'Though He was a Son, yet He learned obedience by the things which He suffered. And having been perfected, He became the author of eternal salvation to all who obey Him.' Heb. 5:8-9.

CHAPTER **6**

Pressing Beyond the First Principles of the Gospel, the Author Warns his Readers that Returning to Judaism Puts Christ to Open Shame and Leaves them Without Hope of Repentance, Balancing this Warning with his Confidence in their Salvation, and with God's Immutable Promise and Oath in Christ, which Brings them into God's Presence Behind the Veil

> 'Thus God, determining to show more abundantly to the heirs of promise the immutability of His counsel, confirmed it by an oath, that by two immutable things, in which it is impossible for God to lie, we might have strong consolation, who have fled for refuge to lay hold of the hope set before us. This hope we have as an anchor of the soul, both sure and steadfast, and which enters the Presence behind the veil, where the forerunner has entered for us, even Jesus, having become High Priest forever according to the order of Melchizedek.' Heb. 6:17-20.

CHAPTER **7**

The Author Further Exhorts them to Persevere in the Faith by Showing that, as an Eternal Priest with an Eternal Priesthood After the Order of Melchizedek, Christ Can Make Believers Perfect while the Law of the Levitical Priesthood Could not

> 'For such a High Priest was fitting for us, who is holy, harmless, undefiled, separate from sinners, and has become higher than the heavens; who does not need daily, as those high priests, to offer up sacrifices, first for His own sins and then for the people's, for this He did once for all when He offered up Himself. For the law appoints as high priests men who have weaknesses, but the word of the oath, which came after the law, appoints the Son who has been perfected forever.' Heb. 7:26-28.

CHAPTER **8**

The Main Point is that Christ is a Permanent Minister in the Heavenly Sanctuary, Making the Earthly Temple Obsolete,

Fulfilling the Promise of the New Covenant from Jeremiah 31 in Bringing the Forgiveness of Sins

> 'Now this is the main point of the things we are saying: We have such a High Priest, who is seated at the right hand of the throne of the Majesty in the heavens, a Minister of the sanctuary and of the true tabernacle which the Lord erected, and not man ... In that He says, "A new covenant," He has made the first obsolete. Now what is becoming obsolete and growing old is ready to vanish away.' Heb. 8:1-2, 13.

CHAPTER **9**

The Old Covenant and its Ordinances, Including the Day of Atonement, was not Designed to Bring People Fully into God's Presence, Christ alone Doing so Through Offering His Blood to God by the Spirit in the Heavenly Sanctuary, Showing the Testamentary Character of the New Covenant Through His Death, Offering Himself Once Only to Save those Who Eagerly Wait for Him to Return

> 'For if the blood of bulls and goats and the ashes of a heifer, sprinkling the unclean, sanctifies for the purifying of the flesh, how much more shall the blood of Christ, who through the eternal Spirit offered Himself without spot to God, cleanse your consciences from dead works to serve the living God?' Heb. 9:13-14.

CHAPTER **10**

Not Only Were the Priesthood and Tabernacle Insufficient, but the Blood of Bulls and Goats Could not Take Away Sins, Christ Alone Fulfilling God's Will Completely by Keeping the Law Fully, Culminating in His Death, the Author Exhorting His Readers to Persevere in Faith, Continue to Endure Persecution, and not Return to Judaism

> 'But this Man, after He had offered one sacrifice for sins forever, sat down at the right hand of God, from that time waiting till His enemies are made His footstool. For by one offering He has perfected forever those who are being sanctified.' Heb. 10:12-14.

CHAPTER **11**

The Author Encourages his Readers to Persevere in Faith, Teaching them What Faith is and Illustrating it through Numerous Old

Testament Examples, Assuring them that They Will Inherit God's Promises Through Faith

> 'But without faith it is impossible to please Him, for he who comes to God must believe that He is, and that He is a rewarder of those who diligently seek Him.' Heb. 11:6.

Chapter 12

Jesus' Perseverance in Faith Under the Cross is the Final and Highest Example, Pressing the Readers to Persevere, Remembering that their Suffering and Pressure to Return to Judaism is the Father's Loving Hand of Discipline, Strengthening One Another While Pursuing Holiness, Being Confident That they Belong to the Heavenly Mount Zion and Unshakable Church in Heaven, Lest they Fall Away

> 'Therefore we also, since we are surrounded by so great a cloud of witnesses, let us lay aside every weight, and the sin which so easily ensnares us, and let us run with endurance the race that is set before us, looking unto Jesus, the author and finisher of our faith, who for the joy set before Him endured the cross, despising the shame, and has sat down at the right hand of the throne of God. For consider Him who endured such hostility from sinners against Himself, lest you become weary and discouraged in your souls.' Heb. 12:1-3.

Chapter 13

As these Jewish Believers Persevere in Faith Under Hardship, they Must Maintain Hospitality and Purity, Being Confident that God Will Supply All of their Needs, Honoring their Rulers in the Church and Looking to a Continuing City in Heaven Only, While Relying on the Christ who is the Same Yesterday, Today, and Forever, the Author Concluding with a Combined Benediction and Doxology

> 'Jesus Christ is the same yesterday, today, and forever ... Now may the God of peace who brought up our Lord Jesus from the dead, that great Shepherd of the sheep, through the blood of the everlasting covenant, make you complete in every good work to do His will, working in you what is well pleasing in His sight, through Jesus Christ, to whom be glory forever and ever. Amen.' Heb. 13:8, 20-21.

James

God shows that faith without works is dead, in order to prevent the rich from abusing the poor in the church

Chapter 1

Likely Writing to Jewish Christians, James Counsels the Poor in the Church to Seek Wisdom from the Lord to Endure Trials at the Hands of the Rich, Whose Wealth Shall Perish, While God Uses Temptation for their Good, and the Rich Should Seek to be Doers of the Word and not Hearers Only

> 'Do not be deceived, my beloved brethren. Every good and every perfect gift is from above, and comes down from the Father of lights, with whom there is no variation or shadow of turning. Of His own will He brought us forth by the word of truth, that we might be a kind of firstfruits of His creatures.' James 1:16-18.

Chapter 2

James Continues to Warn the Church not to Show Partiality to the Rich to the Neglect of the Poor, Reminding them that Doing so Violates the Sixth Commandment, and the Whole Law with it, and that Faith Without Works Justifying that Faith is a Dead Faith

> 'You believe that there is one God. You do well. Even the demons believe – and tremble! But do you want to know, O foolish man, that faith without works is dead?' James 2:19-20.

Chapter 3

In Particular, they Must not Bless God and Curse Others Made in God's Image, Taming their Tongues, not Judging Others, and Pursuing Peace Through Heavenly Wisdom

> 'But the wisdom that is from above is first pure, then peaceable, gentle, willing to yield, full of mercy and good fruits, without partiality and without hypocrisy. Now the fruit of righteousness is sown in peace by those who make peace.' James 3:17-18.

Chapter 4

Their Pride Results in Wars and Fights Among them, and they Either Fail to Pray or Don't Receive What they Pray for Due to their Selfishness, James Exhorting them to Humble Repentance, Particularly in Relation to Speaking Evil of Brethren and Boasting about Plans for Tomorrow

> 'Adulterers and adulteresses! Do you not know that friendship with the world is enmity with God? Whoever therefore wants to be a friend of the world makes himself an enemy of God … Humble yourselves in the sight of the Lord, and He will lift you up … Therefore, to him who knows to do good and does not do it, to him it is sin.' James 4:4, 10, 17.

Chapter 5

James Concludes by Urging the Rich to Weep and Howl Over their Sins Against the Poor, and the Poor to Look Patiently to Christ's Return, Taking Courage from the Examples of Job and Elijah, Believing that the Lord Will Hear their Prayers, Including Those for the Sick, Closing with a Final Exhortation to Turn Back those who Wander from the Truth

> 'Confess your trespasses to one another, and pray for one another, that you may be healed. The effective fervent prayer of a righteous man avails much. Elijah was a man with a nature like ours, and he prayed earnestly that it would not rain; and it did not rain on the land for three years and six months. And he prayed again, and the heaven gave rain, and the earth produced its fruit.' James 5:16-18.

1 Peter

God encourages suffering believers through Peter not to be ashamed to suffer as Christians, knowing that the Spirit of glory and of God rests upon them, as they follow Christ's pattern of suffering, and look to Him as Redeemer and Judge

Chapter 1

Peter Greets Dispersed Christians as Elect by the Father, Sanctified in the Spirit, and Sprinkled with Christ's Blood, Blessing God for the Certainty of their Inheritance in Christ in Spite of their Trials, Showing that Christ is the Central Focus of Scripture, in Whom God Calls Believers to Holiness Through His Word

> 'Of this salvation the prophets have inquired and searched carefully, who prophesied of the grace that would come to you, searching what, or what manner of time, the Spirit of Christ who was in them was indicating when He testified beforehand the sufferings of Christ and the glories that would follow. To them it was revealed that, not to themselves, but to us they were ministering the things which have now been reported to you through those who have preached the gospel to you by the Holy Spirit sent from heaven – things which angels desire to look into.' 1 Pet. 1:10-12.

Chapter 2

Peter Presses the Church Towards Holiness as the True Israel, Temple, and Priesthood, Living as Pilgrims and Strangers in the Earth, While they Submit to Earthly Authority, Imitating Christ by Enduring Persecution

> 'For this is commendable, if because of conscience toward God one endures grief, suffering wrongfully. For what credit is it if, when you are beaten for your faults, you take it patiently? But

when you do good and suffer, if you take it patiently, this is commendable before God. For to this you were called, because Christ also suffered for us, leaving us an example, that you should follow His steps.' 1 Pet. 2:19-21.

Chapter 3

Wives Likewise Submit to God by Submitting Even to Harsh Husbands, While Husbands Must Avoid Harshness, and All Christians Must Bless those who Persecute them, Being Prepared to Suffer for Doing Good Instead of Evil, Taking Encouragement from the Spirit of Christ's Witness Through Noah and God's Judgment on his Persecutors

'For Christ also suffered once for sins, the just for the unjust, that He might bring us to God, being put to death in the flesh but made alive by the Spirit.' 1 Pet. 3:18.

Chapter 4

Christ, Who Brings Life to the Dead, Teaches Believers to Live for the Will of God Rather than the Lusts of Men, Peter Exhorting them to Love and Hospitality, not Thinking their Persecution a Strange Thing, but a Normal Aspect of Christian Living

'If you are reproached for the name of Christ, blessed are you, for the Spirit of glory and of God rests upon you. On their part He is blasphemed, but on your part He is glorified.' 1 Pet. 4:14.

Chapter 5

Peter Exhorts his Fellow Elders to Shepherd the Flock as Witnesses to Christ's Sufferings and Partakers of His Glory, Urging Persecuted Believers to Cast their Cares on the God Who Cares for them, Concluding with Greetings and Two Benedictions

'Therefore humble yourselves under the mighty hand of God, that He may exalt you in due time, casting all your care upon Him, for He cares for you.' 1 Pet. 5:6-7.

2 Peter

God, through Peter, presses believers towards assurance of their election in Christ, by holding to the teaching of Scripture, as they face the dangers of false teachers and anticipate Christ's return in judgment

Chapter 1

Peter Exhorts Believers to Grow in Grace and Assurance of Election in Christ in Light of God's Great Promises and their Fellowship with Him, Securing a Reminder of these Things After his Death, and Testifying to them of Christ's Transfiguration and the More Sure Word of Scripture

> 'By which have been given to us exceedingly great and precious promises, that through these you may be partakers of the divine nature, having escaped the corruption that is in the world through lust ... for prophecy never came by the will of man, but holy men of God spoke as they were moved by the Holy Spirit.' 2 Pet. 1:4, 21.

Chapter 2

While False Teachers Secretly Bring in Destructive Heresies, and they Are in the Church that Christ Bought with His Blood, God will Judge them as He Always Has, Opposing their Ungodliness and Stopping their Deception, Showing that Departing from the Truth is Worse than Never Coming to Know it

> 'But there were also false prophets among the people, even as there will be false teachers among you, who will secretly bring in destructive heresies, even denying the Lord who bought them, and bring on themselves swift destruction ... For it would have been better for them not to have known the way of righteousness, than having known

> it, to turn from the holy commandment delivered to them.' 2 Pet. 2:1, 21.

Chapter 3
In the Meantime, God's Promise Regarding Christ's Return for Judgment and Salvation is not Slack, but they Must Remain Steadfast While the Day of the Lord Will Come Unexpectedly, Closing with a Doxology

> 'But beloved, do not forget this one thing, that with the Lord one day is as a thousand years, and a thousand years as one day. The Lord is not slack concerning His promise, as some count slackness, but is longsuffering toward us, not willing that any should perish but that all should come to repentance.' 2 Pet. 3:8-9.

1 John

Through John, God teaches believers how to know that they have fellowship with the Father and the Son, through the effects of the Spirit's anointing, warning them against Antichrists and idolatry

Chapter **1**
John Reminds His Readers of His Testimony to Christ, Who Is Eternal Life, that they May Know that they Walk with God and are Forgiven by Him

> 'If we say that we have no sin, we deceive ourselves, and the truth is not in us. If we confess our sins, He is faithful and just to forgive us our sins and to cleanse us from all unrighteousness. If we say that we have not sinned, we make Him a liar, and His word is not in us.' 1 John 1:8-10.

Chapter **2**
Jesus is the Propitiation for Our Sins, We Know that We Know Him When We Keep His Commandments, We Must Persevere in Faith and Watch Against Antichrist by the Anointing of the Spirit from the Son and the Father, as We Seek to Have Confidence at Christ's Return

> 'They went out from us, but they were not of us; for if they had been of us, they would have continued with us; but they went out that they might be made manifest, that none of them were of us. But you have an anointing from the Holy One, and you know all things. I have not written to you because you do not know the truth, but because you know it, and that no lie is of the truth.' 1 John 2:19-21.

Chapter **3**
Our Future Hope Consists in Being Like Christ When we See Him as He Is, Experiencing the Full Fruits of our Adoption,

Fleeing from Sin and Loving our Brethren in Light of our Hope, Praying Confidently that Christ Who Died for Us Will Continue to Give Us His Spirit

> 'Behold, what manner of love the Father has bestowed on us, that we should be called the children of God! Therefore the world does not know us, because it did not know Him. Beloved, now we are children of God; and it has not yet been revealed what we shall be, but we know that when He is revealed, we shall be like Him, for we shall see Him as He is. And everyone who has this hope in Him purifies himself, just as He is pure … Now he who keeps His commandments abides in Him, and He in him. And by this we know that He abides in us, by the Spirit whom He has given us.' 1 John 3:1-3, 24.

Chapter 4

Believers Must Know the Difference Between the Spirit of God and of Antichrist, and Live in Love to God and Others in Light of God's Love to Us in Christ

> 'No one has seen God at any time. If we love one another, God abides in us, and His love has been perfected in us. By this we know that we abide in Him, and He in us, because He has given us of His Spirit. And we have seen and testify that the Father has sent the Son as Savior of the world. Whoever confesses that Jesus is the Son of God, God abides in him, and he in God. And we have known and believed the love that God has for us. God is love, and he who abides in love abides in God, and God in him.' 1 John 4:12-16.

Chapter 5

We Know that we Love God's People When we Love God and Keep His Commandments, Receiving the Witness of God Over the Witness of Men, Having Confidence When we Pray According to God's Will, and Being Assured of Eternal Life in Christ as we Reject Idolatry

> 'By this we know that we love the children of God, when we love God and keep His commandments. For this is the love of God, that we keep His commandments. And His commandments are not burdensome … And we know that the Son of God has come and has given us an understanding, that we may know Him who is true; and we are in Him who is true, in His Son Jesus Christ. This is the true God and eternal life.' 1 John 5:2-3, 20.

2 John

CHAPTER 1

As John Writes to the Elect Lady (Likely the Church) and Her Children, God Exhorts Believers Through Him to walk in the Truth and Keep Christ's Commandments, Watching Against Deception from Antichrists

> 'Whoever transgresses and does not abide in the doctrine of Christ does not have God. He who abides in the doctrine of Christ has both the Father and the Son.' 2 John 9.

3 John

Chapter 1

Through John, God Exhorts Gaius to Receive Christ's Servants, Rejecting those Seeking Preeminence, and Following What is Good Instead of What is Evil

> 'Beloved, do not imitate what is evil, but what is good. He who does good is of God, but he who does evil has not seen God.' 3 John 11.

Jude

Chapter 1

Jude Warns the Church to Contend for the Faith Against False Teachers, Giving Examples of Perseverance and of God's Righteous Judgments, Closing with a Doxology

> 'But you, beloved, building yourselves up on your most holy faith, praying in the Holy Spirit, keep yourselves in the love of God, looking for the mercy of our Lord Jesus Christ unto eternal life.' Jude 20-21.

Revelation

God encourages persecuted Christians to look to the reigning Christ, who washed them with His blood and is Ruler of all the kingdoms of the earth, so that they might keep a heavenly perspective under their sufferings on earth, by heeding the Spirit's message to them, as they hope for the heavenly Jerusalem

Chapter **1**

Filled with the Spirit on the Lord's Day on the Island of Patmos, John Writes to the Seven Churches of Asia Minor Concerning the Vision He Saw of the Glorified Christ, who is Lord of the Nations and Who Can Help Persecuted Christians Like John

> 'Grace to you and peace from Him who is and who was and who is to come, and from the seven Spirits who are before His throne, and from Jesus Christ, the faithful witness, the firstborn from the dead, and the ruler over the kings of the earth. To Him who loved us and washed us from our sins in His own blood, and has made us kings and priests to His God and Father, to Him be glory and dominion forever and ever. Amen.' Rev. 1:4b-6.

Chapter **2**

Christ Addresses the Seven Churches, in a Chiastic Structure, Rebuking Ephesus for Losing their First Love in Spite of their Sound Doctrine, Encouraging Smyrna to Persevere Under Persecution, Confronting Pergamos with its Idolatry and Immorality, Urging the Faithful Few in Thyatira to Endure to the End, as a Pattern for the Rest of the Book

> 'Now to you I say, and to the rest in Thyatira, as many as do not have this doctrine, who have not known the depths of Satan, as they say, I will put on you no other burden. But hold

fast what you have till I come. And he who overcomes, and keeps My works until the end, to him I will give power over the nations.' Rev. 2:24-26.

Chapter 3

Paralleling the Letters to Pergamos, Smyrna, and Ephesus, Christ Urges the Dead Church of Sardis to Repent, the Faithful Church of Philadelphia to Endure, and the Lukewarm Church of Laodicea to Hear Christ's Voice

> 'To him who overcomes I will grant to sit with Me on My throne, as I also overcame and sat down with My Father on His throne.' Rev. 3:21.

Chapter 4

John Sees the Father Seated on His Throne, Surrounded by the Holy Spirit, Twenty-Four Elders, Likely Pointing to the Twelve Tribes of Israel and the Twelve Apostles, and Four Living Creatures, Likely Pointing to All Creation, All Praising God for His Holiness, Creation, and Preservation

> '"Holy, holy, holy, Lord God Almighty, who was and is and is come!" Whenever the living creatures give glory and honor and thanks to Him who sits on the throne, who lives forever and ever, the twenty-four elders fall down before Him who sits on the throne and worship Him who lives forever and ever, and cast their crowns before the throne, saying, "You are worthy, O Lord, to receive glory and honor and power; for You created all things, and by Your will they exist and were created."' Rev. 4:8b-11.

Chapter 5

Christ Appears as the Lion of the Tribe of Judah, Who is the Lamb Who Was Slain, to Take the Scroll from the Father, to Open it, and to Unfold Coming Events as the God of Providence and Lord of the Nations, Every Creature in Heaven and Earth Bowing Before Him

> 'You are worthy to take the scroll, and to open its seals; for You were slain, and have redeemed us to God by Your blood out of every tribe and tongue and people and nation, and have made us kings and priests to our God; and we shall reign on the earth.' Rev. 5:9b-10.

Chapter 6

Opening the First Six Seals, the Four Horsemen Appearing in the First Four, Christ Shows that He is Lord of All, Repaying those Troubling His Church with Tribulation, Conquering them, Setting them Against Each Other, Bringing Famine, and Death, While His Martyrs in Heaven Cry out for Justice, and the Nations Cry to Rocks and Hills to Hide them from the Wrath of the Lamb

> 'And they cried with a loud voice, saying, "How long, O Lord, holy and true, until You judge and avenge our blood on those who dwell on earth?"' Rev. 6:10.

Chapter 7

God Seals His People on their Foreheads, Alluding to Ezekiel 9, Using the Number 144,000 in Order to Show that the Church Inherits the Blessings of the Twelve Tribes of Israel and their Armies, and that God Will Remove All of their Sorrows

> 'So he said to me, "These are the ones who come out of the great tribulation, and washed their robes and made them white in the blood of the Lamb. Therefore they are before the throne of God, and serve Him day and night in His temple. And He who sits on the throne will dwell among them. They shall neither hunger anymore nor thirst anymore; the sun shall not strike them, nor any heat; for the Lamb who is in the midst of the throne will shepherd them and lead them to living fountains of waters. And God will wipe away every tear from their eyes."' Rev. 7:14b-17.

Chapter 8

The Seventh Seal Introduces the Second Cycle Describing Judgment and Salvation Through Seven Trumpets, Culminating in Christ's Return, Starting with Striking Vegetation, the Seas, the Waters, and the Heavenly Bodies

> 'And I looked, and I heard an angel flying through the midst of heaven, saying with a loud voice, "Woe, woe, woe to the inhabitants of the earth, because of the remaining blasts of the trumpet of the three angels who are about to sound!"' Rev. 8:13.

Chapter 9

At the Sounding of the Fifth Trumpet, Locusts Come from the Bottomless Pit, Followed by Four Angels Who Kill a Third of Mankind, Ushering in an Army of Horsemen, as Mankind Stubbornly Refuses to Repent

> 'But the rest of mankind, who were not killed by these plagues, did not repent of the works of their hands, that they should not worship demons, and idols of gold, silver, brass, stone, and wood, which can neither see nor hear, nor walk. And they did not repent of their murders or their sorceries or their sexual immorality or their thefts.' Rev. 9:20-21.

Chapter **10**

John Next Hears Seven Thunders, but the Angel Orders him not to Recount what he Heard, but the Angel Announces the End with the Sounding of the Seventh Trumpet, Alluding to Ezekiel 3 by Instructing John to Eat the Little Book he Gives to him, Which Contains both Bitter Judgments and Sweet Promises

> 'Then I took the little book out of the angel's hand and ate it, and it was as sweet as honey in my mouth. But when I had eaten it, my stomach became bitter. And he said to me, "You must prophesy again about many peoples, nations, tongues, and kings."' Rev. 10:10-11.

Chapter **11**

Drawing Imagery From Zechariah 4, John Sees Two Witnesses, which are Two Olive Trees and Lampstands Before the Lord, Shutting up Rain from Heaven Like Elijah, and Representing the Old Testament Prophets Generally, as the Nations Rejoice in their Deaths and Despair When God Raises them, Concluding the Sixth Trumpet and Preparing for the Seventh

> 'We give You thanks, O Lord God Almighty, the One who is and who was and who is to come, because You have taken Your great power and reigned. The nations were angry, and Your wrath has come, and the time of the dead, that they should be judged, and that You should reward Your servants the prophets and the saints, and those who fear Your name, small and great, and should destroy those who destroy the earth.' Rev. 11:17b-18.

Chapter **12**

John Sees a Vision of the Church as a Woman, Christ as her Child, and Satan as a Dragon with Seven Heads and Diadems, with Ten Horns, as Christ Defeats Satan, and God Protects when the Church from Satan's Persecution, Explaining the Present Persecution of the Church and Christ's Imminent Victory

> 'Then I heard a loud voice saying in heaven, "Now salvation, and strength and the kingdom of our God, and the power of His Christ have come, for the accuser of our brethren, who accused them before our God day and night, has been cast down. And they overcame him by the blood of the Lamb and by the word of their testimony, and they did not love their lives to the death. Therefore rejoice, O heavens, and you who dwell in them! Woe to the inhabitants of the earth and the sea! For the devil has come down to you, having great wrath, because he knows that he has a short time."' Rev. 12:10-12.

Chapter **13**

The Beast From the Sea Resembles the Dragon's Heads and Horns from the Preceding Chapter, one Head Being Wounded and Healed, Evoking the Worship of the Nations as he Blasphemes God, While Another Beast Arises from the Earth, Mimicking the Lamb's Mark on the 144,000 by Placing his Mark of Ownership on the Hands and Foreheads of Mankind

> 'So they worshiped the dragon who gave authority to the beast; and they worshiped the beast, saying, "Who is like the beast? Who is able to make war with him?"' Rev. 13:4.

Chapter **14**

By Contrast, the Lamb Appears on Mount Zion with the 144,000, as He Sends Three Angels to Proclaim the Gospel of God's Glory to the Nations, Warning of the Fall of Babylon, and Announcing God's Wrath Against Those Worshiping the Beast and Receiving his Mark, While the Lamb Blesses Those Dying in the Lord While He Brings God's Harvest and Wrath

> 'Here is the patience of the saints; here are those who keep the commandments of God and the faith of Jesus. Then I heard a voice from heaven saying to me, "Write: Blessed are the dead who die in the Lord from now on. Yes, says the Spirit, that they may rest from their labors, and their works follow them."' Rev. 14:12-13.

Chapter **15**

The Seven Bowls Introduce the Last Cycle and the Seven Last Plagues of God, Completing His Wrath, Coming from the Temple and God's Presence in Heaven

'They sing to the song of Moses, the servant of God, and the song of the Lamb, saying: "Great and marvelous are Your works, Lord God Almighty! Just and true are Your ways, O King of the saints! Who shall not fear You, O Lord, and glorify Your name? For You alone are holy. For all nations shall come and worship before You, for Your judgments have been manifested."' Rev. 15:3-4.

Chapter 16

The First Six Bowls Curse Every Part of Creation through Sores, Turning the Sea to Blood, then the Waters, the Sun Scorching Men, Bringing Painful Darkness, and Drying up the Euphrates, While Babylon the Great is Shattered at the Seventh Bowl in a Great Earthquake

'And men were scorched with great heat, and they blasphemed the name of God who has power over these plagues; and they did not repent and give Him glory … They blasphemed the God of heaven because of their pains and their sores, and did not repent of their deeds … And great hail from heaven fell upon men, each hailstone about the weight of a talent. Men blasphemed God because of the plague of the hail, since that plague was exceedingly great.' Rev. 16:9, 11, 21.

Chapter 17

The Harlot Rides on a Scarlet Beast, Resembling the Dragon and Persecuting the Saints, Pointing to the Seven Mountains on Which Rome Was Founded, as the Lamb Promises to Lead His Saints to Victory

'These will make war with the Lamb, and the Lamb will overcome them, for He is Lord of lords and King of kings; and those who are with Him are called, chosen, and faithful.' Rev. 17:14.

Chapter 18

Christ Calls His People Out of Babylon the Great, Lest they Share in her Judgments, as the World Mourns her Fall and Heaven Rejoices, her Sudden Fall Signifying the Fall of All of Christ's Enemies

'Therefore her plagues will come in one day – death and mourning and famine. And she will be utterly burned with fire, for strong is the Lord God who judges her … And in her was found the blood of the prophets and saints, and of all who were slain on the earth.' Rev. 18:8, 24.

Chapter 19

Heaven Rejoices over God's Saving His People Through Destroying Babylon the Great, and Preparing the Church for the Marriage Supper of the Lamb, While Christ Rides on a White Horse, Bringing Final Victory Over all His and our Enemies as King of kings and Lord of lords

> 'Now out of His mouth goes a sharp sword, that with it He should strike the nations. And He Himself will rule them with a rod of iron. He Himself treads the winepress of the fierceness and wrath of Almighty God. And He has on His robe and on His thigh a name written: KING OF KINGS AND LORD OF LORDS.' Rev. 19:15-16.

Chapter 20

Satan is Bound and Cast into the Bottomless Pit for a Millennium, as the Saints Reign with Christ, Satan Released Immediately Before Christ's Second Coming, Drawing from the Depiction of Gog and Magog from Ezekiel 38-39 to Illustrate Christ's Final Victory Over Everything Opposing His Church, Casting All into the Lake of Fire

> 'Then Death and Hades were cast into the lake of fire. This is the second death. And anyone not found written in the Book of Life was cast into the lake of fire.' Rev. 20:14-15.

Chapter 21

John Sees the Heavenly Church, which is the New Jerusalem and the Lamb's Wife, Coming Down From Heaven, Founded on the Apostles and Prophets, Signified by her Gates and Foundations, God Fulfilling the Temple Promises by His Direct Presence, with the Lamb Serving as the Light of His People

> 'But I saw no temple in it, for the Lord God Almighty and the Lamb are its temple. The city had no need of the sun or the moon to shine in it, for the glory of God illuminated it. The Lamb is its light.' Rev. 21:22-23.

Chapter 22

The Curse of the Fall is Reversed Fully, the Blessings of Eden in the Tree of Life and the Rivers of the Garden Fulfilled in Heaven,

God's Face Shining on the Saints Fully in Final Benediction, Urging All on Earth Now to Hear the Spirit's Call to Repent, All of God's Covenant Promises Being Fulfilled in Christ, Warning Neither to Add to nor Subtract from the Words of this Book, as John Closes his Book and the Bible Longing for Christ's Return

> '"I, Jesus, have sent My angel to testify to you these things in the churches. I am the Root and the Offspring of David, the Bright and Morning Star." And the Spirit and the bride say, "Come!" And let him who hears say, "Come!" And let him who thirsts come. Whoever desires, let him take the water of life freely.' Rev. 22:16-17.

Appendices

The Stages of the Covenant of Grace

The Covenant with Adam. Gen. 3:15.

The Covenant with Noah. Gen. 6–9.

The Covenant with Abraham. Gen. 12, 15, 17, 21.

The Covenant with Moses. Exod. 19–24.

The Covenant with David. 2 Sam. 7, 1 Chron. 17, Ps. 89.

The New Covenant in Christ. Jer. 31, Matt. 26, Heb. 8.

How the Books of the Bible Point to Christ

All God's promises are summed up in Christ (2 Cor. 1:20) and all the Scriptures point to Him (John 5:39). Therefore, this section lists some key ideas from every book of the Bible, giving clues as to how they point to Christ. Limited in scope, the summaries point to Christ by types, foreshadowing, and by promises. Many of these summaries require some explanation, but coupled with the summary of God's covenants in the preceding appendix, and following the narrative established by the main text above, they present some clues regarding what to look for while reading the Bible. It helps to remember that the Old Testament ordinances and promises were often defective by design, or fulfilled only partially, in order to keep the eyes of believers on the horizon for Christ's coming.

Genesis – Christ is the Seed of the Woman, who crushes the serpent's head

Exodus – Christ is Redeemer

Leviticus – Christ is High Priest, who makes atonement for sins

Numbers – Christ chastens His people for their sins and preserves them

Deuteronomy – Christ will circumcise the hearts of believers and their children

Joshua – Christ is the Commander of the armies of the Lord

Judges – Christ is the Angel of the Lord, who disciplines His people

Ruth – Christ is the Kinsman Redeemer

1 and 2 Samuel – Christ is the Anointed King and Son of David

1 and 2 Kings – Christ is the Faithful Son of David

1 and 2 Chronicles – Christ preserves His People in exile and restores them

Ezra – Christ is our worship Leader

Nehemiah – Christ dwells with His people in distress

Esther – Christ is the God of Providence, saving His people from all enemies

Job – Christ is the Savior, who will resurrect His people

Psalms – Christ is Prophet, Priest, and King, who represents and saves His people

Proverbs – Christ is the eternal Wisdom of God

Ecclesiastes – Christ gives meaning to life by leading us to fear God

Song of Solomon – Christ is the Bridegroom of His church

Isaiah – Christ is the Branch of David and the suffering Servant, defending God's holiness

Jeremiah – Christ rebuilds the remnant under the new covenant

Lamentations – Christ shows God's great faithfulness in the worst times

Ezekiel – Christ is the Lord who is there among His people by the Spirit

Daniel – Christ is King over an everlasting kingdom

Hosea – Christ is the Bridegroom, saving His unfaithful bride, bringing salvation to the nations

Joel – Christ pours out His Spirit on all flesh

Amos – Christ restores the fallen booth of David

Micah – Christ is the everlasting King born in Bethlehem

Nahum – Christ defends His people by upholding God's Name in Exodus 34

Habakkuk – Christ teaches His suffering people to live by Faith

Zephaniah – Christ rejoices over His People with singing

Haggai – Christ is the true and greater temple

Zechariah – Christ is a Priest crowned King

Malachi – Christ is the Angel of the Covenant

Matthew – Christ fulfills Scripture and has all authority in heaven and earth from the Father

Mark – Christ is the God who does wondrous things

Luke – Christ calls the nations to repentance and faith

John – Christ is the eternal Son of God who became man

Acts – Christ is ascended and reigning, spreading the gospel to the nations by His Spirit

Romans – Christ is the heart of God's gospel

1 Corinthians – Christ is the wisdom and power of God for salvation

2 Corinthians – Christ is the substance of the ministry of the new covenant

Galatians – Christ is the only way of justification

Ephesians – Christ is the centerpiece of the work of the Triune God

Philippians – Christ is the form of God and the form of a servant

Colossians – Christ is the divine and human head of the church

1 Thessalonians – Christ is the hope of believers in death

2 Thessalonians – Christ is the Judge of all people

1 Timothy – Christ is Lord of the church, caring for His government

2 Timothy – Christ is the focal point of Scripture

Titus – Christ is zealous for the godliness of His people

Philemon – Christ brings true freedom

Hebrews – Christ perfects the old covenant in the new covenant

James – Christ reconciles rich and poor Christians

1 Peter – Christ is the true Prophet, who spoke by the Spirit in every prophet

2 Peter – Christ defends His church from false teachers

1 John – Christ is the true God and eternal life

2 John – Christ is true man

3 John – Christ is the pattern of goodness

Jude – Christ preserves His people in everlasting life in spite of false teachers

Revelation – Christ is ruler of nations and defender of His persecuted people

The Ten Commandments

'And God spoke all these words, saying:

"I *am* the Lord your God, who brought you out of the land of Egypt, out of the house of bondage.

You shall have no other gods before Me.

You shall not make for yourself a carved image—any likeness *of anything* that *is* in heaven above, or that *is* in the earth beneath, or that *is* in the water under the earth; you shall not bow down to them nor serve them. For I, the Lord your God, *am* a jealous God, visiting the iniquity of the fathers upon the children to the third and fourth *generations* of those who hate Me, but showing mercy to thousands, to those who love Me and keep My commandments.

You shall not take the name of the Lord your God in vain, for the Lord will not hold *him* guiltless who takes His name in vain.

Remember the Sabbath day, to keep it holy. Six days you shall labor and do all your work, but the seventh day *is* the Sabbath of the Lord your God. *In it* you shall do no work: you, nor your son, nor your daughter, nor your male servant, nor your female servant, nor your cattle, nor your stranger who *is* within your gates. For *in* six days the Lord made the heavens and the earth, the sea, and all that *is* in them, and rested the seventh day. Therefore the Lord blessed the Sabbath day and hallowed it.

Honor your father and your mother, that your days may be long upon the land which the Lord your God is giving you.

You shall not murder.

You shall not commit adultery.

You shall not steal.

You shall not bear false witness against your neighbor.

You shall not covet your neighbor's house; you shall not covet your neighbor's wife, nor his male servant, nor his female servant, nor his ox, nor his donkey, nor anything that *is* your neighbor's.'" Exodus 20:1-17.

Other Proverbs for Meditation

'A wise man will hear and increase in learning, and a man of understanding will attain wise counsel.' Prov. 1:5.

'Turn at my rebuke; Surely I will pour out my Spirit on you; I will make my words known to you.' Prov. 1:23.

'For the upright will dwell in the land, and the blameless will remain in it; but the wicked will be cut off from the earth, and the unfaithful will be uprooted from it.' Prov. 2:21.

'Let not mercy and truth forsake you; bind them around your neck, and write them on the tablet of your heart, and so find favor and high esteem in the sight of God and man.' Prov. 3:3-4.

'Keep your heart with all diligence, for out of it spring the issues of life.' Prov. 4:23.

'Go to the ant you sluggard! Consider her ways and be wise.' Prov. 6:6.

'For the commandment is a lamp, and the law a light; reproofs and instruction are the way of life.' Prov. 6:23.

'Wounds and dishonor he will get, and his reproach will not be wiped away.' Prov. 6:33.

'The LORD possessed me at the beginning of His way, before His works of old. I have been established from everlasting, from the beginning, before there ever was an earth. When there were no depths I was brought forth, when there were no fountains abounding with water. Before the mountains were settled, before the hills, I was brought forth; while as yet He had not made the earth or the fields, or the primal dust of the world.' Prov. 8:22-26.

'Then I was beside Him as a master craftsman; and I was daily His delight, rejoicing always before Him, rejoicing in His inhabited world, and my delight was with the sons of men.' Prov. 8:30-31.

'Whoever is simple, let him turn in here! As for him who lacks understanding, she says to him, Come, eat of my bread and drink of the wine I have mixed.' Prov. 9:4-5.

'Whoever is simple, let him turn in here; and as for him who lacks understanding, she says to him, Stolen water is sweet, and bread eaten in secret is pleasant.' Prov. 9:16-17.

'He who keeps instruction is in the way of life, but he who refuses correction goes astray.' Prov. 10:17.

'In the multitude of words sin is not lacking, but he who restrains his lips is wise.' Prov. 10:19.

'The fruit of the righteous is a tree of life, and he who wins souls is wise. If the righteous will be recompensed on the earth, how much more the ungodly and the sinner.' Prov. 11:30-31.

'A righteous man regards the life of his animal, but the tender mercies of the wicked are cruel.' Prov. 12:10.

'A fool's wrath is known at once, but a prudent man covers shame.' Prov. 12:16.

'Lying lips are an abomination to the LORD, but those who deal truthfully are His delight.' Prov. 12:22.

'The righteous should choose his friends carefully, for the way of the wicked leads them astray.' Prov. 12:26.

'There is one who makes himself rich, yet has nothing; and one who makes himself poor, yet has great riches.' Prov. 13:7.

'By pride comes nothing but strife, but with the well-advised is wisdom.' Prov. 13:10.

'He who walks in his uprightness fears the LORD, but he who is perverse in his ways despises Him.' Prov. 14:2.

'Where no oxen are, the trough is clean; but much increase comes by the strength of an ox.' Prov. 14:4.

'The backslider in heart will be filled with his own ways, but a good man will be satisfied from above.' Prov. 14:14.

'The sacrifice of the wicked is an abomination to the LORD, but the prayer of the upright is His delight.' Prov. 15:8.

'The heart of the righteous studies how to answer, but the mouth of the wicked pours forth evil.' Prov. 15:28.

'The fear of the LORD is the instruction of wisdom, and before honor is humility.' Prov. 15:33.

'In mercy and truth atonement is provided for iniquity; and by the fear of the LORD one departs from evil. When a man's ways please the LORD, He makes even his enemies to be at peace with him.' Prov. 16:6-7.

'A man's heart plans his way, but the LORD directs his steps.' Prov. 16:9.

'Pride goes before destruction, and a haughty spirit before a fall. Better to be of a humble spirit with the lowly, than to divide the spoil with the proud. He who heeds the word wisely will find good, and whoever trusts in the LORD, happy is he.' Prov. 16:18-20.

'He who is slow to anger is better than the mighty; and he who rules his spirit than he who takes a city. The lot is cast into the lap, but its every decision is from the LORD.' Prov. 16:32-33.

'Rebuke is more effective for a wise man than a hundred blows on a fool.' Prov. 17:10.

'He who justifies the wicked, and condemns the just, both of them alike are an abomination to the LORD.' Prov. 17:15.

'He who has knowledge spares his words, and a man of understanding is of a calm spirit. Even a fool is counted wise when he holds his peace; when he shuts his lips, he is considered perceptive.' Prov. 17:27-28.

'A fool has no delight in understanding, but in expressing his own heart.' Prov. 18:2.

'He who answers a matter before he hears it, it is a folly and shame to him.' Prov. 18:13.

'The first one to plead his cause seems right, until his neighbor comes and examines him.' Prov. 18:17.

'A man who has friends must himself be friendly, but there is a friend who sticks closer than a brother.' Prov. 18:24.

'There are many plans in a man's heart, nevertheless the LORD's counsel – that will stand.' Prov. 19:21.

'Cease listening to instruction, my son, and you will stray from the words of knowledge.' Prov. 19:27.

'It is honorable for a man to stop striving, since any fool can start a quarrel.' Prov. 20:3.

'An inheritance gained hastily at the beginning will not be blessed at the end.' Prov. 20:21.

'The spirit of a man is the lamp of the LORD, searching all the inner depths of his heart.' Prov. 20:27.

'The plans of the diligent lead surely to plenty, but those of everyone who is hasty, surely to poverty.' Prov. 21:5.

'The righteous God wisely considers the house of the wicked, overthrowing the wicked for their wickedness.' Prov. 21:12.

'The sacrifice of the wicked is an abomination; how much more when he brings it with wicked intent!' Prov. 21:27.

'The eyes of the LORD preserve knowledge, but He overthrows the words of the faithless.' Prov. 22:12.

'Make no friendship with an angry man, and with a furious man do not go, lest you learn his ways, and set a snare for your soul.' Prov. 22:24-25.

'Do you see a man who excels in his work? He will stand before kings; he will not stand before unknown men.' Prov. 22:29.

'Buy the truth and do not sell it, also wisdom and instruction and understanding.' Prov. 23:23.

'If you faint in the day of adversity, your strength is small.' Prov. 24:10.

'For a righteous man will fall seven times, and rise again, but the wicked shall fall by calamity.' Prov. 24:16.

'By long forbearance a ruler is persuaded, and a gentle tongue breaks a bone.' Prov. 25:15.

'If your enemy is hungry, give him bread to eat; and if he is thirsty, give him water to drink; for so you will heap coals of fire on his head, and the LORD will reward you.' Prov. 25:21-22.

'Whoever has no rule over his own spirit is like a city broken down without walls.' Prov. 25:28.

'Do not answer a fool according to his folly, lest you also be like him. Answer a fool according to his folly, lest he be wise in his own eyes.' Prov. 26:4-5.

'Do you see a man who is wise in his own eyes? There is more hope for a fool than for him.' Prov. 26:12.

'The lazy man is wiser in his own eyes than seven men who can answer sensibly.' Prov. 26:16.

'A lying tongue hates those who are crushed by it, and a flattering mouth works ruin.' Prov. 26:28.

'Open rebuke is better than love carefully concealed. Faithful are the wounds of a friend, but the kisses of an enemy are deceitful.' Prov. 27:5-6.

'As iron sharpens iron, so a man sharpens the countenance of his friend.' Prov. 27:17.

'One who turns away his ear from hearing the law, even his prayer is an abomination.' Prov. 28:9.

'He who covers his sins will not prosper, but whoever confesses and forsakes them will have mercy.' Prov. 28:13.

'He who rebukes a man will find more favor afterward than he who flatters with the tongue.' Prov. 28:23.

'He who is of a proud heart stirs up strife, but he who trusts the LORD will be prospered. He who trusts in his own heart is a fool, but whoever walks wisely will be delivered.' Prov. 28:25-26.

'He who is often rebuked, and hardens his neck, will suddenly be destroyed, and that without remedy.' Prov. 29:1.

'A fool vents all his feelings, but a wise man holds them back.' Prov. 29:11.

'The rod and rebuke give wisdom, but a child left to himself brings shame to his mother.' Prov. 29:16.

'Do you see a man hasty in his words? There is more hope for a fool than for him.' Prov. 29:20.

'Who can find a virtuous wife? For her worth is far above rubies.' Prov. 31:10.

The Beatitudes

And seeing the multitudes, He went up on a mountain, and when He was seated His disciples came to Him. Then He opened His mouth and taught them, saying:

'Blessed *are* the poor in spirit,
For theirs is the kingdom of heaven.

Blessed *are* those who mourn,
For they shall be comforted.

Blessed *are* the meek,
For they shall inherit the earth.

Blessed *are* those who hunger and thirst for righteousness,
For they shall be filled.

Blessed *are* the merciful,
For they shall obtain mercy.

Blessed *are* the pure in heart,
For they shall see God.

Blessed *are* the peacemakers,
For they shall be called sons of God.

Blessed *are* those who are persecuted for righteousness' sake,
For theirs is the kingdom of heaven.

Blessed are you when they revile and persecute you, and say all kinds of evil against you falsely for My sake. Rejoice and be exceedingly glad, for great *is* your reward in heaven, for so they persecuted the prophets who were before you.'

Matt. 5:1-12.

The Lord's Prayer

'In this manner, therefore, pray:

Our Father in heaven,
Hallowed be Your name.
Your kingdom come.
Your will be done
On earth as *it is* in heaven.
Give us this day our daily bread.
And forgive us our debts,
As we forgive our debtors.
And do not lead us into temptation,
But deliver us from the evil one.
For Yours is the kingdom and the power and the glory forever.
Amen.' Matt. 6:9-13.